ROMANIFESTO

"A witty and learned tour through the hall of mirrors that Roman history provides us in the age of Brexit and Boris."

TOM HOLLAND, AUTHOR OF *DYNASTY: THE RISE AND FALL OF THE HOUSE OF CAESAR*

"Asa Bennett's delightful book reminds us that though the Romans may have left our shores in 410 AD, they never left our hearts and minds. They are with us today in more or less everything we think or speak or do, and nowhere more so than in the sphere of politics. Tremendous fun!"

STANLEY JOHNSON

"A sharp, smart and frighteningly familiar portrait of political power. If you think our politicians are bad, wait until you meet the Romans in Bennett's lively guide."

DAISY DUNN, CLASSICIST AND AUTHOR OF *OF GODS AND MEN: 100 STORIES FROM ANCIENT GREECE AND ROME*

"In unpretentious prose our contemporary politicians are measured against the unscrupulous leaders of the ancient world and found morally to be even worse. There are arresting reminders of just how low the bar is now, with shameful deeds excused by the removal of shame from the equation altogether. Contemporary politicians who fancy themselves as classically inspired orators would do well to read this hugely entertaining and lively book. Asa Bennett has your number."

IAN MARTIN, WRITER FOR *THE THICK OF IT* AND *THE DEATH OF STALIN*

"Part entertaining-but-erudite romp through the political shenanigans of Ancient Rome, part well-informed take-down of those who vie with each other to rule over us today, Asa Bennett's book draws a whole host of parallels between the ancient and the modern that are both insightful and instructive. Hugely enjoyable."

TIM BALE, PROFESSOR OF POLITICS AT QUEEN MARY UNIVERSITY OF LONDON

"Troublesome Britons rebelling against self-important pan-European rulers. Radical career politicians invoking the many against the few. Bosom allies turning on one another, daggers drawn, to grab the top job. Asa Bennett's incisive and amusing odyssey through classical politics reminds us that the ancient world is a lot closer than we might imagine."

MARK WALLACE, EXECUTIVE EDITOR OF CONSERVATIVEHOME

ROMANIFESTO

MODERN LESSONS FROM CLASSICAL POLITICS

ASA BENNETT

Biteback Publishing

First published in Great Britain in 2019 by
Biteback Publishing Ltd
Westminster Tower
3 Albert Embankment
London SE1 7SP
Copyright © Asa Bennett 2019

ISBN 978-1-78590-519-3

10 9 8 7 6 5 4 3 2 1

A CIP catalogue record for this book is available from the British Library.

Set in Bulmer

Printed and bound in Great Britain by
CPI Group (UK) Ltd, Croydon CR0 4YY

MIX
Paper from
responsible sources
FSC® C020471

DEDICATIO

Cui dono lepidum novum libellum?
Uxori formosae, tibi namque tu solebas
Meas esse aliquid putare nugas
Quare habe tibi quidquid hoc libelli

CONTENTS

INTRODUCTION

Friends, Romans, readers, lend me your ears! It might seem rather grand to begin this by ripping off Shakespeare's Mark Anthony to my own end, but there is no better way to start this than by adapting the words put in the mouth of one of Rome's best known politicians.

Despite the Roman Empire crumbling many centuries ago, it still casts a large shadow over the present day. And nowhere is this more evident than the world of politics.

Anything that seems remotely chaotic these days ends up being compared with the last days of Rome, whether it is Donald Trump's rollercoaster presidency or Theresa May's equally bumpy leadership in Britain. When leaders become too arrogant, they can expect to be compared to egomaniacal emperors. Any moment of betrayal inevitably invites comparisons to Brutus' notorious plot against Julius Caesar. And any strong female British leader cannot avoid being hailed as the new Boudicca.

Why do we find it so irresistible to hark back to the Romans? It is not simply because of how long ago they had reached their political peak. If age was the only thing that counted, we would be constantly looking for lessons in the oldest known civilisations like those who settled in the eastern Mediterranean region of Mesopotamia. But it is safe to say the deeds of ancient Sumerians like Gilgamesh interest far fewer people than great Romans like Caesar, and all those who vied to follow him.

Their allure has been helped enormously by how much the Romans left behind. They had a vast amount of the world to leave their mark on because their Empire ended up covering most of Europe, as well as spanning across northern Africa and western Asia. The masses of material they produced have spoiled archaeologists rotten, allowing us to piece together so much of what went on in Rome, as the doyenne of classical historians Dame Mary Beard relates: 'We not only have their poetry, letters, essays, speeches and histories, but also novels, geographies, satires and reams and reams of technical writing on everything from water engineering to medicine and disease ... We have notes sent home, shopping lists, account books and last messages inscribed on graves.'

Such an archaeological treasure trove enables us to understand what made the Romans tick, and how they built a huge Empire. Running such a vast operation required them to develop a sophisticated approach to government and democracy, so we can see what smooth political operators they had to become in the process.

Indeed, we would not think of politics as it is without our classical ancestors. The word comes directly from the Ancient Greek word *polis* – which refers to a city or state. Someone who had to take charge came to be known as a *politikos*. That was a worthy thing to be at the time, unlike those who preferred to mind their own business, the so-called *idiotes*. Like most good Greek ideas, their term for a politician was stolen by the Romans. And so a public representative came to be known as a *politicus*. When they stood for elections, they made sure to stand out by wearing gleamingly white togas. Their word for white (*candida*) gave us the term 'candidate' – neatly describing the political hopefuls who aspire to impress voters with their equally gleaming electoral offer. And we expect them to be as candid as possible about what they will do in office, no matter how shiny their toga might be.

Politics is leaving many people breathless about all the apparently new and unprecedented events going on. But in truth, it has barely changed from Roman times, with the only real differences being the standard of technology and the cast list.

Roman politics was fuelled by ambition, ego and self-interest. People sought to get ahead by striking backroom deals. Rivalries were rife, but were shelved if there was an alliance to be had, even if it was so shaky it would soon fall apart. Those on their way up attracted fame, power and glory, while those on their way down were shunned and ostracised. Good leaders would be revered for years, while those who alienated their allies and went power-mad rarely had a dignified exit. The ruling elite had to deal with populist demagogues stirring up revolution. And those who took charge had to be aware of public opinion, and would pander and bribe voters to ensure their goodwill. All the while, they had to shrug off the slurs, gossip and fake news pushed by their enemies. The cut and thrust of their politics is timeless, which makes it easy to follow nowadays.

Some politicians are rightly aware of how much there is to learn from the Romans. Labour's shadow Chancellor John McDonnell sought to improve his colleagues' public speaking by giving a lesson in classical rhetoric – handing his fellow frontbenchers a copy of the great orator Marcus Tullius Cicero's thoughts on how to win an argument. One of the books he consulted to better understand the current state of politics, besides Karl Marx's *Das Kapital*, was Robert Harris' book *Imperium*, which tells the story of Cicero's rise to the top in the turbulent world of Roman politics through the eyes of his personal attendant Tiro. The hurly-burly it contained evidently astounded McDonnell, as when asked who he found to be the most sympathetic character in it, he quipped: 'The poor guy Cicero employs to write all this up.'

Other politicians are even more evangelical about the Romans. Boris Johnson rarely passes up a chance to show off his penchant for classics, a subject he studied at university, to enliven what he wants to say. In his early days as a politician, Johnson compared his desire to climb the political ranks to that of a Roman seeking to complete their own 'order of honours' (*cursus honorum*). Speaking on BBC Radio 4's *Desert Island Discs* in 2005, the then mere Tory backbencher said: 'My ambition silicon chip has been programmed to try to scramble up this *cursus honorum*, this ladder of things, so you do feel a kind of sense you have got to.' Three years later, he became Mayor of London. He compared the reaction to his victory among the media to a 'ravening Hyrcanian tiger deprived of its mortal prey', referring to a now extinct species that was much mentioned in Latin literature, especially Virgil's *Aeneid*.

He owed the Romans as mayor, not least because the city would not have had the importance of being a capital if they had not designated it as such. And he tried to recognise that by banging the drum for the teaching of Latin, saying it could do a 'huge amount' to improve the quality of life for disadvantaged young people in the capital.

His biggest tribute to the Romans by far came in 2006, when he devoted an entire book – and accompanying television documentary series – to explaining why the European Union sought to pick up where the Roman Empire left off in its quest for Europe-wide homogeneity. His thesis in *The Dream of Rome* ended with him declaring his eagerness to see the 'great moment' when Turkey joined the EU as it would see the entire Roman Empire 'at last reunited in an expanded European Union', recommending that the President of the European Commission declare himself a god to help speed the process up. That Euro-expansionist call to arms came back to haunt him a decade later, when he led the official Brexit campaign, which had warned as one of its main arguments during the referendum about the perils of Turkey joining the bloc.

As enthusiastic as politicians like Johnson are to bring up the Romans, they do not always get their references right. A classical reference was one of the many things he argued about with his London Mayoral rival, Ken Livingstone, in 2012. The Labour politician pounced after Johnson claimed in an interview with the BBC to have been influenced by Shakespeare's Pericles, billing him as the first mayor of Athens, rather than ruler of Tyre in Phoenicia (ancient Lebanon). 'I never thought I would catch him out on classical things as I did not do Latin,' Livingstone recounted in the *Evening Standard*. 'But I immediately said Shakespeare's Pericles was a completely different Pericles. He was not mayor of Athens. And Boris just said, "I know, but it was a good point to make."'

Johnson is not the only politician who feels they can make a good point by reaching for the Romans and Greeks. Fellow Conservative politician Jacob Rees-Mogg is famous for mining the past for snappy Commons quips and one-liners outside the Chamber. That should be expected from someone who read history at Cambridge, although he has confessed to regretting he did not study classics instead. 'All the really clever people do that,' he admitted to *The Times*. I discovered shortly after how he had sought to make up for it, spotting during a meeting in his parliamentary office a large book of historical quotations that he admitted to liberally consulting.

Rees-Mogg and his Brexiteer colleagues have found much comfort during their skirmishes with Theresa May over her Brexit deal by looking to ancient texts for inspiration. Those who held out the longest in opposing her deal began to refer to themselves as 'Spartans', in reference to the legendarily hardy people who fought against vastly greater numbers of Persians at Thermopylae in 480 BC – until they were all slaughtered. This immortalised them as formidable warriors, drawing fans from such groupings as the Tory European Research Group of Brexiteer MPs. But they might not have realised that the Spartans were regularly defeated in battle, and eventually gobbled up by the Roman Empire in the second century BC. After that, Sparta became a kitsch vassal state, which rich Romans were able to enjoy like an ancient theme park, staying at a special tourist hostel and getting a taste of the harsh military lifestyle during their stay, with exercises specially put on to impress the tourists.

Brexiteers did not just seek out Spartan bravado for encouragement. Clwyd West MP David Jones tried to stir up his fellow

Eurosceptics in the middle of March 2019 by quoting from Roman historian Tacitus' accounts of the ancient Britons' battles with the Roman Empire at a meeting of the European Research Group. The words chosen by the former Brexit minister were, he later told me, what the Caledonian chieftain Calgacus was reported to have told his troops before doing battle. Calgacus did not hold back in his rhetoric against the 'deadly' Romans, scathingly describing them as people who were so destructive they would 'leave behind a wasteland and call it peace'. Did Jones feel that Theresa May would lay similar waste to Brexit with her deal? Perhaps. It fell to his fellow ERG colleagues, especially the classicists in the room such as Johnson, to point out the big problem with casting them as the plucky Britons fighting against the Romans. As one shouted back: 'They all got annihilated!'

Despite these mixed results, the Ancient Romans would be pleased, and hardly surprised, to be treated as authorities by Britain's political class. They saw Britons in their day as brutish Neanderthals who needed to be civilised. Those who dealt with the locals around Hadrian's Wall in northern England described them as *Brittunculi* ('nasty little Britons'). They may well have assumed we would still be studying what they did. And so we should. Of course, as a keen classicist who was lucky to study them, I would say that. I was so nerdy I went as far as voting for 'the Roman party' in the 2009 European elections due to their promises to make everyone in the EU wear togas and speak Latin. Sadly, they only won 5,450 votes. The voters of South East England missed out on a truly populist revolution. Two years later, I had the chance to work with one of the writers behind *The Thick of It*, translating into Latin some characteristically colourful words he had put in the mouth of Boris Johnson for his satirical *The Coalition Chronicles*, who declared he wanted to drag David Cameron around London from the back of a chariot in the same way Achilles did to Hector around Troy. So I've become acutely aware of the relevance of our ancient ancestors to modern politics.

It has been tempting to roam across modern history to trace the influence of the Romans across many great political events. But I've chosen to focus on the past few decades, drawing on my job at the *Daily Telegraph*, where I inevitably analyse every twist and turn of the Brexit process, so I've paid particular attention to what has been going on in the United Kingdom. So, for those who would prefer to suffer the fate of Emperor Claudius' son Drusus – who died after choking on a pear – instead of hearing more about Brexit, I should admit now that the subject does creep into this work. But rest assured, this book goes far beyond the Brexit process and the British political realm. Although, the events leading up to and following the 2016 referendum have sent politics into hyperdrive, and mean the past decade has given us almost a century's worth of examples to study.

Of course, it would be wrong to treat Roman politics as simply the same as the present day, but with everyone wearing sandals and togas. There are ways we can be grateful that politics has changed since the days of Ancient Rome. For one, politics is not an all-male activity anymore. Women are able to be fully involved, whereas their Roman counterparts were simply expected to support their husbands as they worked their way up the rungs of power.

Politics is now also much less bloody. Whenever modern politicians are stabbed in the back, it thankfully tends only to be metaphorically.

That is in part why the murder of Labour MP Jo Cox during the 2016 referendum was so horrifying, and why Tory MPs were publicly horrified when one of their own told a reporter just a few years later – when Theresa May's leadership was at threat – that 'the moment is coming when the knife gets heated, stuck in her front and twisted'. At the time, one senior Tory backbencher expressed his shock to me about the language, and then coolly told me how if his colleagues were 'going to shoot her in the head … it's best not to get blood on the carpet, otherwise it'll be embarrassing for everybody'. On realising what he had uttered, he panickedly apologised for his tone.

His mortification is understandable given that politicians no longer resolve their differences with bloodshed. Nor do they solve problems by leading private armies into battle against each other. When they come to blows or indulge in cut-and-thrust, you can usually expect such exchanges to be merely verbal, no matter how rowdy Prime Minister's Questions gets. We can chalk that up, at least, as progress.

But in many other ways, politics is still the same. The same motives drive people to scrabble up the ladder as they did back in Rome. What they would insist is public service, cynics would conclude is a lust for power, and glory. Only a select few make it to the top, hence the ever-present jostling for position. In our rush to keep on top of events, it is worth looking back to the Romans to understand how to best make sense of it all. They have dealt with much of this already, and so we can learn from their approach.

For centuries, the Romans campaigned, plotted and fought against each other. Their politicking packed in more farce than the TV series *Yes, Minister* and more intrigue than *House of Cards*.

Those unfamiliar with Roman politics should be able to come away from this book understanding why those who studied it, like Boris Johnson, cannot resist talking about it so much. While those already familiar with the past can see how relatable it is to the present. That is why this book is called *Romanifesto*, as I aim to see what – with our Roman ancestors holding up the mirror – we can learn about modern politics.

There is a lot to ponder. How did they woo the public and climb the greasy pole? How did they handle the rough and tumble of political campaigning and debate? How did they manage their appearance, their finances, and their behaviour in order to get on most effectively? There are heavier matters we can be informed on by looking to the Romans. What can Britain's iconic rebel queen, Boudicca, teach us about Brexit in her fight against the Empire? What could Emperor Hadrian teach President Trump about building walls? What could political plotters learn from Brutus? No longer should answers to questions like these be monopolised by those who were lucky to study classics.

It's about time such wisdom was democratised and given a wider airing. Let this book be as trusty for you as Jacob Rees-Mogg's historical quotes compendium. Not only will it mean politicos can learn from Roman mistakes and successes, but also politicians can avoid making fools of themselves with half-remembered references. They should pay particular attention, in fact, as those of you who don't want to scrabble up the political ladder will come away better able to catch them out. So read on to find out how to do politics as the Romans did.

PART ONE

TAKING OFFICE

Before entering any occupation, diligent preparation is to be undertaken. (*In omnibus autem negotiis priusquam adgrediare, adhibenda est praeparatio diligens.*)

MARCUS TULLIUS CICERO, *DE OFFICIIS*

MASTER YOUR MYTHOLOGY

It's not where you come from that counts, politicians like to say, but where you're going. How you handle where you came from can shape how far you're able to go. Anyone who wants to get on tends to work out the right spin to apply to their origins.

The upper echelons of Roman society were full of people with great political stock. The Senate was stuffed with old men who could boast that they were the latest in a long line of public servants. That was to be expected in a chamber that owes its name to the old age of its members – '*senex*' is Latin for an old man. But it was shaken up by the arrival of 'new men', a term used for those, like Cicero, who were the first in their family to serve. By not coming from the political establishment, they could show off their independence and fresh approach.

'New men' emerge all the time in politics. On 15 May 1987, Neil Kinnock explained in moving terms to British Labour Party members, as their party leader, how far he and his wife had come, without any special family connections to help them:

Why am I the first Kinnock in a thousand generations to be able to get to university? Why is Glenys the first woman in her family in a thousand generations to be able to get to university? Was it because all our predecessors were thick? … Does anybody really think that they didn't get what we had because they didn't have the talent, or the strength, or the endurance, or the commitment? … Of course not. It was because there was no platform upon which they could stand.

The genetic implausibility of a thousand generations of Kinnocks notwithstanding, the then opposition leader wanted to show how much the welfare state had helped his family, which he felt was at risk of being dismantled by his right-wing opponents, by showing with brio how it had helped him go even further in life. He had pulled himself up from humble beginnings and strived, against the odds, to become a potential Prime Minister.

His tale proved to be as powerful as any aspirational 'rags-to-riches' tale that Hollywood might have dreamed up, with the added bonus that it was entirely true, at least in spirit. So it was no surprise that politicians across the Atlantic noticed. A few months after Kinnock's emotive performance, an ambitious Delaware senator, one Joe Biden, chose to round off his pitch to be the Democratic party's candidate for the American presidency by deciding to show how imitation can be the sincerest form of flattery. He declared:

Why is it that Joe Biden is the first in his family ever to go to a university? Why is it that my wife … is the first in her family to ever go to college? Is it because our fathers and mothers were not bright? … Is it because they didn't work hard? My ancestors, who worked in the coal mines of northeast Pennsylvania and would come home after twelve hours and play football for four hours? It's because they didn't have a platform on which to stand.

The flagrant plagiarism forced Biden to withdraw from the 1988 presidential race, a time when the bar for disqualification was rather lower than it is today. Still, Biden's inability to resist Kinnock's rhetoric shows that politicians realise voters want to feel their leaders are remarkable individuals, so they try to offer backstories to meet their expectations. Modern politicians sought to make the reality of their beginnings sound inspiring, in the same way that Cicero milked his special status as a *novus homo* in his pursuit of the consulship. Those who went further, by securing supreme power – whether it be as a dictator or emperor – seemed to require an even more impressive origin story to show the average Roman why they were destined for such high office.

Julius Caesar's political career began pretty conventionally, working his way along the *cursus honorum*, but the turning point was said to have come when he had been sent to Spain on official duties. There, in the year 69 BC, he was struck on visiting a temple in Cadiz by a statue of Alexander the Great. The thirty-year-old could not resist comparing himself to the Greek hero, who died at the age of thirty-two, having conquered swathes of the known world, and wept on realising he had done little by contrast. This moment has been widely seen as the point where Caesar decided on his return to Rome to throw everything he could at getting to the top.

Politics continues to hinge on such turning points. Tony Blair showed his own determination to secure power by how he handled his friend and potential leadership rival Gordon Brown over dinner in 1994. Their decision, which came to be known as the Granita Pact due to the name of the restaurant they were in, was hotly disputed for years, as Brown came away believing he would be handed over the reins much sooner than Blair was willing. Several decades later, the makeup of the leadership of the victorious Brexit campaign can be traced back to a dinner on 16 February 2016 at Boris Johnson's house, where Michael Gove persuaded the London mayor to join his project. Gove tried to exploit that three years later, facing off against Johnson in a debate as contenders for the Tory leadership, when he sought to pose as the leading Brexiteer by thanking him for 'join[ing] me on that campaign'.

The Romans went much further than Gove in what they were willing to seize on to build a compelling political narrative, and did not stop with their political career. Those who rose to greatness like Julius Caesar even made political capital out of their birth. His Julian clan claimed to be able to trace themselves back to Iulus, son of the war hero Aeneas, who, as Virgil told in his epic poetry, fled Troy to Italy where he laid the groundwork for Rome. Aeneas' mother, according to popular legend, happened to be the goddess Venus.

His successor tried hard to take after him. The man known first as Gaius Octavius Thurinus chose to recognise his adoption as Julius' son and heir by taking his father's full name as his own. Rome's ruling family was not big enough for two people called Gaius Julius Caesar, so people began to call him informally 'Octavian' (Octavianus) to avoid any mix-ups. Octavian's move to ingratiate himself with Julius Caesar's fans by taking on his name was as unsubtle as Gordon Brown would have been if he had decided to woo Blairites by taking on their idol's name wholesale and becoming Anthony Charles Lynton Blair. But Octavian had to convince everyone that he was Julius' rightful heir. Otherwise, he risked being sidelined by rivals like Julius Caesar's lieutenant, Mark Anthony.

Octavian sought to strengthen his claim by building a temple dedicated to his adoptive father, adding the title *'Divi Filius'* (Son of the divine [Caesar]) to his name. But Mark Anthony knew how to play familial politics, shacking up with Caesar's former lover Cleopatra as the race to succeed him got going. The Egyptian queen had something that could have sewn up the succession for Anthony: being mother of Caesar's only biological son. She was adamant that the boy was the result of an affair with Julius Caesar, going as far as to name him 'little Caesar' or 'Caesarion' to ram home that point. The man himself had refused to publicly acknowledge whether the boy was legitimately his own, with Caesarion subject to his own *Jeremy Kyle Show*-esque paternity dispute. He was said to have his alleged father's looks and manner, and heralded as 'Pharaoh Caesar' in Egypt, although a prominent Caesar supporter wrote a pamphlet arguing that he could not have possibly been the father. Octavian sought to draw a line under this debate in 31 BC by defeating Anthony and Cleopatra in battle, which left no question over who should then succeed Julius Caesar.

The ultimate proof that Octavian's name-change worked came

from the fact that Caesar became more than a name on his accession, but a title in itself. Roman rulers thereafter tended to follow his example by taking on the name 'Caesar' on becoming emperor, with it manifesting as a term for rulers several centuries later in Germany as 'Kaiser' and Russia as 'Tsar'. Besides taking Julius' name, Octavian also tried to claim similar divine heritage, although as his great-nephew and adopted son, he could not claim to be so directly descended from Venus. That might be why people came to entertain alternative myths, such as his being the son of Apollo, who – it was said – had visited his mother Atia in the middle of the night after she fell asleep in a temple dedicated to his worship.

Other emperors attracted different tales, which weren't solely confined to having divine parents. When assassins came for the young Nero and prepared to butcher him in his bed, Suetonius records a 'bit of gossip' that they were 'frightened away by a snake which darted out from under his pillow'. Nero helped spread that tale when he grew up by publicly wearing a gold bracelet on his arm, which was said to have incorporated the snakeskin it left behind. He was 'not over-modest' about this, Tacitus says in backhanded praise.

While modern politicians would hate to be associated with slippery creatures like snakes, it was savvy for Nero to do so in Rome. Many Romans would have known the legend of Hercules, and indeed worshipped him for his heroic acts. As a baby, he was said to have seen off two snakes that had been put in his bed to kill him. So Nero would have hoped reports of his own brush with serpents in his youth would lead Romans to think of him as another Hercules.

Origin stories did not just matter to emperors. Julius Caesar's lieutenant Mark Anthony liked to claim descent from Hercules, through one of his sons, Anton. He would try to make this seem more credible by dressing and carrying himself in public in ways that Hercules was said to do. He would wear his tunic belted low over his hips, have a large sword swinging at his side and wear a cloak as thick as the lion Hercules was said to have killed and draped around himself, all in order to emulate the legendary hero.

Meanwhile, the conspiracy to kill Caesar might never have got off the ground if Marcus Junius Brutus had not taken a leading role in it. 'What the plot needed most of all was the reputation of a man such as Brutus,' the historian Plutarch explained, suggesting that his involvement would 'ensure' it was a just cause. He had a formidable pedigree as a conspirator, as plots against the state were his family's bread and butter. Brutus was descended through his father from Lucius Brutus, who had been credited with overthrowing the last king of Rome and paving the way for the Republic, while he could hark back through his mother to Servilius Ahala, who in the fifth century BC helped save Rome by foiling a plot by a man called Spurius Maelius to seize power by taking a dagger and cutting him down in the Forum. When Caesar's enemies feared that he was acting like a tyrant, they knew that Brutus would be the man they needed – he had revolution in his blood.

The plotters against Caesar piled pressure on Brutus to join them by appealing to his revolutionary heritage. Graffiti began to appear on the courthouse, deliberately so that Brutus would see it while doing official business as a praetor, offering provocative messages like 'Are you asleep?' and 'You are no true Brutus'. Further writing appeared on the statue of his ancestor, Lucius, reading: 'Oh, if only we had you now!'

The power of a politician's backstory can help determine the next few chapters they get to write about their own career. The Romans knew that all too well, and modern politicians have grasped it too in their efforts to seem more relatable, and equally more remarkable, to the electorate. The Conservatives made a virtue of John Major's background, running posters during the 1992 general election with a picture of his face and the slogan: 'What does the Conservative Party offer a working class kid from Brixton? They made him Prime Minister.' Major himself was recorded for an election broadcast going back to his childhood neighbourhood of Brixton, complete with footage of him buying kippers, to ram his ordinary origins home.

As soon as a politician starts telling voters about their backstory, it is as unsubtle a sign as any that they're vying for the top job. Two Conservative Cabinet ministers effectively fired the starting gun in 2018 on the leadership campaigns they went on to mount the following year when they spoke at their party's conference in Birmingham about where they had come from. Dominic Raab went first by telling Tory members about his Czech-born Jewish refugee father:

Eighty years ago – 1938 – Nazi Germany invaded Czechoslovakia.
The lucky few fled. Some of them to Britain. One Jewish family
arrived in England with a little boy called Peter. He was six years

old and he spoke no English. That little boy grew up knowing that his grandmother, grandfather, most of his relatives, the loved ones left behind, had been systematically murdered for no other reason than that they were Jews. That little boy learnt English. He got into a grammar school. And grasped the opportunities and embraced the tolerance that our great country offers. He became a food manager at Marks and Spencer…

Raab rounded off by pledging to honour his father's memory 'by fighting the scourge of antisemitism and racism until my last breath'. The fervent applause he sparked showed how much his fellow Conservatives had warmed to him. A day later, Sajid Javid told voters about his own father:

Abdul-Ghani Javid left Pakistan and landed in Heathrow. He spent what little he had on a coach ticket, had his first night here in Birmingham, then continued up north to Lancashire to find work in a cotton mill. After standing outside the mill for weeks, he got that first job, and started a family. Eventually, there were seven of us living in a two-bedroom flat on what the papers called 'Britain's most dangerous street'. That's my story.

Javid went on to add his own twist to the Conservatives' Major-era slogan, telling the party faithful: 'So, what does the Conservative Party offer a working-class son-of-an-immigrant kid from Rochdale? You made him Home Secretary.'

Both men sought to introduce themselves to voters by telling them more about themselves, at the same time showing off how remarkable their families had been in triumphing against the odds. They might have struggled to encourage rumours that they had emulated Hercules as babies, or been descended from gods, so settled for focusing on how far they had come to get up on that stage. As Javid put it: 'If you'd have told me back then what I'd be doing now, I'd have told you that it was less believable than any TV drama.'

This was not the first time Javid blended his personal story with his politics. Earlier that year, he distinguished himself as Home Secretary with his response to revelations of how his department had been handling people who had come to the UK as part of the Windrush generation. The slew of stories about British subjects being wrongly detained, denied legal rights and deported by the Home Office required a deft response from the minister in charge. Javid sought to prove that he was not just going to go through the motions by drawing on his experience as a second-generation migrant to show his revulsion at this mistreatment, telling the *Sunday Telegraph* in April: 'When I heard about the Windrush issue I thought, "That could be my mum … it could be my dad … it could be my uncle … it could be me."'

Javid built on his personal story as Home Secretary, using it to show in speeches how deeply he understood the social problems affecting the UK. In April 2019, he addressed the topic of knife crime, drawing on his youth growing up in a two-bedroom flat above a street in Bristol that was known as the 'most dangerous in Britain'. 'It's not so difficult to see how, instead of being in the Cabinet, I could have actually turned out to have a life of crime myself,' he warned starkly, thanking his 'loving and supporting parents' for keeping him on the right side of the law.

The power of personal stories cuts across party lines. When Labour's Sadiq Khan campaigned, ultimately successfully, to be Mayor of London in 2016, he would regularly tell voters about how he was the 'son of a bus driver'. It was repeated so often that it started to become an in-joke during the campaign. After his victory, Javid expressed his congratulations on Twitter – 'from one son of a Pakistani bus driver to another'.

Does that mean aspiring politicians are doomed without a tough upbringing? Far from it. Donald Trump was not able to pretend he had a hard life, claiming that he had built his property empire on a 'small' loan of $1 million from his father. The tycoon put together an image as someone who turned that million dollars into many more millions, paying back the original sum with interest. The four bankruptcies he declared on the way did not lessen his appeal as a charismatic strongman, nor the fact that he could have been twice as rich – according to Bloomberg's calculations – if he had ploughed his inheritance into an investment fund and then did nothing else for the rest of his life. Trump's entrepreneurial story was central to his political pitch, as he pledged to run America like he ran his businesses. And American voters took him up on that dubious offer, electing him as their president in 2016.

Across the Atlantic, Jeremy Hunt tried in vain to build on Trump's success in how he approached his campaign to succeed Theresa May as Conservative Party leader and Prime Minister in 2019. As the son of an admiral, and alumnus of the eminent private school Charterhouse, the only way he could claim to have ever had to fight against the odds was by talking about his success building up the educational publishing business Hotcourses. His entrepreneurial journey played a key part in his campaign pitch. Hunt regularly promised to 'turbo-charge' the economy, pointing to the decisions he made and deals he struck in his business career as proof of his potential. In fact, he seemed to speak about his time as an entrepreneur as often as Sadiq Khan talked about his bus-driving father. Still, it was not enough to stop Boris Johnson pipping him to the post.

Of course, some politicians have not had the most compelling pasts. But if they aspire to national leadership, they will need to find a way to persuade voters that they are dynamic enough to lead them into a bright future. If they cannot do that by drawing on how they got there, they will have to be remarkable salespeople to enthuse the electorate.

DO GOOD AND BE CREDITED

Doing the right thing does wonders for a politician's reputation, which is why they do all they can to be associated with worthy causes. Some of us might chuckle on getting a leaflet from our local Member of Parliament plastered with images of them doing worthy deeds around the constituency, but it matters in politics. If they're a political novice, such behaviour helps them build the good name they need to advance. If they've been around for a while, it ensures their career longevity and can even give it a new lease of life if flagging. As one veteran Conservative Member of Parliament put it to me: 'I've seen shits of the first order become good politicians as time goes by.'

Some manage to make good names for themselves without having to go through a stage of being perceived as badly as that. Labour MP Stella Creasy came to prominence due to her spirited campaigning against notorious high-cost loan companies such as Wonga. The popularity she built up meant it was a short time before she joined her party's front bench under then leader Ed Miliband.

Miliband's leadership may have ended in tears after he lost the general election in 2015, but this has seen him go on to reinvent himself as a witty backbench politician who stars in podcasts and popular comedy shows. Though that does not mean his time as leader should be forgotten. In Parliament, he did show promise, at one point catching David Cameron out for trying to claim credit for Labour's investment in the National Health Service. Grilling the Prime Minister on 11 May 2011, he asked David Cameron to hold forth on how it had been doing after a year under his watch. Cameron responded by boasting, among other things, about the growing number of doctors, but he had fallen into Miliband's trap, as shown by his quick, and cutting, response: 'In case the Prime Minister did not realise, it takes seven years to train a doctor, so I would like to thank him for his congratulations on our record on the NHS.' Normally, Cameron would be ready with a comeback during such exchanges. But not on this occasion. He had been caught trying to take credit for the achievements of a different party in government, and was duly chastened.

The Romans knew how important accomplishments were to establishing oneself as a great leader. A clear way they could make their mark would be by building something impressive. In the early days of the Empire, Roman grandees and the wealthy commonly erected big buildings, such as temples, so they could be admired and lauded for their generosity. They were soon pushed out of such works by the emperor, with all major projects built in Rome by the end of Augustus' reign firmly identified with the State – leaving it beyond doubt whom citizens had to thank for their swish facilities. Modern politicians have cottoned onto this, with Sadiq Khan making sure to be as closely associated as possible with anything good London's City Hall was doing under his watch. He starred in adverts about how '#London-IsOpen'. He also ensured posters about what his administration was up to credited 'Mayor of London Sadiq Khan', as a visible reminder to voters about who was in charge. That move made his predecessor Boris Johnson seem positively shy and retiring for being happy to be credited without his name, and just his job title.

Roman leaders knew how great deeds could shape reputations and confound critics. Claudius found it hard to command respect when he became emperor in 41 AD because of his disabilities, namely a limp and speech impediment. His head and hands would shake slightly too. He was widely mocked, even by his own family. His mother, according to the imperial historian Suetonius, would often call him a 'monster of a man' and was fond of insulting people by saying they were a 'bigger fool than her son'. His advisers ran rough-shod over him, so much so that one evening they invited a large crowd to dinner at his palace and then spent the whole time ignoring him. When his close circle did interact with him over dinner, they rarely did so kindly. If he nodded off after dinner, they would pelt him with olive stones and dates, or wake him up by having someone crack a whip. Sometimes, they would put slippers on his hands as he snoozed, so that they would have more fun watching him wake up and absent-mindedly rub his face with them on.

Such abuse undoubtedly led Claudius to want to prove himself as leader by doing something bold. In Rome, one of the best ways to do that was by expanding the Empire by conquering new territory. And so he decided to target Britannia (as Britain was then known), a land so far away that the Romans regarded it in almost mythic terms. Britannia was the northernmost part of the known Roman world, with continental travellers forced to cross a body of water they only knew as 'the ocean' to get there. The people who lived there, as the poet Catullus wrote, were the 'terrifying, most remote, Britons'.

Julius Caesar had been the first Roman leader to lead an expedition to Britain back in 55 BC, but he did not make serious in-roads. All he achieved by crossing the Channel was to inflict a punishment beating on the Britons for helping the Gauls resist his conquest and bring back more booty to Rome from his British adventure. Unlike Gaul, Britain remained uncolonised by the Romans. But that was not because the Britons were too tough for Caesar; as writers like the geographer Strabo are keen to argue in his defence. 'Although the Romans could have held Britain, they scorned to do so, because they saw that there was nothing at all to fear from the Britons,' he wrote, 'and they saw that there was no corresponding advantage to be gained by seizing and holding their country'.

If that was true, successive Roman leaders did not believe it. Caligula, Claudius' predecessor, drew up an invasion force on the shores of the English Channel, but his troops refused to go any further, fearing that their ships would not make it across such a body of water. That left Caligula at an impasse, as he faced mutiny by pushing on and humiliation if he returned to Rome empty-handed. And so, Suetonius wrote, he immediately declared victory and doled out money to his troops to celebrate their supposed triumph. There are some suggestions that he tried to fake the spoils of conquering Britain, going as far as having some of his most northern-European-looking soldiers roughed up so they could pass as British prisoners when paraded through Rome. It fell to his successor, Claudius, to do it properly, accomplishing nearly a hundred years after Caesar's expedition and three years after Caligula's beach jaunt what neither man could do.

His initiative, in 43 BC, turned out to be the start of the Roman conquest of Britain, with future emperors building on what Claudius started. He made sure to link himself firmly with the successes, travelling from Rome to join the army in order to be seen when it had taken the city of Camulodunum, now known as Colchester. He then personally oversaw a swathe of British kings pledging their submission to Rome, showing a mastery of photo opportunities long before cameras came about. The emperor only stayed in Britain for sixteen days before returning to Rome, but that was enough to prove that, under his watch, the Romans had finally started to colonise Britain.

Other Romans built fantastic reputations by managing to be credited for much more than they had actually done. Claudius' brother Germanicus was widely acclaimed for his supposed military success against the Germans. Indeed, he was dubbed that because of how much he fought them. After he died, while on campaign in the East, his ashes were brought back to Rome in a solemn procession, under imperial guard. But how great a war hero was he? He lost large numbers of his own troops and gained not a single inch of new territory for Rome. After every sally into German lands, he would march his troops back out so they could spend winter safely in the Roman camps on the other side of the Rhine nearby, leaving them free for the Germans to take back. His military brainwaves were questionable. At one point, he decided to sail a fleet of ships up Germany's rivers, but disaster struck when a storm broke out, leaving him and his crew washed up in enemy territory all the way across the North Sea, ranging from Germany to Britain.

Despite this, Germanicus was showered with praise and honours because he was able to take credit for sticking it to the Germans. He did also secure two of the three military standards left by three legions who had been slaughtered by the Germans when ambushed in Teutoburg Forest. Varus, the general defeated that day, fell on his sword. That incident left a scar on the Roman psyche, with Suetonius writing that the news so upset the then Emperor Augustus that he could be heard crying out in his house: 'Varus! Varus! Give me back my legions!' Germanicus might have been a better salesman than a general, but at least he brought Rome some closure. Tony Blair must wish he could inspire the same cultish fervour to make up for his controversial military record.

The constant expansion of Roman territory meant that there was a steady stream of new prisoners of war to boost the number of slaves in Italy. By the first century BC, slaves are estimated to have made up as much as 40 per cent of the total population in Italy. They played a variety of roles in Roman society, with the men – especially those able to fight – providing ideal entertainment as gladiators. One of Rome's major problems in having armies of slaves, many of them former soldiers, was that if they wanted to fight back, they could pack a punch. Their uprisings came to be known as the Servile Wars, with the third – and final one – by far the most famous. The Thracian gladiator behind its notoriety has the American film director Stanley Kubrick to thank for making his name part of Hollywood history: Spartacus. Even those who did not watch Kubrick's 1960 blockbuster will know its standout scene, when the slaves are captured by the Romans and defy orders to identify their rebel leader by all standing up and shouting, 'I am Spartacus!'

Their act of defiance is not rewarded with a happy ending in this film, as the Romans go on to promptly crucify every single one of the rebel slaves along the Via Appia between Rome and Capua. The only glimmer of hope Spartacus felt in his dying moments on the cross comes in the knowledge that his son will grow up aware of his father's heroism. All this makes for powerful cinema, with the cry 'I am Spartacus' now fixed in popular culture as a mark of solidarity. But Kubrick's ending for Spartacus is mere movie magic. In reality, he was never captured. By most accounts, the Thracian was killed in battle, although the writer Appian claims that – like an ancient Lord Lucan – his body was never found. However, that would have made for a rather anticlimactic film ending.

I am Spartacus! © EMMA DOUBLE

Spartacus has been immortalised for his struggle against the Romans. However, much less known is the struggle among Rome's aspiring leaders to be the one who could boast that they had stopped him.

Spartacus' revolt began in 73 BC with an estimated seventy slaves, and then snowballed as vast numbers joined in. They repelled a militia that had been sent out from Rome to stop them, and saw off a second force of better-armed legionnaires. Their growing success encouraged more slaves to join up, causing the rebel forces to balloon to around 70,000. After twice failing to crush Spartacus, the Senate knew it could not allow his forces to maraud around Italy for much longer. Who could they ask to face him down? Many contenders chickened out, which forced senators to turn in their hour of need to the plutocrat Marcus Licinius Crassus. It was as unconventional a move as if the US Senate called in Elon Musk to take on the Taliban (although the maverick rocket and submarine enthusiast tech entrepreneur would have undoubtedly given it a crack, if asked). In their defence, Crassus was able to dip into his own finances to equip, train and lead his troops. That is the least one could expect from the richest man in Rome.

There were others who could have taken on the task, but they were too far away to be of immediate help to Rome. Crassus wanted as much support as possible to ensure Spartacus was crushed, so he asked the Senate to call in extra troops from various corners of Europe. But he realised that rival generals risked coming in late and stealing his thunder. As Plutarch writes: 'He made all the haste he could to finish the war before these generals arrived, knowing that the credit for the success would be likely to go not to himself but to the commander who appeared on the scene with reinforcements.'

Crassus had to move quickly. One of those inbound was the general Gnaeus Pompeius Magnus, also known as Pompey the Great. Just the news that Pompey, already a rising star, was on his way back from Spain sparked some worrying chatter for Crassus. As Plutarch reports: 'A number of people were already loudly proclaiming that the victory in this war belonged to him; it only remained for him to come and fight a battle, they said, and the war would be over.'

Crassus' speed paid off, as he eventually faced down Spartacus' forces in southern Italy, on the banks of the modern-day Sele River. The Battle of the Silarius River in 71 BC proved to be a decisive victory for Crassus, with an estimated 36,000 slaves slaughtered on the open battlefield. Six thousand were captured and, in an attempt by Crassus to show how emphatically he had defeated Spartacus, they were crucified along the Appian Way. Anyone who went down it in the aftermath of Crassus' battle, running along the south-east of Italy from Rome to Capua, would not have been able to avoid the line of crucified slaves – as it was 130 miles long. Yet despite his 'excellent generalship', Plutarch reports that it was Pompey who took the glory.

How so? Pompey did not fight alongside Crassus. Instead, he arrived in time to mop up the stragglers. His men seized and swiftly crucified around five thousand as they fled from battle. While he could not claim to have dealt with more rebel slaves than Crassus, he more than made up for it in the speed with which he moved to cast himself in the key role. Pompey wrote a note back to the Senate boasting that while Crassus had defeated the slaves in open war, he himself had finished it off for good. And the Romans, who already had a soft spot for Pompey, lapped up his take on events. They believed it so emphatically that Plutarch records that no one suggested, even as a joke, that anyone else could have crushed Spartacus besides Pompey.

At least Kubrick's film makes sure, in giving Spartacus a glorious finale, to pick the right Roman as his conqueror, casting Laurence Olivier as Crassus, with Pompey not even making an appearance. But in the eyes of the Roman people, Pompey was the one to thank for putting an end to Spartacus' revolt, not Crassus. He already had renown for his military exploits, with his brutal suppression of anti-government rebels in the early first century BC as a young general earning him the gruesome nickname '*adulescentulus carnifex*' – teen-age butcher. With such a reputation to trade on, it was easy for him to steal Crassus' thunder.

Credit matters in politics, as it helps those in power to protect and improve their reputation. President Trump showed his almost para-noiac fear of this in March 2019 when he publicly acknowledged the help of his national security adviser John Bolton in overseeing recent airstrikes on Syria. The President responded to the audience's rau-cous standing ovation for his aide with a mixture of bonhomie and ill-concealed menace. 'I didn't expect that. I'm a little jealous,' he told the crowd. 'Are you giving him all the credit? Uh oh, you know that means the end of his job.'

What about those who haven't ascended so far up the ladder? Aspiring politicos need to be seen as rising stars to accomplish even greater things. How else are leaders meant to tell who are the rising stars they should want to surround themselves with? Bernard Donoughue, who distinguished himself as a chief adviser to Prime Minister Harold Wilson, returned to government two decades later as one of Tony Blair's junior ministers. But it emerged that he very nearly didn't make that comeback, as Blair sheepishly admitted that he had been accidentally put through by the No. 10 switchboard to a similarly named Labourite when he was trying to ring to appoint him. Donoughue recounted it in his diaries as follows: '[Tony] apologised for what he called "my cock-up" – he'd offered my job first to Brian Donohoe. He said he asked for B. Donoughue and forgot about Brian. He clearly doesn't know Labour MPs very well, as Harold Wilson always did.'

If Blair had known his Labourites better, perhaps he would not have mixed his Donohoes up with his Donoughues. Crassus should be lucky that Pompey had not been called something just as similar to provide extra confusion over who really crushed Spartacus. Imagine the mayhem if he had been called something like 'Crasus' or 'Cresus'.

Pompey milked the acclaim for all it was worth, while his plutocrat rival never forgave him for stealing his thunder. Crassus learned a lesson that all politicians should remember. If only Nick Clegg had learned from the likes of Pompey, his time in coalition with the Tories could have been less painful. As Deputy Prime Minister, he was quickly seen as a passenger in the government, rather than someone actively driving for what he and his fellow Liberal Democrats wanted. He was banned from making any official announcements or addressing the press from outside the front door of No. 10, an iconic symbol of government authority as the Prime Minister's residence, as the Tories feared it would bestow far too much credibility on him. Once out of office, he admitted that his coalition partners had been 'bloody right to do so', as he acknowledged ruefully that they 'realised much more than I did that the trappings and physical orchestration of power is immensely important'. The result was that Clegg may have been in office, but he was not able to show that he was in power. And he struggled to show his Lib Dem supporters that he was delivering enough for them to justify compromising on their principles to take office.

Credit is crucial in politics, as Pompey found to his success and Clegg to his cost. The Lib Dem may well have been one of those who scoffed at MPs waving bumf at voters about all they have been up to – with images to prove the claims – but his comparative political modesty has left him with little to laugh about now.

If you do something good in politics and someone steals your thunder, did it really matter? Certainly not to the public, who already know who to praise – even if it isn't the person who deserves it.

But all that glitters is not gold
Credit may be like oxygen for ambitious politicians, something they need in order to thrive. But that does not mean they need to act like magpies, taking every shiny bit of credit they possibly can. Before Tony Blair swept to power in May 1997, the then Conservative Deputy Prime Minister Michael Heseltine pleaded with him to back

the special project that had already been decided upon to mark the new millennium by building an enormous dome. Blair was at first reluctant, then gave in and agreed to take it on once in office.

Why did he go for it? Blair must have thought that such a massive structure would act as a fitting tribute to the significance of his premiership. That thinking is understandable given that Roman leaders could not resist showing off by having something big built. Plenty of triumphal arches and columns dedicated to various emperors can still be found in Rome today, and across the expanse of where its Empire used to be. The largest amphitheatre ever built was overseen by three emperors, Vespasian, Titus and Domitian, who were all part of the Flavian family. They made sure the Roman people were in no doubt who to thank for the entertainment their masterpiece would end up hosting, as it was known officially as the 'Flavian Amphitheatre' (*Amphitheatrum Flavium*). We now know it as the Colosseum, a name that derived from the colossal statue, constantly remodelled to depict whichever emperor was in charge, that stood nearby. Buildings were a big part of a political PR programme, as Donald Trump recognises. The man who was notorious as a property developer for slapping his surname on anything he built reportedly quipped as President in April 2018: 'You've got to put your name on stuff or no one remembers you.'

However, any dream Blair had of him being for ever remembered for 'Tony's Dome' were swiftly dashed after it was opened. Despite the initial fanfare, his government had to sink many hundreds of millions of pounds into a project that was widely panned and written off as a white elephant. Their funds went into its construction, maintenance and then eventual sale. One can only imagine how dearly Blair must regret listening to his Tory predecessors, given that the hot potato they left him to handle brought him little credit, and a lot of flak instead.

MAKE THE SYSTEM WORK FOR YOU

Rules are meant to be followed, but politicians can't help bending them at their convenience. As Speaker of the House of Commons, John Bercow has had to uphold parliamentary procedures as MPs grappled with Brexit. But he has shown a merrily independent approach to deciding how closely it needs to be followed.

On 9 January 2019, Speaker Bercow astonished the government by allowing MPs to debate something unhelpful to Theresa May, which he justified by declaring that 'if we only went by precedent, manifestly nothing would ever change'. Around two months later, he manifestly changed his attitude by drawing on a parliamentary convention 'of long standing, dating back to 2 April 1604' to stop the Prime Minister from putting her Brexit deal to Parliament again unless it changed in substance.

His edict provoked bemusement elsewhere in Europe, with the former Belgian Prime Minister Herman Van Rompuy musing that 'in every normal country, Theresa May would have already resigned a long time ago'. Yet Monsieur Van Rompuy's own career had been littered with instances of dirty procedural tricks to pursue his own aims. Six months before assuming office in 2008, he exploited his position as Speaker of the Belgian Parliament to stop a politically awkward debate, ensuring that parliamentarians would not be able to get into their own Parliament by having the locks on the chamber's doors changed, leaving the opposition politicians raging about his 'coup d'état'.

His other schemes were no less daring. As Belgium's speaker, a role which meant he decided what politicians would discuss, Monsieur Van Rompuy did not turn up to his office for a week to avoid opening a letter from Members of Parliament demanding a debate he did not like. This behaviour is to be expected from the man who, as part chairman, was involved in a plot to suspend the King of Belgium for a day to ensure a Bill on abortion could be passed that the monarch personally refused to sign. This was, he insisted, 'an exceptional solution to an exceptional situation', the second time since World War II that a Belgian monarch was removed (albeit temporarily) as head of state.

The Romans were not afraid to pursue their own exceptional solutions to political problems. In 59 BC, Julius Caesar – then a consul – was trying to pass into law a controversial Bill. He was prevented from doing it in the Senate because Cato the Younger led his fellow senators in a walkout to prevent it being heard. So Caesar took his legislation to another assembly that could approve it, but found his fellow consul Marcus Calpurnius Bibulus was determined to frustrate his efforts.

Bibulus sought to block Caesar's Bill by demanding that the vote be suspended for religious reasons. He claimed to have been consulting the heavens and feared that the omens were not favourable. But

Caesar ignored him, in part as he happened to be Rome's chief priest as well, so felt he had the religious authority to shrug off his rival's gloom. That drove Bibulus to sharpen his opposition by stepping up to publicly denounce the Bill, but he was cut short by Caesar's supporters pouring excrement on him. As he got over his humiliation, the assembly went on to pass the Bill.

Refusing to accept defeat, Bibulus tried to persuade the Senate to annul the law but was ignored. So Bibulus stayed at home, in part to avoid further points of ordure, claiming he was watching for any further bad omens. That move ground the year's legislation to a halt, to the fury of Caesar's supporters, who blamed it on Bibulus for manipulating religious rites to scare a superstitious Senate. Bibulus dogged Caesar over the following months, trying to block Caesar from being appointed governor of Gaul by declaring that no public business could happen as he continued to watch the heavens for ill omens. But he was overruled. Ironically for the procedural saboteur, when he later tried to defend his actions as consul, he was forced to shut up by a tribune, who used his veto to prevent him from saying anything further.

Theresa May was lucky that Speaker Bercow only went back as far as the seventeenth century to make life awkward for her. Although after his various interventions she would have undoubtedly wished that he suffered a similar comeuppance to the consul Bibulus: whether it was by being showered with faeces or just being prevented from speaking any more. Knowing how to work the system is crucial for a politician not just to accomplish their agenda, but also to advance themselves up the ladder.

Only the remarkable can rewrite the rules

Aspiring politicians know they cannot usually expect to be able to vault into the highest of offices in one leap. That is why the ascents to power of people like Tony Blair and David Cameron were so re-markable, as each man managed after entering Parliament to become Prime Minister without having to spend years working their way up the ministerial ranks beforehand. An ambitious politician would be typically expected to serve their time working as a ministerial aide in the hope they might get their break as a junior minister. Then, if they are lucky enough to be seen as a promising talent, they could be rewarded with an elevation to Cabinet, with any major office of state guaranteeing that they would be viewed as a future potential Prime Minister in their own right.

But Blair and Cameron avoided that career route, instead man-aging to take over their parties in opposition and lead them into government. The age both men managed to pull that off made their ascent all the more remarkable, with Blair setting a new record by becoming Prime Minister in 1997 at the age of forty-three, only to have it beaten by Cameron in 2010 when he took office as a slightly younger 43-year-old premier. Breathless comparisons were made about how Britain had not had so young a Prime Minister for nearly two centuries, when Lord Liverpool took office in 1812, the day after his forty-second birthday. The fact both men replaced much older men as they swept to office made their youth even more noteworthy.

Despite the excitement these 43-year-olds caused by taking power at such a tender age, Ancient Romans would not have treated them like the modern wunderkinds they seem to be now, as they expected men of that age to be aiming for one of the highest offices they had: the consulship. They would have been more bowled over by their lack of previous experience in office, as Roman politicians normally needed it on their way to the top. That was the essence of their so-called '*cursus honorum*', which set out the official order of public offices people were expected to work their way through.

After spending a few years in the military, a politically ambitious Roman was meant to start at the bottom of the ladder as a lowly quaestor. Then they could move on to greater offices, striving to be elected as an aedile, a praetor and a consul. Each post came with more power, such as the right to command soldiers, and a growing entourage to match their level of influence as they went about their business. On entering Rome's political big leagues, they could expect to rule over part of the Empire as a provincial governor. If they had distinguished themselves, they could aspire for the final step on the '*cursus honorum*' by being elected to uphold public standards as censor. In the days of the Roman Republic, a senior statesman could expect in an emergency to be given supreme power as a dictator. Later on, the emperor took that on full time.

What was there to stop Roman candidates aiming much higher in the hope of skipping the junior jobs? Official age requirements were put in place to ensure that an ambitious politician knew where they should be focusing on their climb up the political ladder. Quaestors needed to be at least thirty years old, while aediles had to be at least thirty-six, praetors at least thirty-nine and consuls forty-two. Anyone who achieved office at the youngest possible age allowed earned bragging rights, as they could claim to have done it in his 'own year' (*suo anno*).

Such a pipeline meant that those who wanted more power, prominence and the entourage of flunkies that came with higher office had to bide their time. Some rulers sought to exploit these rules to stop challengers rising up too fast. During the first century BC, a turbulent time in Rome, Lucius Cornelius Sulla rose up the ranks to become consul, and then secured dictatorial powers. With such power, he sought to gold-plate the *cursus honorum*, banning people from taking on any senior office such as praetor or consul until they had served in the junior posts. He also forbade any man from serving in the same office for a second time until ten years had elapsed, a perfect amount of time to blunt their political momentum by ensuring any popularity they had been building through achievements in office had waned.

If he hoped that would be enough to stop anyone else getting too big, he was proven sorely wrong. Pompey the Great, fresh from helping Crassus see off Spartacus' slave revolt as one of his military achievements, showed he was unafraid to flout Sulla's rules by standing with the tycoon to be consuls in 70 BC. Their joint candidacy proved to be an electoral juggernaut, bringing together two men with successful military records, Pompey's personal chutzpah and Crassus' money. But Pompey had never stood for any elected office before, and was technically ineligible for the consulship because he was just thirty-five, so he had to be given special dispensation by the Senate. It was painfully obvious from the beginning of his consulship how unfamiliar Pompey was with the system of Roman government.

When he had to chair debates in the Senate, one of his responsibilities as consul was to ask a friend to bail him out by writing a handbook on senatorial procedure.

Being an outsider did not stop Pompey from working with Crassus to tear up Sulla's rules once he got into office, as part of their own reform agenda for the Republic. Pompey turned the system on its head, defying the *cursus honorum* as he blazed his own trail. That is the same spirit leaders like Blair and Cameron have followed in their pursuit of high office. Nigel Farage's success at the helm of a rag-tag outsider UK Independence Party (UKIP) showed that people could still make a historic impact on British politics without even being elected to Parliament. He tried to do that seven times, most recently in the constituency of Thanet South, but his failure to break into the House of Commons did not stop him from harrying party leaders like Cameron and shaping public debate on Europe in his favour.

Many politicians will be impatient to get on, and be straining under the system. They need not worry as their time will come – as long as they are impressive enough to deserve it.

WORK YOUR NETWORK

Politics is a people business at heart. Elections are won by whoever best persuades people to vote for them. They cannot do it all by themselves, so have to work out how to inspire others to go out and campaign for them. This requires politicians to find ways to persuade people that it is in their interests to stick with them.

Roman politics was brazenly transactional. That was the inevitable result of a society where there were lots of voters who needed money, and monied people who wanted votes. They could court supporters by acting as a 'patron', securing their loyalty as 'clients' in exchange for offering protection and regular help. That could come in the form of money, great legal minds could offer free advice, and otherwise patrons could dole out food.

Some modern politicians have tried to offer potential supporters basic incentives like food, but the law ensures such endeavours tend not to end well. In the 2015 UK general election, a parliamentary candidate for the UK Independence Party was questioned by local police after hosting an event in which sausage rolls and sandwiches were given away, as it invited allegations that he had been trying to improperly influence voters by appealing to their gut. Instead of offering tasty treats, candidates have to rely on the successful digestion of their message. Douglas Carswell got the balance right by hosting fish-and-chip suppers in Clacton for voters, where they could pay to tuck into a nice meal and a political discussion with their local MP. This was part of his wider electoral approach that saw him elected to Parliament four times – twice as a Tory and twice under the UKIP banner.

So what did a Roman patron hope to gain by being so generous? In the worst-case scenario, such as if they had to stand trial, they could expect to be accompanied to the courthouse. Such an entourage, dressed in mourning gear and wailing their patron's fate, could persuade a jury to look on them much more sympathetically. After all, if the defendant had so many fans, they hoped the jurors would end up wondering, what could be wrong with them?

At election time, patrons could expect to see their clients marching out to cast their votes in support. It was hard for Roman voters to renege on their promises to back their benefactor, as in the early days they had to announce how they would vote orally to a teller, so it was easy for everyone to see who they were backing. That changed in the second century BC, when a tribune brought into law secret ballots for the election of Roman magistrates. Their introduction in 139 BC caught on, with the rest of Rome's voting systems moving to secret ballots over the following decades. Allowing the electorate to make their decisions in secret made it harder for the rich to buy votes. Romans could be particularly crafty by sucking up to more than one candidate at election time in order to see who could make them the best offer for their support. And candidates could not be entirely sure those who had promised to vote for them would actually do so, just as Tory MPs found in recent leadership elections, as they tried to take advantage of their own secret ballots. So it was just as important in Rome, as it is now, for successful politicians to build extensive support networks they could rely on.

Romans were just as obsessed as modern campaigners with reaching out to as many supporters as possible to try and get them out to vote. Marcus Tullius Cicero, who made his name as a star lawyer, had a lot of advice from his brother on how to successfully get elected as consul. Luckily, Quintus wrote it all down, so we can judge how effective his suggestions were. A key part of the Ciceronian playbook was that Marcus, as the outsider candidate, needed to build up his network so he could call on enough support to help him win. He was urged to 'call in all favours' from those he knew to ensure they came through. 'Make it clear to each one under obligation to you exactly what you expect from him. Remind them all that you have never asked anything of them before, but now is the time to make good on what they owe you,' Quintus suggested. For those who didn't owe his brother anything, he added that they could still be won around with the promise of great rewards if they helped him win. His message should be tailored to whoever he was speaking to, in order – his brother said – to 'show them that the more they work for your election, the closer your bond to them will be'.

The aspiring consul was urged to 'diligently' cosy up to Rome's movers and shakers to ensure they all thought well of him. The envisaged upside was that 'even if they don't actively back you they will confer prestige on you by mere association'. That advice is still followed by campaigners to this day when they rush to sign up celebrity supporters, whether it be those like Hillary Clinton's campaign trumpeting endorsements from megastars like Beyoncé and Lady Gaga, or the so-called People's Vote campaign boasting about how the likes of Delia Smith and Patrick Stewart were funding coaches to ferry supporters to their marches.

The Ciceronian charm offensive did not just target the elite, but anyone else with influence, such as Roman tribal leaders, whose opinion would be looked to by many of their compatriots for an indication on how to vote. 'Do whatever it takes to make them support you sincerely and enthusiastically,' Cicero was told. Politicians still follow that when seeking high office as they try to sign up big names as backers, knowing that their support will encourage others to follow suit. Donald Trump showed that in 2016 by trying to win the votes of Christian Americans by wooing evangelical leaders, which led to ridiculous scenes of him avoiding questions over what part of the Bible he liked best and even signing copies like he had written it himself.

Such brazen electioneering will have weighed on Cicero's mind. His angst was clear when he lamented in a philosophical treatise that 'true friendship is very difficult to find among those who engage in politics and the contest for office'. He had found that to get ahead in politics, you have to make as many people as possible your friend – even if you barely know, or like, them. That is what drives this system of tribal politics, which remains alive and well, as Anthony Scaramucci lamented when recalling the eleven days he served as communications director in the White House under his friend, President Trump: 'The first pill you take is the "anti-friendship" pill. You can be my friend for thirty years, but I'm gonna stab your eyeball out with an ice pick if it gets me more power.'

Politicians are always on the hunt for supporters, especially those who can inspire others in their 'tribe' to join them. They still pursue – just as Cicero was advised – the big names and big hitters. That leaves those with influence and support to offer in a powerful position, which they can exploit to the utmost.

Perhaps the most striking example has been Theresa May's efforts to keep the Democratic Unionist Party on her side. The Northern

Irish party managed to extract £1 billion from her as a price for propping up her government after the 2017 election, and after that made sure to consistently drive as hard a bargain as possible for the votes of its ten MPs. The government narrowly avoided a vote of no confidence in Parliament at the beginning of 2019, seeing it off by a margin of nineteen votes. The DUP's leader in Westminster, Nigel Dodds, wasted no time in reminding May that DUP votes helped to 'make the difference', a subtle warning that their ten MPs could have brought her down if they had turned against her then. May's marriage of convenience with the DUP ended up becoming anything but convenient, despite her government's efforts to appease the Irish Unionists with even more promises.

Cicero was urged to approach his election in a similarly mercenary way. Anyone who might support him was to be seen as a friend, as Quintus put it: 'For a candidate, a friend is anyone who shows you goodwill or seeks out your company.' But, in appropriate advice from his brother, he was urged not to 'neglect' his family as a potential source of support. 'Make sure they are all behind you and want you to succeed', he was urged. Modern politicians know that well, with some having to learn the lesson the hard way. If David Miliband had been able to be sure his brother was behind him and wanted him to succeed in the race for the Labour leadership, he would have easily won. As Labour leader, he could have done what his brother failed to do in 2015 and become Prime Minister. Instead, he was pushed into second place, with defeat paving the way for his eventual exit from British politics altogether.

The soap opera around the Miliband brothers haunted the

winner, Ed, throughout his leadership of the Labour Party. Jacob Rees-Mogg had his own family drama when his sister, Annunziata, decided to stand as a candidate for Nigel Farage's Brexit Party in the 2019 European elections. 'It's odd that we should be in different parties, to some extent uncomfortable for us both,' he admitted on LBC radio about the woman he had once described as his 'Brexit conscience'. Outcomes like that are why politicians take pains to ensure their family members are supporting, rather than opposing, their campaign.

That support can come in the form of having their partner and children pose with them publicly and be seen at their election count. But some politicians go much further to bring their family into the campaign. The Kennedys were the first twentieth-century example of politics being treated like a family business, with Robert managing his brother John F.'s campaign for the Senate and presidency, bank-rolled by their father Joe, United States Ambassador to the United Kingdom under Franklin D. Roosevelt. Boris Johnson and his clan took it to another level, campaigning together in elections and con-stantly fighting each other's corner in public.

When he was elected London Mayor in 2008, Boris Johnson's journalist sister Rachel promised 'many years of Boris-induced sun-shine' for the capital. His father, Stanley, told me in March 2018 that he thought he would be a 'superb' Prime Minister. As the Johnson *paterfamilias*, Stanley took pride in the rise of his son Boris, along-side the political rise of another of his sons, Jo, who entered Down-ing Street in 2013 as David Cameron's policy chief. He wrote in the

Mail on Sunday that the idea of them facing off to be Tory leader and Prime Minister 'would be tremendous fun'.

Donald Trump has had even more fun climbing the political ladder, not least as his wife and children have been on the campaign trail with him too. Testament to his familial approach to politics is the fact that his daughter Ivanka and son-in-law Jared are senior White House aides, and his sons Donald Jr and Eric constantly campaign for him at political rallies and defend him on television and social media.

There are occasions when a politician can find themselves hindered by their nearest and dearest, especially if they are also in elected office. Two Conservative politicians, Andrea Jenkyns and Jack Lopresti, were on different sides of the debate over Theresa May's Brexit deal (against and pro respectively), which was awkward as they happened to be married to each other and have a child together. Tensions reached such a height that one Tory MP told me they found Lopresti – clutching the baby – pleading with government whips for understanding about missing a key vote as he had been unable to arrange childcare.

Rome's patrons and clients unwittingly established the model behaviour for politicians, which they have been following to this day. The same self-interest and back-scratching powers. Aspiring leaders establish themselves as political patrons, grooming lots of new talent for the senior jobs. These rising stars reward their patron with steadfast loyalty, believing that their careers are destined to benefit by sticking with such big fish.

Michael Gove and Boris Johnson's political partnership reached its peak during the 2016 EU referendum, but it had been built many years ago at university. Gove freely admitted to Johnson's biographer Andrew Gimson that he became 'Boris' stooge ... a votary of the Boris cult' after meeting him in the 1980s in the student bar. 'He seemed like a kindly, Oxford character, but he was really there like a great basking shark waiting for freshers to swim towards him,' Gove recalled. Johnson acknowledged the part he played in an essay for a book his sister Rachel edited called *The Oxford Myth*, advising aspiring young politicians to assemble 'a disciplined and deluded collection of stooges' for support. 'The tragedy of the stooge is that ... he wants so much to believe that his relationship with the candidate is special that he shuts out the truth,' he wrote. 'The terrible art of the candidate is to coddle the self-deception of the stooge.'

The people Johnson referred to as 'stooges' were what the Romans classed as 'clients': ambitious strivers looking for a patron to stick with who would most benefit them. Some will be alarmed by Johnson's apparent cynicism, but he is describing how political patronage works with the same candour employed by Cicero's brother, demonstrating how little the system of back-scratching and *realpolitik* has changed. Johnson's political peers would not be so blunt, but have been just as keen to foster their own clients (or, as Johnson calls them, 'stooges') in order to push themselves along. In 2005, Theresa May helped set up a campaign aimed at encouraging more Conservative women into Parliament. Over ten years later, the result was that by the time she was standing to be party leader and

Prime Minister, there were many women who sided with her – not least out of recognition for the work she did to get them into elected office. Similarly, Tim Farron spent so much time as Liberal Democrat chairman campaigning with party members across the country that it was no surprise he swept in as leader in June 2015. It was widely joked at the time that he had shaken the hand of every single Lib Dem in the country.

Others political patrons behave as talent scouts. Tony Blair pushed the likes of David Miliband (whom he once hailed as the 'Wayne Rooney' of his Cabinet) up the ladder, while Gordon Brown worked to install his own supporters. Whenever Blair as Prime Minister conducted a reshuffle, the results would be keenly watched by journalists to see how many of his own allies he had moved up, and how many Brownites had benefited. Whichever faction was growing in number and influence was to the benefit of their political master.

Why did Blair and Brown bother to indulge in such patronage? Partially because it pays to surround yourself with loyalists, but also they would have had an eye on the longer term: managing the line of succession. While they did not have the luxury of being able to simply anoint their heir, like a Roman emperor would by adopting a rising star as their son, they could still try to ensure their favourites were in the best position possible to take over from them when the time came. That was worthwhile in both cases as it allowed the best chance of their agenda being continued long after they depart the stage, as Blair tried to do by lining up David Miliband, only to have to leave his legacy in the hands of Gordon Brown to build on.

George Osborne showed a meticulous grasp of the patronage system in his own political career, filling the Treasury under his watch with ministers who would go on to even greater things in government. Nicky Morgan, Sajid Javid and Andrea Leadsom all started out as junior members of his Treasury team before rising up to become full Cabinet members in their own right. Matt Hancock started out as Osborne's chief of staff before winning a safe parliamentary seat, a series of ministerial jobs and then breaking into the Cabinet. Osborne joked about this in March 2019, revealing in an article for the *Spectator* magazine that he had set up a WhatsApp group around the time Theresa May took over as Prime Minister and demoted his former aide titled 'Make Hancock Great Again': 'Now she depends on him and others she fired or relegated as her last line of defence – an irony not lost on them … Our WhatsApp group has achieved the ambition in its name without even trying.' Hancock tried to pursue further greatness by launching his own bid to be Prime Minister in 2019, only to withdraw and back Boris Johnson. His decision bemused some of his supporters, given the vigorous disagreements they'd had over how to handle Brexit, but he is alleged to have candidly told friends at a drinks reception that he had done so because 'he's going to win and needs good people around him'.

Anyone close to Osborne could expect to be promoted in Cabinet reshuffles, a sign of the sway their patron wielded in David Cameron's administration. His influence, represented by how widely his wards were scattered across government, led to him being called the 'Octopus Chancellor', as he had tentacles firmly embedded in every department.

People have few natural friends in politics. When reading any story about a British politician that quotes an unnamed 'friend' of theirs saying something highly relevant, journalists know that it is actually, more often than not, themselves holding forth, or an adviser paid to speak on their behalf. But if politicians cultivate their colleagues, they won't need to be so desperate that they have to talk themselves up, as their allies will be happy to do it for them.

Building a political support network can pay off handsomely later on. Theresa May first broke into politics as a local councillor in the London borough of Merton. She became friends with a fellow Conservative councillor called Chris Grayling, and the pair stuck together over the years that followed as they entered Parliament and government. In 2016, Grayling managed May's ultimately successful campaign to be Conservative Party leader and Prime Minister. He was rewarded with a job in her Cabinet as Transport Secretary, paying her back by becoming one of her most loyal defenders during the Brexit negotiations. His loyalty was worthwhile, as she refused to sack him despite all the controversies that broke out under his watch. And there were a good few, such as the chaotic introduction of new railway timetables, shelving plans to regulate drones just before they brought Gatwick Airport to a standstill, giving a £14 million contract to a ferry firm that did not own any ferries as part of his preparations for a no-deal Brexit, only then to have to pull the plug on it, and even being caught on camera hitting a cyclist when opening his ministerial car door without looking – and rushing to blame that on the cyclist for going too fast. Despite all this, May stuck by the man widely mocked as 'failing Grayling'. Grayling was out of the door once May's successor took over, a clear sign that their friendship helped keep him in post so long.

Osborne had reason to be thankful for his own networking when in 2008 he faced calls to be sacked as shadow Chancellor over allegations he had been trying to solicit money from a Russian oligarch during a yacht party in Corfu. The 'Deripaska affair' left his political future hanging by a thread, but he was saved by his party leader. If he had not been a close friend of David Cameron, his career could have been over before he had even been able to enter government.

Perhaps William Hague had this in mind when he paid tribute to then Chancellor Osborne at his fortieth birthday party by revealing what he saw as his four rules of politics. The first rule was to work out who the next Tory leader was going to be and to 'stick to them like glue'. Rule two? See rule one. The third one was 'don't fuck it up', while the fourth rule was, again, to not forget the first rule. As much as Hague was joking in his tribute, Osborne showed how much his gags had the ring of truth. In the 2019 Tory leadership contest, the former Chancellor decided to throw the *Evening Standard* – the newspaper he edited – behind Boris Johnson. Despite previously criticising him regularly in the pages of his newspaper, the outlet concluded archly that 'opportunism knocks'.

His near-death political experience over the Deripaska affair shows the danger that money, and those who have it, poses in politics. Politicians are drawn to riches like moths to a flame. These days that is because they are constantly on the lookout for ways to raise funds for their party, or for their own personal political operation.

It gives donors a considerable say on how those they support should behave. One of the clearest signs that May's leadership was on borrowed time at the start of 2019 was the news that many donors had refused to spend more money until she was gone. The idea that donors were able to choke off a politician's time in office by starving them of cash might rankle, but in the Roman times the rich were much more flagrant with their interventions. Bribes were notorious, and there were no enforceable limits on campaign spending. There had been so much money thrown at candidates at election time by the rich, Cicero claimed that the interest rate in Rome temporarily doubled. Such behaviour went on unashamedly, despite the legal penalty for '*ambitus*' being ten years' exile.

Politics has long been transactional, with people choosing to stick with those who could – or do – benefit them. That principle applies as much to voters as it does to fellow politicians. Those who remember that and approach politics in such business-like terms tend to thrive. After all, that's how the host of *The Apprentice* with an autobiography entitled *The Art of the Deal* became President of the United States.

STAY CLOSE TO SUCCESS

Success acts like a magnet in politics, which means anyone who might be going places finds they naturally attract supporters. Those supporters do not just include voters keen to back them at the ballot box, but other aspiring politicos looking to be on the winning team.

If a candidate, or campaign, looks dynamic and popular enough, their popularity can end up snowballing. That is why ambitious campaigners try to get there as fast as possible by talking up how many people they can draw to support them.

Donald Trump can't resist boasting – and often exaggerating – the size of the crowds at his rallies, with that habit most notoriously apparent when his administration went out of its way to claim that his inauguration as President attracted the biggest audience in history – even though photos suggested the turnout paled in comparison to the numbers that came to watch Barack Obama being sworn in. Campaigners for another referendum on Brexit have drawn plenty of people out on marches, boasting that more than 700,000 people came out in October 2018 and around a million did in March 2019. But academic estimates later emerged that suggested the actual turnout had been as much as three times smaller than had initially been made out.

This temptation to rhetorically highball crowd sizes and popularity is irresistible, given that the aura of popularity makes it even easier to persuade wavering people. The Romans knew how important it was for an ambitious politician to be seen drawing crowds, with Quintus Cicero advising his brother: 'Voters will judge you on what sort of crowd you draw both in quality and numbers.' That maxim even applies on a smaller scale, such as in manoeuvring ahead of a contest for the leadership of a major political party.

A few weeks before the British people voted in the 2016 referendum on the United Kingdom's membership of the European Union,

I sat down with an ambitious Conservative politician to talk about how he thought things would pan out after the referendum result. He had already concluded that the Remain campaign had victory in the bag, not unreasonably given the overwhelming indication from the polling that had been carried out.

That meant George Osborne, David Cameron's friend and close ally as Chancellor in his government, was effectively next in line to be Prime Minister. Such a result would have been ideal in the eyes of the backbencher I was speaking to, as he had spent the past few months cosying up to Osborne. 'I've backed the winning horse,' he told me chirpily at the time, 'so I'm feeling optimistic about my prospects.'

Like many in Westminster, he was blindsided by the actual referendum result. Remain's defeat boded ill for Osborne's future, given that he had staked his political and economic credibility on it. The ambitious MP tried to put on a brave face about the result when I caught up with him during the fallout, but even he could not deny that his preferred candidate had been damaged: 'He does need a repair job.' Osborne faced up to reality within days, announcing he would not throw his hat into the ring to succeed Cameron. He was sacked soon after by the person who did become Prime Minister, Theresa May, while the MP who had bet his political future on Osborne is still languishing on the back benches. And he is far from alone as a politician who bet his fortunes on someone he thought would be the winning horse, only for that gamble to backfire.

As much as politicians might claim to fight for their principles, they can be more than ready to put them aside if it might benefit their career. Soon after Jeremy Corbyn was elected Labour leader in 2015, a rising star in the party wailed to me about the 'joke of a leader' that the membership had picked. That Labour politician has since become a stalwart member of Corbyn's frontbench, clearly realising that swallowing her pride was the only way to get ahead given that he was not going to depart anytime soon. Meanwhile, Sajid Javid, an Osborne protégé, joined his mentor in backing Remain during the referendum. But the then Business Secretary could have easily backed Brexit, as he acknowledged during the campaign when he insisted that he only advocated Remain with a 'heavy heart and no enthusiasm'. 'I am still a Brussels basher and will remain so,' he added. Javid's motives were regarded widely with suspicion. Iain Duncan Smith, a Conservative politician who was so happy to bash Brussels that he wanted the UK to leave, claimed that he had been reassured by Javid that he felt the same way. 'I'm deeply disappointed in him,' he told BBC Radio 4's *Today* programme, in a claim that Javid's team rushed to insist was not true. Other Eurosceptics began to refer to him as 'Slippery Saj'.

Some ministers serving in Cabinet believed that Javid's Eurosceptic flirtation was a ploy that would mean he could serve as the perfect deputy in a future Osborne leadership. James Kirkup explained why ministers suspected this in the *Telegraph*, explaining that 'the Osborne–Javid ticket would thus become a symbol of Tory reunification and harmony after the referendum, able to speak for both Remain and Leave supporters'. But Javid was left exposed by backing the losing side, although he tried to cover himself by carrying himself as a 'reluctant Remainer'. Since then, he has been trying to repair relations with Brexiteers by acting as a staunchly Eurosceptic voice in Cabinet.

Jacob Rees-Mogg backed the winning Brexit side during the referendum. But he did not have the same luck finding the right person to support as the UK's next Prime Minister. He supported Boris Johnson at first, moved on to Michael Gove and then Andrea Leadsom, backing the eventual winner, Theresa May, when she was the only one left in the race. The fact she backed Remain, albeit with the same reluctance as Javid did, was undoubtedly the key reason Rees-Mogg supported everyone else he could besides her.

When Rees-Mogg appeared on the BBC comedy show *Have I Got News for You* shortly afterwards, he tried to laugh off the jibes over his run of backing losers. 'My predictions during the Conservative leadership campaign were not always correct,' he deadpanned. The Conservative backbencher went on to claim he was 'absolutely' a fan of May, explaining that 'there is greater zeal in a convert than there is in somebody who starts off down the road'. The problem for Rees-Mogg with his belated support was that when May came to draw up her government, he was swiftly overlooked for any major jobs. If he had thrown his weight behind her from the beginning, she would have looked much more kindly on him. Instead, the only hope he had of entering government was if he had been happy to take on a junior job, which left him cold judging by his public dismissal of serving as a mere 'minister for paperclips'. He did not join the government until May's successor, Boris Johnson, invited him to be the man steering his government's agenda through Parliament. That gave him the job titles of Leader of the House of Commons and Lord President of the Council, evidently much more serious than whatever he had been offered by May. 'The Prime Minister kindly offered me a very interesting job to do,' he trilled in an explanation as to why he had accepted.

Liam Fox, however, was a Brexiteer who benefited by backing the winning candidate early on. He entered the Tory leadership race in his own right, but swiftly backed May after he was knocked out in the first round of voting. His decision to throw his weight behind her was not a surprise to those who knew how close they were. Just days before, May and Fox had been spotted having lunch in an up-market Italian restaurant around Westminster. But some Brexiteer MPs were astonished, because they had been promised by him that he would only support a Brexit-backing politician in the race. 'I've never forgiven him for that,' one veteran Tory Eurosceptic MP told me. Fox was rewarded by May for getting behind her early with a plum job in her government soon after she won the leadership and took power, jetting off around the world as her International Trade Secretary.

The Brexit deal May ended up negotiating was rejected the first time she presented it to Parliament for its approval on 15 January 2019 by a historically huge majority. The day after, Labour MP Clive Lewis did not hold back in how he described that defeat in the House of Commons: 'Yesterday's vote was not just a defeat but a complete and utter rout. Some members have talked about historical parallels but, if yesterday's vote had been a battle, it would compare with the battle of Cannae, in which Hannibal annihilated the Roman army.'

The Romans may have lost the battle, but they ended up winning the war. What helped them clinch victory in the end? People sensing which way the wind was blowing and defecting from the Carthaginian side. Their general Hannibal enjoyed great success in his battles against the Romans in Italy, such as at Cannae in 216 BC, thanks to his use of light cavalry from the North African kingdom of Numidia. They supported them in battle for years, until the Carthaginians suffered a setback in 206 BC at Ilipa (near modern Seville). That marked a turning point for the Numidians, who decided to pull their support and fight alongside the Romans. They picked the right time to defect, as four years later Hannibal was crushed in a battle near Zama, in modern-day Tunisia. Their commander Masinissa was allowed to command the combined Roman and Numidian cavalry. Their cavalry vastly outnumbered the numbers on the Carthaginian side, so the Numidian support proved decisive. Their forces helped the Romans win the Second Punic War. In thanks, the Romans let the Numidians thrive, with Masinissa becoming the first king of Numidia, showing how much it can pay off to be on the winning side.

By contrast, the Carthaginians were humiliated in defeat, with Rome forcing them to pay a vast quantity of silver, to limit their navy to just a tiny force of ten ships – just enough to fend off pirates – and being banned from raising an army without Roman permission. Carthage had become a vassal state, which is why Boris Johnson sought to evoke its plight in one of his many colourful ways of criticising the Brexit deal Theresa May had agreed. 'They think that in the end we will sign up to these Carthaginian terms,' he huffed in the pages of the *Telegraph* on 10 March 2019. Later that month, a Conservative member of the House of Lords tried to offer him some historic consolation. Viscount Ridley told peers on 27 March: 'After the second Punic War, which imposed the Carthaginian peace that Mr Boris Johnson likes to talk about, there was a third Punic war. That did not end well either, but perhaps this one will end better – for the Carthaginians, that is.'

Viscount Ridley was right to hope for a better ending for the British than what the Carthaginians suffered, as the aftermath of the second Punic War left them unable to defend themselves from the Numidians, Rome's allies in the area. When they raised an army to defend themselves from their neighbours' raids, Rome swiftly moved in to destroy Carthage, annexing its lands as a result of the third – and final – Punic War.

The Numidians were not the only ones to show a skill for finding the winning team to support, which in their case was the Romans. The Romans knew how shamelessly careerists worked to side with anyone successful, and, as the historian Plutarch noted, this tended to be what military commanders found when they defied their doubters: 'The very strategy, which before the battle had been condemned as passive and cowardly, now came to be regarded as the product of a superhuman power of reasoning, or rather of a divine, almost miraculous intelligence.'

Despite his cynicism, ambitious Romans were just as shameless in politics as they sought to remain close to power. The veteran politician Lucius Vitellius, who served as consul three times, stayed at the top tier of politics under three different emperors. He survived that long by going out of his way to suck up to anyone in power. When it was Caligula, he marked himself out as the first person to treat him like a living god, putting on a great show of daring to approach him with a veil over his head and throwing himself to the floor in reverence. When Claudius was in charge, Vitellius exploited the fact that the emperor was known to be someone who took the opinion of his wife seriously by subjecting her to a special charm offensive. The historian Suetonius records how far he went in his crawling: 'He begged of Messalina as the highest possible favour that she would allow him to take off her shoes; and when he had taken off her right slipper, he constantly carried it about between his toga and his tunic, and sometimes kissed it.'

Such sycophancy was later exposed as a sham when Messalina fell out of public favour and he suddenly had no time to fuss about with her shoes. His greasy self-promotion kept him in the upper echelon of Roman politics for many years, and he was recognised at his funeral for being 'steadfast in loyalty to the emperor'. His efforts to keep the Vitellius clan close to power paid off when his son, Aulus, became emperor in 69 AD (even if it was just for a few months).

The Romans got the art of self-aggrandisement down to a tee, even practising it in their love lives. The poet Ovid advised Roman men that, if they saw the target of their affections at the races, they should find out which competitor they were backing, and 'whoever she favours, you should follow suit'. Getting in with the right person could deliver life-changing results in Roman society. A slave would normally be treated as the lowest of the low, effectively denied basic human rights by being treated as an object in law. But if owned by the emperor, they could rise to the highest levels of the Imperial civil service. As part of his staff, they read the documents he had to deal with, and advised – and undoubtedly had a hand in drafting – the responses he made as a judge of petitions and disputes throughout the Empire. They would have been handling so much correspondence that the emperor would have likely done little more than skim through each item before giving it his seal of approval. They were as useful to the emperor as the officials in Downing Street handling the Prime Minister's reams of correspondence. That proximity to power gave them influence, which was so great that even senators would defer to them. That led freeborn Romans to conclude that they were missing out by staying away from the civil service, having previously believed that doing so would mean they were no better than slaves.

Those with ambition are drawn towards successful people, believing that they'll bring more success for them too. That's why politicians end up putting aside ideology to back people they might not necessarily agree with. If they sided with someone they agreed with, they might remain ideologically pure. But how would they get anywhere near power just by cosying up to the also-rans? That is why when politicians come a cropper, they quickly find out who their real friends are, as their fair-weather allies tend to desert in search of better political prospects. To get ahead, politicians end up having to look for winners so they can share in their glory.

SPEAK FROM THE HEART,
NOT THE TELEPROMPTER

Politicians need to express themselves in public as part of their job. If they cannot put their point across smoothly, they can expect to struggle. That means politicians pull out all the stops to make sure they can seem like confident performers. Some just practise endlessly, others hire coaches. Those that aren't natural wits who can think on their feet tend to resort to planning in advance what they're going to say.

A few proudly insist on writing their own speeches. Many realise that they will need talented writers to supply them with the right words for the moment, giving rise to the speechwriting profession. They now play an integral role, with most top-level politicians tending to read their speeches off a lectern in front of them, or on autocues – positioned just out of shot of the TV camera – so they can seem to viewers like they're speaking off the cuff.

The Romans prized leaders who could speak confidently without having to resort to reams of notes, declaiming speeches off the cuff by way of *ars memoria*, an ingenious mnemotechnic advocated by Cicero and Quintilian. Neither would they have been impressed by the Members of Parliament seen often in the House of Commons reading short two-minute speeches off sheaves of paper, using notes even to make sure they are asking the right question of a minister. Skilled orators could speak without any assistance for hours if needed. Tacitus encapsulates that attitude in summarising why Nero's speaking style stuck out among Rome's recent emperors:

Older men, who spent their leisure in making comparisons with the past, noted that Nero was the first ruler to need borrowed eloquence. The dictator Julius Caesar had rivalled the greatest orators. Augustus spoke with imperial fluency and spontaneity. Tiberius was a master at weighing out his words – he could express his thoughts forcibly, or he could be deliberately obscure. Even [Caligula's] mental disorders had not weakened his vigorous speech; Claudius' oratory, too, was graceful enough, provided it was prepared.

Nero's problem, as the historian saw it, was that he had devoted himself – despite his 'lively' mind – to practising many activities, none of which were public speaking. That is not because he was afraid of the training it required, as he put himself through all sorts of bizarre processes in the hope of being a better singer. He would lie on his back with light weights on his chest to strengthen his breathing, and according to Suetonius, refrain from eating fruits such as apples, as it was believed that they harmed the vocal chords.

Such experiences could have served him well if he had wanted to be an impressive speaker. Perhaps he was put off by what famous orators put themselves through. The Greek orator Demosthenes was known to have filled his mouth with pebbles and recited verses to strengthen his tongue, supposedly breaking his stutter through exercises like this. Another Greek, Molon of Rhodes, taught Cicero and Julius Caesar the art of public speaking. Students could expect to go through a number of exercises to strengthen their voices, modelled on Demosthenes, such as having to shout against the crashing of the ocean waves.

Perhaps the strangest exercise a modern politician has put themselves through in order to speak well on stage is to drink a lot of water before going on stage, in the belief that speaking with a full bladder would give them the required urgency as they spoke. Its pioneer, the politician Enoch Powell, explained in a 1968 documentary why he followed that technique: 'You should do nothing to decrease the tension before making a big speech. If anything, you should seek to increase it.'

One man who watched that documentary was David Cameron, who went on to become leader of the Conservative Party. Two years into the job, in 2007, he delivered a fluid one-hour-long speech without any notes or teleprompter to help him, and just a full bladder to ensure he hurried up. The passion he put into that speech helped safeguard his leadership by scaring the then Prime Minister Gordon Brown off from calling a snap election. He repeated his trick a few years later as Prime Minister in his own right, using it in 2011 during tense negotiations with the European Union. Over the nine hours of formalities and diplomatic horse-trading, he ensured – as a member of his team later put it – that he remained 'desperate for a pee'. He decided that night to veto a controversial increase to the EU budget, which might have been motivated by a desire to bring talks to a close so he could relieve himself.

Politicians go to great lengths to perform well in public. Sajid Javid acknowledged his struggle to be a fluent orator. 'I don't have the oratory of Cicero,' he admitted to the BBC on 18 June 2019, adding self-deprecatingly that his rhetoric was 'less Homer's *Iliad*, more Homer Simpson'. The key identified by Roman orators was to know your subject so well that you can speak knowledgeably and passionately without having to rifle through papers for reference. The arguments they made sought to persuade their audience through interrogation of the issue at hand, rather than merely trite soundbites.

Modern politicians would do well to follow that, instead of robotically reading from a staid script off a teleprompter, or from scribbled notes. The mark of a great speech, as Cameron identified, is to know what you want to say so well that there is no need for this. Sometimes that can backfire, as Ed Miliband found in 2012 when he tried to memorise his own speech but was accused of not caring about the economy because he forgot to mention the deficit. But that is the risk politicians have to take if they want to make a speech their audience will truly remember.

Repeat, repeat, repeat

Only the most arrogant would assume every word they utter will be savoured by their audience and never forgotten. That means politicians can find themselves having to make the same points more than once to hammer their message home. The philosophy behind such repetitiveness was explained by Labour's spin maestro Alastair Campbell, who argued that at the point where an audience is getting sick of hearing a message, it is starting to sink in. But the Romans knew that long before New Labour.

In the second century BC, the Roman senator Cato the Elder found a brutally effective way to remind his fellow Romans that they had still left their rival Carthage standing after the Second Punic War: to constantly mention it. But he did not opt for long-winded explanations, as that would have been a guaranteed way to disengage his audience, so he boiled down his argument into a single sentence: Carthage must be destroyed.

He declared it at the end of every speech, no matter what the topic. The call was short, and could be condensed into three words to get his point across – '*Carthago delenda est*'. Eventually, Rome went to war for a third time and destroyed Carthage once and for all.

That effectiveness inspired one modern Eurosceptic politician to take similar rhetorical action. Daniel Hannan, then a member of the European Parliament, demanded that the European Union's flagship Lisbon Treaty needed to be put to a referendum. In his own Catonian stand, he decided to end his speeches with a similar call – '*Pactio Olisipiensis censenda est*' (the Lisbon treaty must be voted on).

Hannan did not get his wish, as the Lisbon Treaty was signed off in June 2008 without voters in the United Kingdom being asked for their approval. But Hannan could claim to have been vindicated in his Eurosceptic fervour, as eight years later the British people – having not had a say on the latest episode of European integration – voted to leave the EU altogether. Cato had to wait a bit longer than eight years for his wish to be granted, but the result was equally incendiary – Carthage was burned to the ground.

While both men would not claim to have brought about these results by repeating three- or four-word summaries of what they want, their constant rhetorical sloganeering helped reshape the political climate in their favour.

BE READY, AS GREATNESS CAN BE THRUST UPON YOU

As soon as a Roman embarked on their *cursus honorum*, their peers would be watching out for the talented few who showed the drive to be more than a lowly quaestor. And that remains the case for any modern politician working their way up the greasy pole.

It can be a mixed blessing for a politician to have their potential for higher office talked about. On the one hand it is easier to convince people to support someone who is seen as a rising star. After all, why should they invest their political or financial capital in someone who won't get anywhere? But the danger is that some people can shrivel under the spotlight, with their flaws exposed and any slip-ups magnified subject to intense scrutiny. The attention they receive can be a red rag to rivals, driving them to do what they can to thwart their rise.

Consequently, anyone who fancies their chances at greater things tends to do all they can to play down, but never quite dismiss, questions about their ambition. Leadership contenders cannot help but beat around the bush when asked if they might aim for higher office, suggesting they are considering it not out of self-interested ambition but selflessly because of how many people want them to do it. Conservative politician Steve Baker, the self-anointed Brexit hardman, demonstrated that neatly in May 2019, when he suggested that he had to consider standing 'out of respect for colleagues and members of the public' after receiving a level of support he 'could never have foreseen'. He eventually decided to throw his weight behind a bigger Brexiteer figure: Boris Johnson.

Johnson has long been subject to such leadership speculation, so he has become creative in how he handles it. One of his most colourful answers came in 2004 when he compared his chances of becoming Prime Minister to 'the chances of finding Elvis on Mars, or my being reincarnated as an olive'. Nearly a decade later, he compared the leadership jostling to the jostling of a rugby scrum, telling the interviewer Michael Cockerell: 'If the ball came loose from the back of the scrum, which it won't, of course, it would be a great, great thing to have a crack at.'

That same year, Johnson offered a very different, but much more intriguing, response: 'If, like the Roman leader Cincinnatus, I were to be called from my plough to serve in that office I wouldn't, of course, say no.' Some listeners would have been inclined to dismiss that as mere rhetorical fluff, but to do so would be to ignore the significance of Johnson reaching for the life of Lucius Quinctius Cincinnatus to describe his career plans.

Granted, some of those who have dealt with the former Foreign Secretary have come away believing he is a flighty idealist. The Tory politician Rory Stewart, who worked with him at the Foreign Office, told *The Times* in April 2019: 'He's a wonderful lyricist and rhetorician, but I struggled to get him interested in the steps of the journey from A to B. Seriousness … requires moral principles … he reminds me not of a Roman senator, he reminds me more of Catullus.' In other words, Johnson in Stewart's mind was not so much a statesman as a performer who just happened to have a nice turn of phrase.

What Johnson writes can sound as jolly as Catullus' romantic ditties, but even his most controversial output is not as crude as what the poet put his name to. In his most notorious elegy, which wasn't translated fully into English until the twentieth century, Catullus responds to two male critics who think his love poetry makes him 'girly' by telling them he would orally and anally rape them (*pedicabo ego vos et irrumabo*) to prove them wrong. By contrast, the most chest-beating Johnson indulged in came in 2017, when he goaded Labour's election campaign chief Andrew Gwynne into facing him in front of Sky News' camera. 'Come on then, you big girl's blouse!' Johnson teased, throwing his arm around Gwynne once he had approached. The encounter reached its farcical peak when Johnson seemed to stumble, and – with his arm still around his Labour rival – pulled Gwynne down as well.

Away from the rough and tumble of the TV studio, Johnson's decision to cast himself as a new Cincinnatus reveals how he saw himself, and how he saw his rise to the high office panning out.

In the fifth century BC, Rome was in constant peril. Cincinnatus would not have been blind to that. He only became consul in 460 BC because the man who was meant to serve out that year was killed trying to take back control of the Capitoline Hill from a gang of rebellious slaves and outlaws. Cincinnatus stepped up to take on these rebels, and then swiftly retired to his farm once his time in office was over.

Summoned to save Britain: Boris' ideal rise to power © EMMA DOUBLE

But Rome's troubles were far from over. And its next crisis was brewing to the east of the city. The Aequian tribe had signed a peace treaty with the people of Rome in 459 BC, but a year later they rattled on their agreement. Their soldiers marched through the Alban Hills to seize the city of Tusculum, looting and pillaging as they went. The Romans responded by sending out two armies; one to invade Aequian lands while the other set out to rescue the city. But their plan went awry after the army sent to save Tusculum stopped to make camp on its way to the city, and then found they were under siege from the Aequians. The second army was too far away to help, and the Senate would not have known about the dire situation their troops had landed in if five horsemen had not been able to escape and tell them. Meanwhile, another tribe – the Sabines – were making surprise raids on Rome. They were easily rebuffed, but the skirmishes had ruined the crops surrounding the city.

This military misfortune threw Rome into a panic. It was decided unanimously, the historian Livy records, that only one man could restore order: Cincinnatus, the man 'Rome rested all her hope of survival' on. After stepping up to save the city from civil unrest, and having been praised by the Senate for his service, he had retired to work on his little three-acre farm. The group of senators who had gone out to bring him back found him busy at work on the plough. Cincinnatus was surprised, understandably, by their visit. But their response when he asked if everything was OK would have dismissed any doubts that all they wanted was a chitchat. They offered a prayer for divine help as they replied that everything would be fine for both him and the country with him in charge. He did not hesitate to accept their request, calling for his wife to get him his toga. Once he had put it on, they hailed him as dictator. All the power he needed would be in his hands, which were still grimy from his farm work.

Cincinnatus leapt quickly into action. Every man of military age was ordered to gather on the Field of Mars in order to join him in marching to save the trapped Roman army from being besieged by the Aequians. It did not take long for him to triumph. After just fifteen days in command, he disbanded his army, resigned as dictator and went back to his plough. Such a record would have been enough to ensure Cincinnatus would be remembered as a hero. But nearly two decades later, Rome needed him for one last job. In 439 BC, a well-off plebeian called Spurius Maelius had been making waves by deciding – during a severe famine – to buy lots of grain to distribute for free among the poor. That went down a storm among the Roman people, which is what Maelius wanted in order to further his ambitions, as Livy notes:

Such generosity won their hearts, and crowds of them followed him wherever he went, giving him an air of dignity and importance far beyond what was due to a man who held no official position. Their devoted support seemed to promise him the consulship at least, but – so rarely are the fair promises of fortune enough to satisfy the human heart – he was soon nursing a loftier – and a criminal – ambition. Even the consulship he would have had to fight for against the united opposition of the nobility; but it was no longer the consulship he wanted: it was the throne.

The last king of Rome had been overthrown decades before in 509 AD, so it showed how bold Maelius was in hoping to become so popular that he could bring back the monarchy. Reports reached the Senate that he had been building up a cache of weapons in his house, with various suspicious groups – including corn-sellers – seen visiting it. And so senators were both furious, and alarmed, when they met to discuss it. Fierce recriminations flew as politicians bickered over who was to blame for the plot growing this far. Their rows were brought to an end once it was proposed, and decided unanimously, that Cincinnatus would be given all the power he needed to save Rome yet again.

As flattering as it would have been to be so regularly in demand, Cincinnatus had some trepidation, as he was getting on in age. He asked the Senate why it wished, as Livy puts it, 'to expose an old man like him to what must prove the sternest of struggles'. But the senators piled on the flattery, arguing that he had 'more wisdom – yes, and courage too – than in all the rest put together'. That did the trick, as Cincinnatus decided – after praying to the Gods to 'save his old age from bringing loss or dishonour' – to take power once more.

Back in charge, he was just as swift to act as before. Maelius was ordered to appear before him in a court of law. He refused and ran away, trying to fend off Cincinnatus' right-hand man with a knife as he shouted for help. But he was quickly cut down, with the dictator explaining to the Roman people that Maelius deserved his fate for his 'criminal lunacy' in trying to buy himself a kingship. Then, Cincinnatus ordered that Maelius' possessions be sold, with the proceeds going towards the public purse, and that his house be demolished, with the site left empty as a reminder to everyone about the plot that failed. After three weeks as dictator, and with Rome safe yet again, he resigned his post and went back to his farm.

A few years after comparing himself to Cincinnatus, Johnson showed that he had not forgotten the legendary Roman leader. After the EU referendum in 2016, he shocked his supporters by announcing he would not be standing for the Conservative leadership. He knew someone bold was needed to lead Britain into a bright future post-Brexit, but he concluded in dismayed tones that 'having consulted colleagues and in view of the circumstances in Parliament, I have concluded that person cannot be me.'

In a reflective moment on LBC Radio in January 2019, Johnson admitted that he 'regretted' staying out of the race, a move that could have seen him become Prime Minister in 2016. 'In retrospect if I had my time again, I might have done things differently,' he told his interviewer, Nick Ferrari. 'I certainly have engaged with a lot of heart searching about it ever since.'

When asked if he might one day stand for the leadership, Johnson replied coyly that 'the plough, the row I am hoeing now is far more important'. The plough proved to be the safest place for Johnson to be, as he could leave his rivals to exhaust themselves in their efforts to jostle for position. His campaign took off once he entered the race formally on 12 June 2019, with the frontrunner building such a massive lead that the question was not *if* he would win, but by how great a margin. Tory MPs piled in behind him, with even those who were privately sceptical of his abilities putting their doubts aside to back him. This snowballing support culminated with Johnson being crowned on 23 July 2019 as the new Tory leader, almost as if by acclamation.

His in-tray was just as packed as the one Cincinnatus faced. While he did not have to deal with Aequian raiding parties, or a conspiratorial attempt to seize power by manipulating food supplies, the Tories were in just as much turmoil over the threat posed by the Brexit Party and Jeremy Corbyn's Labour hordes. He acknowledged the stakes in his leadership launch, warning: 'Delay means defeat. Delay means Corbyn. Kick the can and we kick the bucket.' After Theresa May's failure to deliver Brexit left the Tories in dire electoral straits, MPs and party members clamoured for Johnson to save them with the same urgency that Roman senators called upon Cincinnatus to take charge.

Both men were seen as the best person in an emergency to bail out their country. Johnson and Cincinnatus can claim a similar political veterancy, with the former having served as Foreign Secretary and Cincinnatus as consul before taking on supreme power. But Johnson can be proud to have not had to wait until his eighties, like Cincinnatus, to achieve it. He has risen to power in the same spirit as his Roman model, prevailed upon by his colleagues to save the country from an urgent crisis. Although his critics can only dream of him following Cincinnatus' example further by bowing out voluntarily after a few weeks.

PART TWO

IN OFFICE

We are not born for ourselves alone; a part of us is claimed by our nation, another part by our friends. (*Non nobis solum nati sumus ortusque nostri partem patria vindicat, partem amici.*)
Marcus Tullius Cicero, *De Officiis*

PERSONALITY CULTS NEED A PERSONALITY

For millennia, personality cults have been the nucleus of political life. The Romans famously made sacrifices for the well-being of their emperor. Medieval kings were at once chieftain, warlord and *paterfamilias*, ruling by divine right. By way of social media hype, today's politicians can attract quasi-religious veneration and even messianic status.

Donald Trump is seen by his supporters as the only man who can 'make America great again'. Meanwhile, the bearded Labour politician Jeremy Corbyn has been compared to another hirsute JC: Jesus Christ himself. Not only do they share the same initials, but they have stirred the same level of devotion from their followers. As the Son of God entered Jerusalem on a donkey, so the allotment-tending leader of the Labour Party pledged to cycle to No. 10 if he became Prime Minister.

Perhaps the first modern British politician to build a personality cult was Alex Salmond. The SNP chief managed to whip up enough popular support to become the most powerful politician in Scotland, becoming its First Minister. In this position of authority, he was able to secure a referendum on Scotland's independence, which he fought in 2014 with verve.

Anyone who argued that the Scottish people would suffer by breaking away from the UK was accused of 'talking down Scotland', with Salmond's supporters eagerly echoing his arguments in person and on social media. Critics of the independence movement, whether they were in politics, media or business, were swamped with abuse by Salmond's supporters. Their fervour led them to demonstrate outside the BBC's Scottish headquarters to demand the sacking of its political editor, Nick Robinson, for what they saw as his biased reporting, as they waved banners with his face on to prove their point. Salmond was accused of tacitly encouraging their fanaticism because of how little he would do to condemn or restrain their actions. He was not immune from indulging the personality cult himself, hosting press conferences where supporters would sit alongside the journalists, eagerly clapping his answers and booing any hostile enquiries their leader received.

Rival Scottish politicians were left exasperated by what was going on. 'It reminds you of the Moonies, or some of the crazy American sects,' then UKIP MEP David Coburn told me. 'They take all their candidates and all the people that speak for them, put them in the cellar, thrash them with rubber hoses in stress positions until they trot out the same story. Nobody says anything wrong!'

Such fervour arose south of the border when Jeremy Corbyn took over as leader of the Labour Party. His supporters would be just as protective of him as the Scottish Nationalists were of Salmond. They developed their own lexicon, with Corbyn critics referred to as 'melts' or 'slugs' while their man was lauded as 'the absolute boy'. Or they would more typically call him by his first name, 'Jeremy', or 'Jez' – as if he was a personal friend to them all. Whenever he spoke at rallies, they would be rapturously received, with every point he made – no matter how mundane – applauded. They would wave signs with his face on them, and chant his name to the tune of the White Stripes' 'Seven Nation Army', which resulted in the Labour leader being greeted on stage at the Glastonbury Festival to chants of 'Oh Je-re-myyy Corrrr-byn' from the crowd. So many instances have arisen where Corbyn fans have shown slavish devotion to their leader, prompting critics to round them up on Twitter under the cutting label '#notacult'.

For example, in early 2019, amid rumblings of a party split, Labour frontbenchers were asked to publicly swear their loyalty to 'a Labour-led government under whatever leadership the members elect'. There was no shortage of critics to such initiatives. 'I joined the Labour Party,' one MP, Mike Gapes, complained. 'I did not sign up to … a Stalinist cult.' He was one of seven parliamentarians to resign, after decades as a party member, in February 2019. Many other MPs and party members who followed him out the door made similar complaints about Labour's cultishness.

Corbyn's Conservative opponent, Theresa May, had a go at building a cult of her own when they competed in the 2017 general election. She campaigned in front of massive posters with her name on them. Her party's candidates all had to boast in their election literature of how they were 'standing with Theresa May', which would feature pictures of them quite literally standing with their dear leader. The trouble was, as one Conservative MP later put it to me, 'you can't build a personality cult if you don't have a personality'.

The Romans took cultish politics to a new level, as any good ruler could expect to be eventually worshipped as a god, with followers sacrificing bulls, or offering up wine and incense in their honour. That was partly a consequence of the might of the imperial propaganda machine, which would help shape an ideal image of the emperor for people to revere. A lot of work went into ensuring consistency, with the imperial bust decided centrally in Rome so that copies would look the same across the Empire. The emperor's head would be embossed on rings and stamped on coins. Alongside the imperial visage, these coins were used to broadcast whatever the emperor wanted to tell the people as a mantra. This reached a propaganda peak in 69 AD – the Year of the Four Emperors – when each man on the throne took their chance to hammer their key message on a fresh load of coins. For example, Galba declared himself 'saviour of the citizens', while Vespasian – the last of emperors that year – preferred to declare on his coins that *'Roma resurgens, libertas restituta'* (Rome rises up again, with freedom restored), which is reminiscent of President Trump's re-election slogan 'Make America Great Again'. The emperor's face even turned up on dining room silverware, pastry moulds and sacrificial cakes, as archaeologists have found. It became the mark of a fashionable Roman family dining room to have a marble portrait bust of the emperor pride of place.

The speed and rigour with which the Roman world was flooded with the emperor's image is best matched by Americans today. Once a president takes office, they have an official portrait painted, which is then hung in airports, libraries and other public buildings across the country while they are in power. Their image may not be shared in as wide a variety of official ways as a Roman emperor would expect, but others will do the job for them as they become one of the most famous people in the world. Trump's supporters marked his inauguration by mocking up their own memorabilia, issuing commemorative coins with his face on them in the same imperial fashion.

In order to assert his importance over Rome, Augustus seized on symbols that would tie him into the nation's story. He lived in the same small house on the Palatine Hill for forty years, right next to an old hut which was said to be the very home Romulus – the city's founder – had lived in. If President Trump wanted to emulate that, the quickest way he could do so would be to move from the White House to set up camp just outside the log cabin Abraham Lincoln was born in.

Still, America's Presidents learned a lot from Roman emperors. The imperial image, just like an American presidential portrait, would tend to be a purposely flattering image. Augustus always looked around nineteen years old whenever he was depicted officially, an extraordinary look for someone who lived to be as old as seventy-six. Statues of the emperors would cast them as much larger than how they looked in real life, providing onlookers with a taste of the awe they were meant to feel in their presence. Commodus went one step further by calling himself the 'Roman Hercules' and having statues depicting him in Herculean garb, such as a lion skin over his head and a club in his right hand, erected all over Rome.

It was not difficult for a Roman emperor to seem supernatural given how much the state machinery would build them up, and how much power they wielded. A worthy ruler tended to be elevated after their death to the status of a divinity, which would be a boon to their successors, who could boast of their special lineage. Cults were so easy to attract that some emperors set themselves apart by refusing the chance to have one while they were still alive. Claudius ruffled feathers with his touch of modesty (as much as one can have as emperor of Rome) by passing on the opportunity to be worshipped as a god, and instead having a cult worshipping his exceptional skills (what the Romans called '*genius*'). He may have even been worshipped in Britain, with a temple in the lands his forces conquered at Camulodunum, known presently as Colchester.

Roman cults did not just spring up for emperors, as some politicians found – if they had any dealings in the Greek peninsula, an area where mysticism was rife – that they could develop their own following. Hadrian, who as emperor enjoyed his own cult following, had a lover called Antinous whose death in 130 AD inspired a city to be named after him ('*Antinoupolis*') and a separate cult that early Christian writers saw as a blasphemous rival to their own belief system. The manner of Antinous' death – falling into the Nile during an Imperial cruise down the river – inspired the credulous to compare him to exotic Egyptian gods like Osiris. All this came decades after Pompey, who enjoyed great military success in the East, inspired worshippers – the so-called '*Pompeiastae*' – on the island of Delos and even new cities in his name, such as '*Pompeiopolis*' (literally, 'Pompeytown'). People at Mytilene on the island of Lesbos even named a month in their calendar after him.

Pompey was not the only one to be venerated. When the Greeks were conquered by the Romans in the second century BC, they built temples to their victorious general Titus Quinctius Flamininus, placed his face on their coins and came up with a goddess, 'Roma', to be worshipped alongside him. A century later, Appius Claudius Pulcher was delighted when he became governor of the province of Cilicia (now part of Turkey) to have a temple built in his honour. He was so pleased to have this level of veneration that when he left office, he complained to his successor – none other than Marcus Tullius Cicero – about how his temple needed to be built faster. Cicero was later offered his own temple but declined, concluding – not unreasonably – that it would make other Romans jealous.

Modern politicians cannot expect to be offered their own cult worship that easily. They have to earn it by being charismatic enough to inspire such fervour. It might be hard to keep their egos in check when faced by crowds of cheering followers and supporters chanting their name, but they must not let it go to their heads. Those who think they are God's gift to politics tend to set themselves up for a fall.

NO HAIR TODAY, GONE TOMORROW

Politics is often said to be described as show business for ugly people. But that does not mean that the public turn a blind eye to matters of appearance. As much as we aspire to be sophisticated in our judgement, the public can be awfully shallow. In searching for someone suitably dynamic, we can be swayed by the simplest things, such as how much hair politicians have on their head. Not to mention how vibrant it might be in colour.

History shows that leaders without luscious locks have found it hard to connect with the electorate. The grey-haired John Major clung onto power in 1992, winning the most votes ever for any political party in a United Kingdom general election as he saw off his bald Labour rival Neil Kinnock. Major was later swept aside in 1997 by the brown-haired Tony Blair, who went on at the next election to easily defeat his bald Conservative challenger, William Hague. Hague tried in vain to draw attention away from his pate by covering it up most notoriously with a personalised baseball cap while plunging down a waterslide. But the waterslide provided a fitting visual metaphor for the Conservatives' plummeting political prospects.

Voters had proven themselves to be partial to a leader who had the thickest head of hair, leading one political commentator, Alan Watkins, to advance that as a grand theory about the electorate, pointing out that the last bald man to be elected Prime Minister was Winston Churchill in 1951. In Churchill's case, he was facing the equally bald Clement Attlee for the post, but was helped to victory by his reputation as a great wartime leader. 'I have to say history is on [Watkins'] side,' Kinnock admitted, years after his own failure to sweep to power.

Hague led the Conservatives to a massive electoral defeat in 2001, prompting *The Guardian* to opine that 'A bald man can never again lead the Conservative Party'. Did they listen? The man they replaced Hague with, Iain Duncan Smith, had the same problem. Namely, as former newspaper editor Kelvin MacKenzie put it, he was 'as bald as a baby's bottom'. Duncan Smith's team was painfully aware of it, as

one of his aides at the time acknowledged to me recently: 'The problem with Iain's hair was he had none of it!' His leadership petered
out so fast that he didn't even get to face voters at election time as
their potential Prime Minister. The Conservatives then picked the
balding Michael Howard, and enjoyed suitably improved prospects
at the 2005 election – but still failed to remove Blair from power. That
only changed once they picked the well-coiffed David Cameron.
His looks were part of his appeal, as he recognised in his pitch for
the leadership: 'We don't just need new policies or presentation or
organisation, or even having a young, passionate, energetic leader –
though come to think of it, that might not be such a bad idea.' And
voters sent the well-coiffed leader into power at the first election
he led his party into in 2010. That ended years in the political wilderness for the Tories under grey-haired or hairless chieftains. The
years Cameron spent in office did take their toll on his thatch. He
joked about it in 2014 to journalists, telling them that his top priority
for the year ahead was 'keeping the bald spot under control'.

Roman leaders could become rather obsessed about being seen
to have a good head of hair, as they knew the mockery they risked
otherwise. If their hair was too short, they were in danger of looking
like a prisoner of war – who would typically be shaven so their locks
could be reused for wigs.

A balding pate was even riskier. Julius Caesar's critics loved to
scoff at him for his baldness. He was 'troubled greatly' by his lack
of hair, the historian Suetonius records, so tried to cover it up by
combing his 'scanty locks' over any patches. A combover was not
his only way of trying to spare his blushes. He also made use of a

strategically placed laurel wreath, granted to him in recognition of military victories, that he wore at every opportunity.

If the follically challenged Roman had been around today, he could well have opted for a Hague-style baseball cap with 'CAESAR' emblazoned on it. That was imagined in 2018 as part of an excellent production of Shakespeare's *Julius Caesar* by Nicholas Hytner, in which audience members were able to buy their own 'CAESAR' caps to fit in with the rally-like stage setting. But these caps were inspired by Donald Trump – whose hair inspires its fair share of speculation – rather than Hague. The President has been fond of wearing red caps at political rallies, typically bearing his slogan 'Make America Great Again' rather than his own name, which showed commendable restraint given his love of plastering his name on everything else associated with him.

Caesar's hair neurosis was surpassed by the Emperor Domitian, who ruled from 81 to 96 AD. He liked to while away time alone in his chamber, focusing for several hours on catching flies and stabbing them with a sharpened pen. When a courtier asked if anyone was in his room, a quick-witted colleague quipped: 'Not even a fly.' His sadistic behaviour, recorded by Suetonius, may well have been a way to vent his frustration about his lack of hair. The emperor showed himself to be extraordinarily sensitive about his pate. It was covered up in his official depictions, with Domitian shown on coins and in statues with flowing locks of hair until the bitter end of his reign. He wrote a book about hair care, which he dedicated to a friend with the cheery message that 'nothing is more pleasing … but nothing shorter-lived' than having hair. And he resorted to wearing wigs in his later years to hide the true state of his own baldness.

Other emperors were not happy to just put on a wig, and instead resorting to draconian punishments. When Emperor Caligula's hair began to thin, he decided to make sure that everyone else was just as bald as he was. 'Any good-looking man with a fine head of hair [he] ran across … had the back of his scalp brutally shaved,' we are told by Suetonius. The imperial biographer also claims that the emperor made it illegal for anyone to look down on him from above, no doubt to protect his pate.

Such sensitivity about hair might seem ridiculous, but the Romans would not hesitate to judge them. The poet Ovid wrote in his work that a bald head was 'ugly', comparing it in appearance to a hornless bull, a field without grass and a tree without leaves. Meanwhile, the poet Martial wrote cuttingly in one of his epigrams: 'On your bald pate no wig you use. You draw hairs on, with no excuse. At least no barber needs to trim it. You can erase it in a minute.'

This mockery is similar to what recent bald Tory leaders endured when trying to win power. Hague was mocked by one newspaper commentator for his 'skinhead version of Toryism', while Duncan Smith was described in one profile piece as 'every bit as bald' as his predecessor. Unlike Caesar, they did not even have a formidable military record to help them shrug off such jibes. Instead, in Duncan Smith's case, he had to fend off accusations that he had exaggerated the achievements on his CV.

Politics can be brutal, especially for those who have distinctive features, like bald men. Voters tend to want someone full of energy as their leader, with a vibrant and full head of hair to match. Those with bald ambition can power through the jibes, but they need the charisma and grit of Churchill and Caesar to do so.

BACK TO BASICS BEGINS AT HOME

In 1993, Britain was in the grip of a moral panic, as government ministers grappled with the rising cost of the welfare state. The Conservative politician in charge of social security policy, Peter Lilley, had insisted he would 'close down the something for nothing society', riffing on a song from *The Mikado* by Gilbert and Sullivan to outline his plans:

> I've got a little list | Of benefit offenders who I'll soon be rooting out | And who never would be missed | They never would be missed | There's those who make up bogus claims | In half a dozen names... They never would be missed | They never would be missed | There's young ladies who get pregnant just to jump the housing queue | And dads who won't support the kids | of ladies they have ... kissed | And I haven't even mentioned all those sponging socialists | I've got them on my list | And there's none of them be missed | There's none of them be missed.

Prime Minister John Major was seen to have stepped up to champion family values by issuing a rallying cry on 8 October to his fellow

Conservatives. Speaking at their annual conference, he argued that it needed to show 'the best of Britain' by rediscovering the 'old values – neighbourliness, decency, courtesy'. Building to his rhetorical peak, he declared: 'It is time to return to core values, time to get back to basics, to self-discipline and respect for the law, to consideration for others, to accepting responsibility for yourself and your family – and not shuffling it off on other people and the state.'

The then Prime Minister's 'back to basics' cry went down well with his audience, but it was a hostage to fortune given he was positioning himself and his party as champions of morality. And the steady revelations over the following months about how his colleagues were failing to show 'consideration for others' and 'responsibility' in their personal affairs caused mounting embarrassment. Members of his government were constantly being forced to resign after being exposed over extra-marital affairs, while other MPs were humiliated by revelations about their secret lovechildren. 'It's getting ridiculous,' one minister complained at the time. 'It seems there's a policy of one bonk and you are out.' No matter how strict Major was on those caught with their pants down, his aspiration to lead a moral administration had been left in tatters.

The bitter irony was obvious to all. Piers Morgan, who as editor of the tabloid *News of the World* oversaw the reporting of many of the sex scandals that humiliated Major's government, noted in his diaries:

Major's brought all these exposés on himself, with that ludicrous 'Back to Basics' speech at the last Tory conference … It strikes me that probably every Tory MP is up to some sexual shenanigans, but we can hardly get them all fired or there will be nobody left to run the country.

Gyles Brandreth, who at the time was a Conservative MP and member of the Major government, was more sympathetic about the Prime Minister's plight. 'You've got to pity the poor PM too,' he wrote in diaries, quoting his wife as lamenting to him: 'That's Back To Basics gone to buggery.'

Contrary to its depiction in popular culture, Ancient Rome was not a non-stop circus of wine, orgies and fighting. Plenty of people had more conservative attitudes, and shared Major's desire to see traditional values upheld. As the satirist Juvenal declares, in a rant about the problems of stopping a loved one from committing adultery by locking them indoors, 'Who will guard the guards?' (*Quis custodiet ipsos custodes?*).

Augustus Caesar fought the moralists' corner as emperor by bringing in a wide range of legislation to enforce high standards of conduct. The '*Leges Juliae*' (Julian Laws) aimed to expand the population by encouraging people to marry and have children. They went much further as an intervention than the measure David Cameron took as Prime Minister, of reinstating a tax break for married couples from 2015. But in his case, he was open about it being a symbolic move to show how much the state approved of marriage as an institution.

Under Augustus' agenda, those who were old enough to marry but refused to were punished with higher taxes and were banned from receiving inheritances or even attending the public games. By contrast, those who produced a lot of children stood to benefit under measures like the so-called 'law of the three sons', which promised rewards for especially fertile citizens. That measure was revived in spirit, perhaps unwittingly, by Hungary's populist Prime Minister Viktor Orbán when he promised to exempt women who have four or more children from ever paying income tax again. Although his motive in encouraging a larger domestic population was motivated by a desire to justify curbing migration, rather than to pose as an arch-moralist.

Augustus did not just want to encourage large families, but the right type of families – giving a million sesterces to Marcus Hortalus, grandson of a famous lawyer, to ensure that his illustrious line would not die out with him. But that left his successor with a problem when Hortalus rocked up at the Senate complaining that he had since married and produced four children, but was struggling to feed his family as he had blown through his grant. His plea drew sympathy from the listening senators, but Tiberius insisted on giving him a lecture. 'If every poor man starts to come here demanding money for their children,' he is recorded by Tacitus as saying, 'we shall never satisfy them and will bankrupt the state.' He went on to harangue him in terms that Conservatives like Peter Lilley would be proud of, warning that 'industry will languish and laziness will thrive if a man has nothing to strive for or fear, and everyone will carelessly sit expecting relief from others, too useless to help themselves and a burden to the state'.

His furious rebuke sparked murmurs of discontent across the

Senate, as senators made their concern known about hearing someone from such elite stock being accused of scrounging. Tiberius
relented by agreeing to give marginally less than Hortalus' original
grant, not to him directly but shared out among his children. That
was the last time Emperor Tiberius was so generous in bailing someone out with public money, Tacitus records, undoubtedly because
his gesture failed to stop Hortalus' family 'sinking deeper into humiliating poverty'.

Augustus' prototype child benefit policy caused his successor
problems, but it paled in comparison with the grief he suffered from
another bit of his moralising agenda. His ban on adultery was by far
his strictest measure. It came with significant legal teeth. Any couple
who broke it had their property confiscated and were banished to
different islands. Fathers were legally permitted to kill their adulterous daughters and whoever they had affairs with. But they had to
be thorough, as if they killed only one of the couple, they would be
charged as a common murderer. The wronged husband could also
take matters into his own hands under the law and kill whoever had
led their wife astray, but then he had to divorce his wife within three
days of doing the deed. The cuckolded man would be duty-bound
to act; if he knew his wife was cheating on him, but did nothing to
stop it, he could be prosecuted for the crime of '*lenocium*' – being a
pimp, in effect.

Admittedly, there was a legal loophole for married Roman women
keen on adultery: they could get around the law by registering themselves as a prostitute. That workaround was closed by Augustus'

successor Tiberius after it became embarrassingly popular with the wives of senators.

Nevertheless, the tough stance Augustus took on adultery set him up for his own 'back to basics' disaster. His best hope of a smooth succession resided in his daughter Julia, whom he sought to marry off to a potential heir, and hoped would give birth to many more potential candidates. After three marriages, she had provided him a successor in the form of her third husband Tiberius, and two sons as potential other heirs. But she presented her arch-moralising father with a massive political problem.

As the Roman historian Velleius put it, Julia was 'tainted by lust'. And so she would reportedly prostitute herself in the Forum, the same place her father used to announce his curbs on adultery, propositioning passing men, even strangers. They would be offered 'every indulgence', as the writer Seneca put it, with 'adulterers welcomed in their droves'. She was said to have had it off with them all over the Forum. Some writers suggest her favourite place for late-night hanky-panky was on the rostra, where speakers like her father would have railed against adultery, while others claimed she preferred it on the statue of Marsyas – the satyr that came to represent liberty and freedom of speech. Such antics, according to the historian Cassius Dio, were all part of the 'revels and drinking bouts' she indulged in. She was supposedly unabashed about her behaviour. According to fourth-century AD writer Macrobius, when Julia was asked why her children all looked like her husband, despite her notorious adultery, she came out with the quip: 'I take on passengers only when the ship's hold is full.' In other words, she would risk it only when pregnant. Her libertine ways were so notorious that the philosopher Pliny the Elder dubbed her 'a model of debauchery' (*exemplum licentiae*) – a title perhaps only Silvio Berlusconi would aspire to claim nowadays.

The interest Julia was attracting around Roman society over her personal peccadilloes posed an excruciating problem for Augustus. How could he demand moral behaviour from his people if he could not secure it from his own family? To be fair, he could hardly pretend to be blameless. Even Augustus' friends couldn't deny his penchant for adultery, Suetonius records, telling of how he once took the wife of an ex-consul from her husband's dining room 'before his very eyes into a bedchamber, and bringing her back to the table with her hair in disorder and her ears glowing'. But such hypocrisy did not stop the emperor from having to uphold his laws, not least as he was meant to serve as 'father of the nation' (*pater patriae*). That role had to be squared with his other paternal responsibilities, as *paterfamilias*, presiding over the imperial family. He could not allow his daughter to get away with flouting his latest measures, especially if her behaviour had become more notorious than anything he might have been getting up to. And so Augustus settled on a way to punish her that would mean no one could accuse him of giving his daughter special treatment: he banished her from Rome.

John Major's errant ministers might have been politically disgraced and lost their jobs in government, but they could still live in London. No one accused Augustus of being a soft touch by exiling his daughter, the historian Tacitus writing that he went 'far beyond' what his own laws required. Julia was exiled to a small volcanic island in the Tyrrhenian Sea just off the west coast of Italy called Pandateria, now known as Ventotene. As pleasant as that might sound, Augustus took steps to ensure she could not enjoy herself in the slightest. She was denied any of the indulgences that had been available to her in Rome, like wine. No men were allowed to be in her vicinity unless they had been granted special permission from the emperor, only then after he had been told everything about them, like how handsome and tall they were. And he needed to know every detail about the appearance of her male visitor, even if they had any marks or scars on their body. While confining his daughter to a glorified house arrest, he meted out similar punishment to the men she had dallied with. Some were banished to their own far-flung destinations. One of them may have been the poet Ovid, who wrote enigmatically in his work about being banished to a town on the Black Sea for what he calls a 'mistake' – a reference that academics still argue over to this day. Others were simply put to death.

Clearly, Augustus decided that the best way to protect his status as Rome's moraliser-in-chief was to be seen coming down hard on those in his household who failed to meet his standards. He used a similar pretext to exile Julia's eldest daughter to a different Italian island, although that could be because her husband had been plotting against Augustus, rather than because of further adulterous allegations hitting the family. He had been aware for a while of his daughter's behaviour, but Cassius Dio writes that he 'refused to believe it', explaining: 'Those who hold positions of command, it appears, are acquainted with everything else better than with their own affairs; and … they have no precise information regarding what their associates do.'

But Augustus could not deny it for long, deciding in his eventual fury to make the scandal public. The Senate was duly informed, and the emperor did not hide his outrage. He was said to be prone to lamenting to confidants that he wished he had died childless, with Suetonius reporting that he made clear his irritation by sighing and getting snappy whenever Julia's name came up. When he did talk about her, he pointedly compared her to one of his ulcers. He cut her out of his life for good, never seeing her again and issuing instructions that her body be barred from his mausoleum.

Despite all this huffing and puffing, the politician Seneca wrote that Augustus' 'anger gave away to shame' later as he came to regret how much he had aired his dirty laundry. He tried to make amends five years after her initial exile by bringing her back onto the Italian mainland, allowing her to have a property in the southern city of Rhegium. She was even able to walk around the town. But she was still not allowed back into Rome, in a sign that her father was not ready to entirely forgive her. No amount of pleading from her friends in the capital could convince him otherwise. His refusal to compromise on his moral crusade meant that the bitterness around her exile remained in the background for the rest of his years.

Moralising legislation is all very well, as long as the politicians behind it are ready to take the necessary steps to respect it. Augustus was not the only Roman ruler who had to make difficult personal decisions for this purpose. The Emperor Claudius had to have one of his sons-in-law put to death after he was caught *in flagrante* with a male lover. Major was lucky as Prime Minister that his own affair with Tory MP Edwina Currie came out years after they had both left office, otherwise it would have scuppered his 'back to basics' agenda altogether.

Tony Blair faced his own challenges in trying to enforce higher standards of behaviour among the public. In 2000, he went on the warpath against drunken youths, proposing powers for the police to levy on-the-spot fines for those caught being disorderly. Just days after the Labour Prime Minister suggested this, his sixteen-year-old son Euan was arrested for being 'drunk and incapable' after going out in London's West End to celebrate the end of his GCSEs. Reports of his arrest, and how he had been found sprawled out on his own in Leicester Square, meant his father could not duck it. 'Being a Prime Minister can be a tough job but I always think being a parent is probably tougher. Sometimes you don't always succeed,' he told religious leaders shortly after.

Augustus will have wished he could have been so sanguine. Instead, his daughter was part of the personal cost he paid to make sure he could set an example to his fellow Romans. His moral laws did not last for ever. The cost of enforcing them, and the eventual advent of Christianity, meant most of these laws became obsolete or were repealed. The only law that lasted the distance was one banning senators from marrying actresses (who, at the time, tended to be tawdry prostitutes).

Augustus was not the only Roman leader who had to make difficult personal decisions in order to maintain public propriety. Julius Caesar's break into the political big league came in 63 BC when he was elected as Rome's chief priest (*'pontifex maximus'*), a role that required high moral standards given that its holder had to preside over state worship. But scandal erupted after a year when his wife Pompeia hosted a solemn women-only religious festival at their home, which was infiltrated by a man. Opinion was divided as to whether the intruder, Publius Clodius Pulcher, was trying to pull a prank, ruffling the feathers of the women amid their ceremonial pomp, or wanted to cavort with Caesar's wife. Tongues wagged for months amid the fallout about them being potential lovers, prompting Caesar to try to draw a line under it. He decided on a firm, but brusque, approach to damage control: divorcing his wife. According to Plutarch, Caesar later offered this public explanation for his course of action: 'I thought my wife ought not even to be under suspicion.' That has given rise to the wider proverb of 'Caesar's wife must be above suspicion'.

By contrast, some modern politicians do not mind if their wives fall under suspicion. The Speaker of the House of Commons is meant to be an impartial chair of parliamentary debates, which meant that John Bercow had to constantly fend off questions about his wife's proudly anti-Brexit and pro-Labour views. The line he stuck to was that while he was obliged to be impartial, that did not apply to his wife – 'who is not my chattel'. Speaker Bercow's egalitarian defence would have struck the Romans as rather emasculating, as they saw marriage as an enterprise where the man was unquestionably in charge.

Despite kicking out his wife in the hope of keeping his name clean, Julius Caesar could not help being subject to gossip. During a fierce debate in the Senate, the historian Plutarch records that a note was brought in and handed to him. Caesar read it without sharing what it said with his fellow senators, which infuriated one of them, a man called Marcus Porcius Uticensis, better known as Cato the Younger. He kicked off, accusing Caesar of reading messages from enemies of Rome. The uproar his accusation sparked forced Caesar to hand over the letter, only for Cato to find out that it was in fact a steamy love letter from his sister, addressed to Caesar. He threw it back at Caesar in fury, barking: 'Keep it, you wino!'

Of course, politicians should stand up for what is morally right. But when they try to enforce these values on the people, they need to make sure their own house is in order.

REMEMBER BREAD AND CIRCUSES

Who could object to bread? It is a mainstay of what we eat. Christians ask as part of the Lord's Prayer for 'our daily bread'. And who could not enjoy a circus? Both are popular by themselves. But when put together, they become a pairing that no one welcomes in politics.

The Roman satirist Juvenal was the first to begin this trend when he railed at the state of popular values. People were no longer driven by their sense of civic duty, he wrote, and instead held back and 'anxiously hope for just two things: bread and circuses' (*panem et circenses*). Instead of impressing voters with achievements and integrity, he warned that rulers could do so far too easily by doling out cheap food and hosting public entertainment. He was not alone in this suspicion, as the historian Plutarch warned that 'the man who first offers banquets and bribes to the people is the first to destroy their liberties'.

Thanks to Juvenal, 'bread and circuses' has become the preferred term to describe an apparent attempt to appease voters with cheap baubles. Labour peer Andrew Adonis tried to argue that Boris Johnson would be willing to make his dreams come true by stopping Brexit, claiming in July 2019 that he was 'the Roman emperor for whom policy is bread and circuses for the little people'. Just over a decade earlier, the veteran Conservative MP Chris Chope used it in his curmudgeonly crusade against the then Labour government's idea of introducing a new bank holiday in the Autumn: 'In my view, bank holidays should be used to mark special days of religious observance or national celebration. They should not be used effectively to provide bread and circuses to a populace that is increasingly disillusioned with this cynical government.'

The Tory government that followed was accused of being just as cynical when it decided to cut taxes on beer and bingo. It trumpeted their decision by boasting that it would help 'hardworking people do more of the things they enjoy'. Critics rounded on the government for its 'condescending' language, while Labour MP Stephen Pound wryly observed in the House of Commons: 'Beer and bingo may not exactly be the bread and circuses of our age.'

Despite the derision 'bread and circuses' attract, they get to the heart of an important political art: showing voters the benefits of keeping you in charge. Julius Caesar delighted the Romans after conquering Gaul by showering them with gifts and entertainment, putting on gladiator fights and staging plays across the city as well as circus races, sporting contests and a mock sea battle. And that is not all, as Suetonius records there were public banquets and gifts

PART TWO: IN OFFICE

of grain and oil. Augustus showed similar public-spiritedness in his enthusiasm for holding games, which he made sure to attend in person, so he could be seen enjoying the same entertainment as the common folk, just as modern politicians rush now to be seen watching football. By contrast, the Scrooge-like attitude taken by Augustus' successor Tiberius to public revels meant that he deserved to be called – as Pliny the Elder put it – the *'tristissimus hominum'*, the saddest or gloomiest of men. He rarely put on games, making sure very few could happen by slashing the budget put aside for them, and the number of gladiators allowed to participate was capped. That ensured Roman citizens would have thought the rare entertainment under Tiberius' watch was a miserly knock-off of what they had become used to seeing under his predecessor. A wise Roman would make sure their people had as much food and entertainment as necessary, otherwise they risked popular discontent. Vespasian found that to his cost after being sent to govern North Africa on the Empire's behalf, when the people of Hadrumetum chose to protest the city's food shortage by pelting him with turnips.

Those in power who wanted to stay in office made their case to the public by giving them all the bread and circuses they could desire. Some Romans sought high office by literally making bread part of their electoral pitch. Among the graffiti in Pompeii, it is possible to see this message from one gourmet voter: 'I beg you to make C. Julius Polybius aedile [magistrate]. He makes good bread.'

Of course, if all a politician needed to get ahead was to bake good bread for voters, Paul Hollywood would be Prime Minister for as long as he wished. But anyone who wants to be in office for a long time needs to give voters as clear an idea as the Pompeiian bread-raving resident about the benefits of them staying in charge. And so leaders have found the quickest way to win the public's love is to spoil them rotten.

The Emperor Nero delighted the Roman people by throwing lots of money around. In 56 AD, he gave each citizen 400 sesterces, which was enough to pay for an average family's food for nearly a year. His move proved so popular, he did it again later in his reign. Nero was an enthusiastic master of revels, bringing his own brand of entertainment to Rome with a festival of artistic performances, gymnastics and equestrian displays. He wanted his name so closely associated with the revelry that it was named after him – the 'Neronia'. It was a gutsy move, as the last rulers who held special games to celebrate – and promote – themselves were Julius Caesar and Augustus. Nero's choice of entertainment upset conservative tastes, with Tacitus aghast at the idea that Roman noblemen 'should defile themselves on the stage under the pretext of delivering an oration or a poem', or that they might 'strip to the skin … put on the gloves, and practise' Greek-inspired wrestling. The historian even fretted that the great and good would be corrupted by listening to 'emasculated music and dulcet voices'. But such quibbles were drowned out by the crowds that came to enjoy the Neronian games.

He was one of the many Roman rulers who delighted the public by knowing how to put on a show. In the second century AD, the Emperor Commodus was so keen on gladiator fights that he took part in them himself. His involvement horrified the upper classes, who felt about it the same way that members of Parliament would today if they had to watch Theresa May cage-fighting, or if President Trump took part in bare-knuckle boxing on the White House lawn.

Commodus was the same man played by Joaquin Phoenix in Ridley Scott's 2000 film *Gladiator* getting into the arena. While we have no evidence that he faced down Maximus Decimus Meridius, or anyone else who looked like Russell Crowe, in a climactic duel, we know that he took on a variety of colourful foes. The emperor once killed a hundred bears in a single day, picking them off in the arena with a spear and pausing only to refresh himself with a drink of wine. He worked his way through a safari of other animals, at other points killing three elephants and a giraffe. The historian Cassius Dio, who was a senator at the time of his reign, watched him behead an ostrich, and then recorded what the emperor did next:

> He came up to where we were sitting, holding the head in his left hand and in his right hand raising aloft his bloody sword; and though he spoke not a word, yet he wagged his head with a grin, indicating that he would treat us in the same way.

Many of the senators were tempted to laugh in response, Dio added, as if keen to suggest they wanted to do so in mockery – although it is perfectly possible they had been getting the giggles in sheer terror. One snort out of place could have seen them put to death immediately for offending the emperor, so Dio notes they had to keep themselves under control by chewing on leaves from their garlands to suppress their mirth.

Those who watched a Union Flag-waving Boris Johnson dangle

from a zip wire during the 2012 London Olympics did not have to fear for their lives if they chuckled. Indeed, they were expected to enjoy everything they saw during the games. The then London Mayor threw himself into the Olympic revels with verve, with his efforts immortalised by his tangle on the zip wire. He knew that the athletes were the main source of delight for the public, telling me soon after that he had tried to persuade them to run naked in tribute to Ancient Greek tradition but had been 'discouraged from doing so'. Nevertheless, Johnson acknowledged the important role the Olympic athletes had played in his own colourful expression of thanks to them: 'Speaking as a spectator, you produced such paroxysms of tears and joy on the sofas of Britain that you probably not only inspired a generation but helped to create one as well.'

The warm glow left by these 'paroxysms' ended up lifting the public's view of Johnson – to his sheer delight. 'I'm hoovering up all the credit!' he was overheard declaring to an Olympic Board member. 'All this credit!' And he was right – it was easy to forget that the 2012 Olympics had been secured by his predecessor Ken Livingstone. His electoral rival did not pass up the chance to remind voters when trying to persuade them to re-elect him, rather than the man who had ousted him, that he had set in train much of the preparation for the games which under Johnson was about to bear fruit.

That Olympic boost in Johnson's reputation was a bittersweet result for David Cameron, who knew he was eyeing his job as Prime Minister. 'If any other politician anywhere in the world was stuck on a zip wire it would be a disaster,' he grudgingly acknowledged. 'For Boris, it's an absolute triumph.' Johnson's Olympic boost was predictable given he was the elected official who had to directly oversee the games. It also vindicated his decision to seize every chance to publicly associate himself in the public's mind with the Olympics, even recording a personal message that was played across the capital's public transportation network. When Mitt Romney, then a contender for the American presidency, suggested the level of preparations before the games kicked off was 'disconcerting', Johnson exploited that criticism mercilessly. Speaking in front of the crowds in London's Hyde Park, he got them going by yelling: 'I hear there's a guy called Mitt Romney who wants to know whether we're ready. He wants to know whether we're ready. Are we ready? Are we ready? Yes, we are.'

The fervent reaction, as the crowds chanted 'Boris, Boris,' showed vividly how the Olympic buzz had translated into greater love for the Conservative politician. Johnson later acknowledged to the interviewer Michael Cockerell for a 2013 documentary of his life that these chanting crowds made him 'understand why Roman emperors put on great games and great spectacle … you suddenly think "Wow!"'. But he stressed that he did not want to become an emperor himself, noting how often they 'came to sticky ends'. At another point, he joked about the Borismania that 'this will all come crashing down, we all know that'.

Politicians do not have to preside over great sporting displays to benefit from them. In 1996, English football fans were thrilled to see their national football team defy years of disappointment in the European championships by making it as far as the semi-finals. Their excitement was captured by the 'Three Lions' footballing anthem that had been released that year, in which Frank Skinner and David Baddiel sang of the winners' trophy 'coming home' after 'years of hurt'. Tony Blair, then fast emerging as the country's likely next Prime Minister, wanted to show voters that he shared their delight by offering his own twist in his pre-election pitch. Speaking at Labour's conference that year, he waxed lyrical to his audience: 'Labour's come home to you, so come home to us. Labour's coming home. Seventeen years of hurt never stopped us dreaming, Labour's coming home. As we did in 1945 and 1964. I know that was then but it could be again.' Tapping into the national mood with his football analogy did Blair no harm at all. Of course, that does not mean all a politician needs to do to guarantee the public's affection is to put on a massive party, or at least be seen keenly participating in it. The reason 'bread and circuses' became notoriously popular is because their benefit was clear to the public. Politicians have forgotten that all too often.

There are countless initiatives politicians indulge in that are dangerously complex, leaving the public in the dark as to what their point is. The High Speed 2 rail project was dreamed up as a way to bring the United Kingdom closer together by allowing even faster travel across the country. But criticism has risen as costs have spiralled, with critics seizing on how the initial estimated cost of as little as £33 billion stands to balloon past £100 billion, which would make it the most expensive railway ever built. With costs going off the rails, critics have argued with increasing vigour that it should be binned as the money could be better spent elsewhere, while its supporters find it harder and harder to defend. Projects like HS2 suffer when they become so gargantuan that their original purpose is forgotten, leaving critics to run riot in shaping how the public sees it. When Theresa May unveiled her plans during the 2017 election campaign to reform social care, they were too complex for her – or her colleagues – to explain neatly. As a result, she had to shelve them quickly to stop what had been swiftly called the 'dementia tax' from harming her electoral prospects any further. A few years earlier, then Health Secretary Andrew Lansley's ambitions for the National Health Service became bogged down in the labyrinthine detail about what he was proposing. One official captured the rage about it inside the Prime Minister's team when they told *The Times* that he should be 'taken out and shot'.

By contrast, politicians have had much greater success with simpler policies. Not just because of them tending to be much less fuss to deliver, but also because they are easier for voters to understand why they are worthwhile. That is why successful politicians try to boil down their offer, as Tony Blair did in 1997 by dishing out a 'pledge card' to the electorate with five key promises in short bullet points, such as smaller class sizes and a freeze on various tax rises.

Imagine if a Roman consul stood for a modern election. They could have summed up their offer to the public in eye-catching terms, such as: 'Free money and more entertainment'. Modern politicians phrase their pledges differently, but they are offering much the same in spirit.

Jeremy Corbyn was accused of trying to tempt voters with free money in 2017, with an electoral pitch that was packed with big promises to spend more money and reverse a swathe of budget cuts. He also promised four new public holidays so voters could enjoy the extra time off work. The Tories ridiculed his largesse as 'magic money tree' politics, although the events that followed forced Prime Minister May to give it a good shake or two. She announced in late 2018 her plans to hold a jolly Brexit-inspired 'Festival of Britain' in order to 'showcase what makes our country great today', with displays of culture, sports and innovation. Ministers pledged to pour £120 million into preparations for the festival, which had been pencilled in for 2022, so it would coincide with the Queen's Platinum Jubilee and the Commonwealth Games in Birmingham. It would have been the spiritual successor to the original 1951 Festival of Britain, which sought to promote optimism and confidence in the future after the Second World War. But May's efforts to enthuse the public turned out to be too little, far too late.

Politicians like to scoff at 'bread and circuses', but they do so at their peril, given that they risk forgetting they have to persuade voters they are not just better off, but happier, under their watch. Ministers may have been mocked for how they sold their cuts to taxes on beer and bingo, but they were cheered in the pubs and bingo halls across Britain.

Politicians do best when they remember how to make the benefits of their side clear to voters. The Remain campaign forgot that during the EU referendum by basing its case against Brexit on studies that suggested it would harm the country's gross domestic product. But their focus on economic theory played into the Brexiteers' hands, as Michael Gove was able to declare that 'people of this country have had enough of experts from organisations with acronyms saying that they know what is best and getting it consistently wrong'. Remain campaigners found to their horror that many voters agreed with Gove. A senior Labour MP had a shock when out campaigning in the north of England, knocking on doors on a council estate where he expected to find lots of poor, albeit loyal, voters, as he was greeted with utter bemusement by one householder. The reply he had, after setting out his case for Remain – drawing on various gloomy economic forecasts – was to the point: 'I'm a single man with a dog, how the fuck does GDP matter to me?'

The public does not depend on their leaders directly for their 'bread' these days, but the same thinking drives voters to look out for politicians who'll most benefit their wallet. That is why politicians continually compete to prove that they can financially benefit voters more than their rivals, and then do their best to prove it in government with spending splurges and tax cuts. Meanwhile, recent events like the Olympics show how much the public continues to love sporting events, and those that help make them a success. Perhaps the reason politicians like to mock 'bread and circuses' is that they know that sums up all too well how they need to appeal to voters.

KEEP YOUR FRIENDS CLOSE

More often than leaders like to think, their main threat comes from people who are supposed to be their biggest supporters. Winston Churchill once made light of that when he was showing a newly elected Tory MP around the House of Commons. 'So that's the enemy?' they asked, pointing to the benches opposite. 'No, that's the opposition,' he replied, before pointing to the benches behind them and adding: 'That is the enemy.'

The main Brexit campaign Vote Leave is remembered as a brutally effective electoral machine, but it could have so easily fallen apart due to the bubbling tensions between the people behind it. As its director Dominic Cummings later recalled on his blog: 'Our biggest obstacle was not the IN campaign and its vast resources but the appalling infighting on our own side driven by all the normal human motivations described in Thucydides – fear, interest, the pursuit of glory and so on.'

Cummings underlined his point about the strains of the campaign by quoting from the Greek historian's account of how society changed on the peninsula during the Peloponnesian Wars:

> Thus revolution gave birth to every form of wickedness in Greece. The simplicity which is so large an element in a noble nature was laughed to scorn and disappeared ... When men are retaliating upon others, they are reckless of the future and do not hesitate to annul those common laws of humanity to which every individual trusts for his own hope of deliverance should he ever be overtaken by calamity; they forget that in their own hour of need they will look for them in vain ... The cause of all these evils was the love of power, originating in avarice and ambition, and the party-spirit which is engendered by them when men are fairly embarked in a contest ... For party associations are not based upon any

established law nor do they seek the public good; they are formed
in defiance of the laws and from self-interest...

The Brexiteers argued endlessly about campaign tactics, with MPs
attached to the Vote Leave campaign trying from the beginning to
remove Cummings due to their fear he would lead them to defeat.
Party associations were strained nearly to breaking point during the
referendum. The Conservative Party itself had to declare neutrality
and insist it would not take a side in the vain hope of keeping the
peace as much as possible. That left the space clear for leading Tory
politicians to knock seven bells out of each other while party members campaigned for both sides.

After the referendum, Theresa May emerged as the person to bring
the party back together. As someone who fought, however weakly,
on the losing Remain side, May argued that she was well-placed to
understand both sides and ensure that 'Brexit means Brexit'. She
decided to exploit her immediate popularity, with polls putting her
leagues ahead of the Labour opposition, by calling a snap election in
the hope of winning a titanic majority to help her get the necessary
legislation through Parliament. But on the morning of 9 June 2017,
the full scale of Theresa May's disastrous gamble became clear. Far
from cementing her authority in the House of Commons by increasing her majority, she lost it, forcing her to beg another party to prop
her up.

Recriminations flew during this humiliating state of affairs,
and May had to show she would govern differently. So her senior

advisers, Nick Timothy and Fiona Hill, resigned within hours of the election result emerging. 'When Caesar is under attack, the Praetorian Guard must sacrifice themselves,' Jacob Rees-Mogg mused to Sky News reporter Lewis Goodall. The Conservative backbencher rightly recalled the principle behind the Praetorians, which came about as an elite guard for Roman generals and magistrates that later would be adopted by Augustus as an imperial entourage. Rees-Mogg was so taken by his historical quip that he repurposed it when we spoke in March 2018, a year after May began the Brexit negotiations. As we spoke about how well he thought she was doing, he sought to demonstrate how supportive he was of his party leader by telling me that he saw himself 'as part of the Prime Minister's Praetorian Guard'.

Such a boast was an attempt by Rees-Mogg to show how much Eurosceptics supported her. He had a good claim to express that given he was chair of the European Research Group of Brexit-backing Tory backbenchers. But I could not resist pointing out to him that the Praetorian Guard had not defended every last emperor to the death. Indeed, they could be held responsible for quite a few emperors dying in their time. 'Um,' Rees-Mogg briefly paused. 'The Praetorian Guard backed the good emperors and Mrs May is a good emperor, or empress I should say…'

Despite leaping to the defence of his 'good empress', Rees-Mogg became one of her staunchest critics. He had only mere weeks before, in January 2018, warned that part of her Brexit plan – pursuing a transition of around two years – would leave Britain a 'vassal state' during that period. This jibe would be often repeated publicly whenever he had the chance. That July, he accused May of trying to recreate 'the worst aspects of the EU' with her approach, panning it as 'the greatest vassalage since King John paid homage to Philip II at Le Goulet in 1200'. That November, he upgraded his beloved 'vassal state' jibe by accusing May of turning Britain into 'not so much a vassal state anymore as a slave state'. For good measure, he added that she had 'surrendered to Brussels and given in to everything they want'.

The mounting aggression in his attacks on May's Brexit plans encouraged people to ask why he still seemingly had confidence in her leadership. 'The PM has my full support,' he told the *Daily Telegraph* in January 2018. 'May the PM live forever, Amen, Amen, Hallelujah, Hallelujah, Amen.' The differences, he insisted, were merely with the approach his party leader was taking towards Brexit, rather than with her continued reign. But by November, with it clear that May had nailed down a deal, he was singing a different tune. 'There comes a point at which the policy and the individual become so intimately connected that it would be very hard to carry on promoting the person who is promoting this policy,' he told BBC *Newsnight* on 14 November. When asked whether he would formally declare he had lost confidence in May's leadership, he replied: 'Not in the next twenty-four hours.'

But, within twenty-four hours, Rees-Mogg was standing outside the Houses of Parliament at the grand St Stephen's Entrance telling journalists why he had no more confidence in May's leadership and wanted someone else to take over 'as quickly as possible'. His letter neatly summarised his already familiar criticisms of her leadership, arguing that a change was needed because the agreement she had hammered out 'has turned out to be worse than anticipated and fails to meet the promises given to the nation'. But it also revealed that his desire for change had not come out of the blue. He had told May's arch-enforcer, the chief whip Julian Smith, 'a few weeks ago' that 'it would be in the interest of the party and the country if she were to stand aside'.

As the tribune of dozens of Eurosceptics, hacks were quick to ask themselves whether his announcement could have been the trigger for fellow MPs to move against May by demanding a change of leader. Turning on his party leader had the potential to bring her down as Prime Minister, and potentially even usher in a new government. But Rees-Mogg strained to make clear that 'a coup is the wrong word' to describe what he was trying to do. A coup, he argued, was an attempt to remove someone through 'illegitimate procedures', whereas he was 'entirely constitutional' by demanding a vote of no confidence, which if lost by May would pave the way for a contest to elect a new party leader.

Rees-Mogg turned out to be right in his insistence that it had not been a coup for a different reason; coups tend to be well co-ordinated. A vote of no-confidence would only happen if forty-eight MPs had written letters demanding a change of leader. But after several days, there was no sign that level had been reached. The group of Eurosceptic MPs Rees-Mogg represented could have easily hit that number if they had all put their pen to paper demanding a contest, prompting speculation among his allies that some of their colleagues had been lying to them. He admitted sheepishly at a public event later that his putsch had gone a 'bit *Dad's Army*', in reference to the ragtag volunteer soldiers of the hit 1970s BBC comedy.

After nearly a month, enough MPs had made their lack of confidence clear for a vote to be held testing whether the Conservative parliamentary party still backed May as leader. Rees-Mogg issued a call-to-arms for his fellow dissidents that morning: 'Theresa May's plan would bring down the government if carried forward. But our party will rightly not tolerate it. Conservatives must now answer whether they wish to draw ever closer to an election under May's leadership. In the national interest, she must go.'

But the contest, announced and held on 12 December, saw her emerge as winner with 200 votes to 117 against her. Despite her winning two thirds of the votes, Rees-Mogg still tried to pressure her into leaving. Soon after the margin of her victory came out, he spent that evening arguing that it had actually been a 'terrible result', so she needed to 'see the Queen urgently and resign'. She did not take up his suggestion, and soon after he had to acknowledge her victory in the Commons, declaring that 'she therefore commands my confidence'. Sky News found him a born-again loyalist, telling their reporter that he supported the Prime Minister 'enthusiastically' because he was a 'a loyal Conservative … This is not hedging about.'

Such an oath meant little, as there was no point in Rees-Mogg calling for her to go any longer given that she was safe, under Tory party rules, from a further leadership challenge for a year. He still kept up his vocal opposition to her Brexit plan, kicking off 2019 by complaining in the *Telegraph* that May's deal would see the British pay '£39 billion for nothing at all'. It was no surprise when he joined 431 other MPs in voting down May's Brexit deal when it came to be voted on for the first time by the Commons in January. He celebrated its historic defeat by inviting his fellow Eurosceptics around later that evening to his house for champagne. That February, he was contrite when confronted by *Spectator* editor Fraser Nelson at an event hosted by the magazine about his past expressions of support for May. Reminded that he had gone as far as to claim she would do a 'fabulous job', Rees-Mogg offered this apology: 'Mea culpa, mea culpa, mea maxima culpa.'

Rees-Mogg's wayward loyalty, swearing allegiance to his 'empress' early on before turning on her, was not forgotten around Westminster in a hurry. He warned May against trying to soften the terms she had agreed for Britain's exit so that it could pass through Parliament thanks to the support of Labour MPs, describing the party as a 'fair-weather friend'. His lecture on loyalty bemused some of his Tory colleagues, with one MP pondering to me whether he was 'speaking from experience' in warning against 'fair-weather' supporters. Given his strident criticism of May's premiership, his attendance at her farewell drinks reception held at Downing Street on 22 July for MPs raised some eyebrows. 'I think the Prime Minister would have reason not to think I was her greatest supporter whilst in office,' he conceded to BBC *Newsnight*, acknowledging her invitation was 'generous and kind'.

Perhaps the Conservative politician wanted everyone to know how hollow his support for May's leadership was when he described his Eurosceptic group as her 'Praetorian Guard', as those Roman legionnaires were fantastically fair-weather friends. Twelve emperors met their end at the hands of their supposed bodyguards: Aurelian, Balbinus, Caligula, Caracalla, Commodus, Elagabalus, Galba,

Gordian III, Numerian, Pertinax, Probus and Pupienus. It is remarkable how often they got their hands dirty. But their motive each time was clear: self-advancement. The emperor's death tended to pan out well for the Praetorians. One of the most notorious examples came in 217 AD when one of Emperor Caracalla's bodyguards took his chance to stick a knife in him as he stopped by the roadside to relieve himself. Guess who took over? The commander of the Praetorian Guard at the time, Marcus Opellius Macrinus. It's no surprise that he was widely speculated to have had a hand in the assassination.

The most outrageously political Praetorian was a soldier called Lucius Aelius Sejanus, who managed to scheme his way into becoming the most powerful man in Rome. After enough years of military service, fighting on campaigns in as far-flung places as Armenia, he was picked by Tiberius to head his imperial guard. That position, serving as the emperor's chief bodyguard and right-hand man, offered a lot of responsibility. But he still hungered for more, possessing what Tacitus described as an 'unbounded lust for power'. But there were several people who stood in the way of him and greater power: Tiberius' heirs.

Sejanus began by plotting to get rid of Tiberius' son, Drusus Caesar. He was targeted first not only because of his importance in the line of succession, but also because they had recently fallen out. Tacitus recounts that they had a spat which culminated with Drusus raising his fist at Sejanus, and then hitting him in the face in their resulting scuffle. In revenge, Sejanus seduced Drusus' wife Livia, persuading her that they could one day be married, and that it would be better if her husband was bumped off. They succeeded in making that happen soon after, with Sejanus picking a slow-acting poison so it would look like Drusus had died of natural causes.

His death left a power vacuum, which Sejanus stepped in to fill. Tiberius had been sharing some responsibilities with his son, Drusus, and so they were taken on by his chief Praetorian instead, whom he began to call his 'partner in my toils' (*Socius Laborum*).

But Sejanus was not yet happy, as Tiberius still had plenty of heirs who could thwart his ambition. The emperor's nephew (and adopted son), Germanicus, could have been a contender, but he died mysteriously after suddenly falling ill while on campaign in Syria. Sejanus was suspected of having a hand in Germanicus' death by his wife Agrippina. And so, on returning to Rome, she started to whip up support among senators for Sejanus' wings to be clipped. As the widow of a publicly respected general, she was able to easily win them around. And her three sons were especially threatening for Sejanus as they – effectively Tiberius' grandchildren – were likely heirs for him to groom.

After eliminating the first Drusus without sparking public suspicion, or calls for his death to be avenged, Sejanus was feeling bold about what he could do next. He considered poisoning Agrippina's three children, but concluded they were too well looked after for that to work. So he was even more dastardly with his next step. Sejanus tried to insert himself directly into the line of succession by seeking to marry Drusus' widow Livia, so he could become part of Tiberius' dynasty. But he was rebuffed by the emperor, who warned him against overstepping his position. Duly put back in his place, the scheming henchman changed tack. He started a whispering campaign against

Agrippina, using his trusted position to make Tiberius paranoid that she (rather than his own bodyguard) was seeking to take the throne from him. He managed to terrify Tiberius so much that he successfully persuaded him to leave Rome to retire to the countryside, and then to the island of Capri. As head of the emperor's close protection, Sejanus controlled all the information that passed to Tiberius, so it was not difficult to keep him convinced that it was best to stay away from the city, leaving its care to his right-hand man.

Tiberius' self-imposed exile bemused many Romans. They had been used to the emperor staying in their palatial home in Rome, in the same way Americans expect their President to live in the White House, rather than Mar-a-Lago, the Florida club owned by President Trump that he likes to refer to as his 'Southern White House'. Tiberius' move was the equivalent of the Prime Minister of the United Kingdom deciding to move out of Downing Street in order to live on the Isle of Wight. It was just not what a Roman ruler did, as Quintus Cicero acknowledged in the political advice to his brother: 'Don't leave Rome! ... There is no time for vacations during a campaign. Be present in the city.'

Tiberius' absence meant that gossip thrived in Rome about what sort of debauchery he was indulging in on his island retreat. The rumour mill went wild, with Suetonius chronicling lurid tales about how he invited prostitutes of both genders to come and have orgies in front of him, while he had an erotic library festooned with filthy images he could point to 'in case a performer should need an illustration of what was required'. The salacious tales he attracted are reminiscent of the stories about Silvio Berlusconi's notorious 'bunga

bunga' parties. Emperor Tiberius was in no position to stamp on such gossip as he never returned to Rome, preferring instead to stay in Capri for the rest of his life.

Left to his own devices, Sejanus was in the perfect position to pursue his own agenda. The soldier, as Cassius Dio wrote, 'himself seemed to be the emperor'. Bronze statues were erected in his honour, and his birthday was celebrated publicly as if he was part of the imperial family. He, like Tiberius, was given a gilded chair in the theatre. And they were both elected consuls together. Religious sacrifices were made to Sejanus with the same reverence given to the man who was actually emperor.

Sejanus seized his chance to crack down on his enemies, namely Agrippina and her children. Many of those close to her were dragged before kangaroo courts to face accusations of treason, sexual misconduct or corruption. She herself was placed under house arrest, and then later exiled along with two of her sons. One of them, a man called Drusus, was accused of plotting against the emperor and locked up. He wasted away in prison, delaying the inevitable – as Tacitus notes grimly – by 'tearing out the stuffing of his mattress' to chew on it. The only son who survived the purges, by moving to Capri with Tiberius, was a young lad named Gaius Caesar, better known by his nickname Caligula.

Sejanus would have gotten away with his coup, if the actual emperor had not found out and intervened. Tiberius could not rely on the rest of his Praetorian Guard, not least because of how rogue its chief had gone. Instead, he had another force set up to counterbalance their influence: the 'urban cohorts'. These troops, who acted as a heavily armed police force, were particularly useful as they were not under Sejanus' command. It was not long before the power-hungry Praetorian was caught, thrown into prison, then put to death.

Despite Tiberius having to stop his chief Praetorian seizing power from him, his imperial guard continued to think about more than the emperor's welfare. Sejanus' successor, a man called Naevius Sutorius Macro, could see that Tiberius – then in his late seventies – was not long for the world. And so it was worth him thinking ahead to who would succeed him, so that he could be sure to have the next emperor's favour. Macro quickly decided to cosy up to Tiberius' adopted grandson Caligula, courting him – Tacitus writes – 'with daily increasing energy'. Suetonius suggests that he was so desperate to get on with Caligula that he even turned a blind eye to his wife having an affair with the aspiring emperor. And when Tiberius was on his deathbed, Macro ensured the succession went as smoothly as possible.

On 15 March of the year 37 AD, it seemed that Tiberius had breathed his last. Once the news spread, Caligula prepared himself to take over as his followers rushed to congratulate him, but there was a last-minute hitch. News emerged that Tiberius was still alive. He had recovered his voice and was now demanding food to help him get over his faintness, which sparked panic among those who had just been celebrating his passing. Caligula was 'extremely apprehensive', Tacitus records, but was saved by the Praetorian Macro, who hurried Tiberius along to his death by ordering him to be 'smothered under a huge heap of clothes'.

Macro helped smooth Caligula's rise to power in another way.

Tiberius had officially anointed him in his will as heir, but sharing the Empire with his young grandson Gemellus. Macro managed to have the will declared invalid, with it being concluded that the late emperor had not been in his right mind when writing it. That meant all the power would go to Caligula, while Gemellus was fobbed off with the title of '*princeps iuventutis*' – effectively, the young people's emperor – and died suspiciously soon after.

The Praetorians relished orchestrating the rise and fall of the emperors they were meant to guard. Some of the guardsmen assassinated Caligula in the year 41 AD, in a plot led by an officer who was reported to have snapped after being relentlessly teased by the emperor. According to Suetonius, he 'suffered every form of insult' for his apparent effeminacy and, above all, his squeaky voice. After he was killed, the soldiers found Caligula's uncle Claudius hiding behind a curtain in the aftermath. And, needing a ruler to justify their own existence, they proclaimed him the new emperor. He thanked them for their decision by showering them with cash, a necessary move for such a mercenary force but one that led Suetonius to complain that he had used 'bribery to secure [their] loyalty'. Many later emperors would follow Claudius' example by paying their entourage handsomely to ensure their fealty.

Some of Claudius' Praetorians retired to their country estates to enjoy their riches, while others like the chief officer involved with the plot – Chaerea – stayed on. But it turned out to be a big mistake, as he and one of his fellow assassins were put to death, after Claudius concluded that their disloyalty to his predecessor needed to be punished to prevent anyone else getting ideas. His new Praetorian Guard were loyal, accompanying him on his trip to Britain in 43 AD, but just as mercurial. After Claudius was poisoned, with it clear he was on his way out, they transferred their support to Nero. But even he was at the mercy of his Praetorians. It was clear his time as emperor was running out when his guardsmen pulled their support and threw their weight behind his emerging rival, Servius Sulpicius Galba. They decided to do so in the belief that Galba would reward them handsomely, but he had clearly missed the memo. 'It's my habit to recruit soldiers, not buy them,' he informed them stiffly on taking over. Short-changing the men tasked with his protection ensured he did not last more than seven months. Once Galba's rival Otho made a better offer, the disgruntled troops declared him the new emperor. That was just the start of what is now known as the Year of the Four Emperors.

After enough decades of politicking, the Praetorians' influence went to their heads. In the second century AD, after they had bumped off Emperor Commodus in 192 AD for a reward of 3,000 denarii and then killed his successor Pertinax three months later, they put the emperorship up for auction to the highest bidder. Titus Flavius Claudius Sulpicianus began bidding for the throne, but he was outbid by Didius Julianus, who offered each soldier 5,000 more than the 20,000 his rival had been willing to offer. After such a bid, the Praetorians were only too happy to declare him emperor, with the Senate playing ball in order to keep the peace. Understandably, other people were not sold on picking the next emperor on the strength of how much they could pay the Praetorians. And so an ugly war for power broke out, in what is now known as the Year of the Five Emperors, in 193 AD. Didius Julianus only lasted sixty-six days in power for that year before he was abandoned in favour of a better prospect, with one of his soldiers delivering the final blow by killing him in his palace. According to Cassius Dio, his last words were: 'But what evil have I done? Whom have I killed?' That sounds like the cry of someone who expected their money to have bought them greater loyalty from their guardsmen.

The Praetorians continued to make and break Rome's emperors until the early fourth century, when it was finally decided that they might be best disbanded. The guardsmen rebelled against an attempt to abolish them and declared that they wanted a man called Maxentius to be the new emperor. But their decision was overruled by Constantine, who crushed them all in battle. After his victory, he exiled the surviving Praetorians and ripped up their headquarters, marking an end to their grip on power.

Jacob Rees-Mogg and his fellow Eurosceptics were in the early days among Theresa May's biggest defenders. They would march into the voting lobbies whenever she was in danger of having her hands tied by Remainer MPs in order to help her out, and would leap to the defence of her negotiating strategy and the red lines she had set out on Brexit. But the clearer it became that their empress would not reward them with the Brexit they wanted, the more sour they became about her leadership.

That is a similar danger countless emperors faced when their Praetorian Guard concluded it was no longer in their best interests to protect them. The Praetorians would risk their lives in order to do their duty, so they would feel it was only wise to pay attention to the political situation, and to ensure they were always backing the best horse, rather than helping a weak one hobble along. The way May has approached Brexit might not have put Rees-Mogg and his fellow Eurosceptics' lives at risk, but they have still had grave reason to worry, fearing the damage it would cause to their parliamentary careers and the Conservative Party's welfare. And so they have felt driven to take matters into their own hands by doing all they could to put an end to her leadership.

May might have been reassured on hearing her Conservative colleagues like Rees-Mogg comparing themselves to the Praetorian Guard in their apparent loyalty to her as Prime Minister. But if she knew her history, it would have been clear that his message was more double-edged. Those who sound ready to defend their leader to the death tend to want something out of it for their loyalty. Boris Johnson will be acutely aware of this, after the support of the ERG 'Praetorians' helped him succeed her as Prime Minister. But they were insistent that he committed to delivering Brexit by 31 October to guarantee their support. 'If he lets us down, I'll fucking kill him myself,' one senior Tory Brexiteer told me.

Loyalty comes at a price, as the Praetorians showed. If they did not have any reason to protect their emperor, they quickly found someone they preferred to have in place. Leaders should bear that in mind when considering those clamouring to be close to them. They should not just keep their friends close, but make sure they are spoiled rotten, in order to stay safe.

Marcus Tullius Cicero © EMMA DOUBLE

BRACE YOURSELF FOR TOUGH WORDS

Has politics ever been ruder than it has been since Donald Trump became President? Many people seem adamant that he has taken public discourse to a new low with his panache for puerile insults and playground name-calling. Certainly, he is much blunter than his American predecessors. People who have left his administration under a cloud have variously been described as 'lazy as hell', 'dumb as a rock', 'lowlife' and 'wacky'. By contrast, when Dwight Eisenhower was asked to name any accomplishments by Richard Nixon, the man who served as his vice-president for two terms, he replied with the comparatively tame, even if still unflattering: 'If you give me a week, I might think of one. I don't remember.' In 1960, that line was seen as stunningly vicious, with Nixon's Democratic rival for the presidency John F. Kennedy using it in his attack adverts.

British politicians struggle to show the same verbal ferocity as Trump. They can certainly dish it out, such as when Gordon Brown was accused of having changed from 'Stalin to Mr Bean' (by Vince Cable) and Jeremy Corbyn was branded a 'mutton-headed old mugwump' (by none other than Boris Johnson). But these examples seem positively genteel compared to Trump once suggesting that the father of his presidential rival, Ted Cruz, whom he liked to call 'Lyin' Ted', had been caught up in JFK's assassination. And Trump is not alone in his rudeness towards the Republican senator. Senator Cruz is a popular target of vitriol incidentally, with fellow Republican politician John Boehner branding him 'Lucifer in the Flesh' and a 'miserable son of a bitch'. British politicians only tend to be so crude outside of the House of Commons, as Winston Churchill's grandson Nicholas Soames showed in 2013 when he collared a Tory MP in the Commons tearoom – who had been attracting speculation over his leadership ambition – to denounce him in no uncertain terms as 'a chateau-bottled nuclear-powered ocean-going shit'. He did not stop there, accusing Adam Afriyie of being 'totally fucking disloyal' and a 'fucking disgrace' for pushing his 'grotesque fucking vanity project' of a leadership campaign.

Despite the sound and fury in Parliament's weekly bout known as Prime Minister's Questions, overly strong insults tend not to be allowed. Everyone is assumed to be 'honourable' in the Houses of Parliament, so that means the 'honourable members' – as they have to refer to each other – cannot be accused of anything negative that might put that into doubt. This genteel side to parliamentary etiquette made itself known on 20 July 1983, when a minister – Alan Clark – turned up to the Commons to take questions as a government representative after popping by a wine-tasting. A new Labour MP caused outrage by openly accusing him of being drunk, telling MPs that she thought 'seriously … that the minister is incapable'. There were 'screams, yells, shouts of "Withdraw", counter shouts. General uproar,' Clark noted in his diary. 'The House was alight.' A line was only drawn under it when the MP, Clare Short, offered to withdraw her remark, although she warned that MPs would realise she 'meant what [she] said'.

Playground-level insults can cause similar outrage. In July 2010, the Labour MP Tom Watson lost his rag with then education secretary Michael Gove, accusing him of being a 'miserable pipsqueak of a man'. That proved too much for the House of Commons, as the Speaker silenced him and he later apologised. Insinuating criminal activity is much more harmful, so it is no surprise the Speaker stamps on it. The outspoken Labour MP Dennis Skinner in December 2005 used a question to the then shadow Chancellor George Osborne to unsubtly allude to tabloid allegations of cocaine use, quipping: 'The only thing that was growing then were the lines of coke in front of boy George and the rest of the Tories.' He was ordered out of the chamber for doing so.

As rough as such exchanges might sound, they pale in comparison

PART TWO: IN OFFICE

to the vitriol Romans could muster. In his early days, Julius Caesar was sent as a Roman representative to the court of Nicomedes IV, the old king of Bithynia, to assemble a fleet of ships. But he stayed so long during his visit that he came to be ribbed over why he had devoted so much time to the project. One Roman politician liked to call him the 'Queen' of Bithynia, the historian Suetonius records, while one of the bawdy songs Caesar's own troops liked to sing in moments of triumph was about how 'Caesar laid the Gauls low, and Nicomedes laid him low'.

Marcus Tullius Cicero, as one of the most gifted orators of first-century BC Rome, was not stuck for words whenever he wanted to lay into someone to mock. Perhaps that is because of the influence of people in his life like his brother Quintus, who advised him at election time to zero in on his opponent's weaknesses. 'Consider Antonius,' he offered by way of example, 'who once had his property confiscated for debt ... then after he was elected as praetor, he disgraced himself by going down to the market and buying a girl to be his sex slave.' Such faults were well worth highlighting, he suggested, so voters were forewarned about the person they risked electing. In what could be the first historical record of opposition research, candidate Cicero was urged to make use of all the dirt he could get: 'It ... wouldn't hurt to remind [voters] of what scoundrels your opponents are and to smear these men at every opportunity with the crimes, sexual scandals, and corruption they have brought on themselves.'

A gifted orator like Cicero knew how to deploy such information to brutal effect in his speeches. And he could go far in his efforts to do so because Roman politics was a rhetorical bear pit. Accusing someone else of lying in Parliament is against the rules, but in Rome it was entry-level sparring. The jibes thrown around could be much stronger, such as accusing someone of incest. Cicero's favourite forms of abuse tended to be to cast his target as effeminate, or a lush. Facing the former consul Lucius Calpurnius Piso Caesoninus in the Senate, he quickly tried to humiliate him by dramatically recalling what a state he'd found him in on a recent visit:

> Do you remember, you scum, when I visited you around the fifth hour with Gaius Piso, how you, in slippers, came out from some hovel, your head wrapped, and, how when you exhaled from your foul mouth the disgusting smell of a tavern, with you using the excuse of poor health, which you said was because you were in the habit of caring for it with medicinal wines?

Cicero was only getting started, as he went on about Piso's 'dirty vices', namely binge-drinking and hosting saucy parties: 'No one was able to say whether he was spending more time drinking or vomiting or urinating.' The Tory bon viveur Alan Clark would have had a field day in this arena, with his wine-tasting that outraged MPs undoubtedly striking a Roman audience as relatively tame. Nevertheless, Cicero did not hold back in the overall portrait he wanted to put together of Piso, depicting him as a slave to his desire, rather than public service. 'Indeed he is accustomed in his discussion to put more weight to the desires of the stomach than the eyes or ears,' the master rhetorician quipped.

Despite Cicero's colourful harangue, Piso managed to close down the row by issuing a pamphlet rebutting his criticisms as breezily as if they had been aired at a comedy roast. The fact he then went on to be elected censor, taking charge of Rome's moral standards, shows that he managed to tough out Cicero's jibes.

But be careful about crossing the line

Boris Johnson landed on an ideal way to make his feelings known in 2016 about the President of Turkey's efforts to prosecute a German comedian for his offensive poem: writing one of his own. The poem was published by *The Spectator*, a magazine he used to edit, as part of a competition it was running to find the best poetic rebuff to Recep Tayyip Erdoğan's attempted clampdown, and won him a £1,000 prize (which had been donated by a reader). His limerick read as follows: 'There was a young fellow from Ankara | Who was a terrific wankerer | Till he sowed his wild oats | With the help of a goat | But he didn't even stop to thankera.'

Johnson defended his prize-winning work, telling an interviewer at a Swiss weekly magazine that 'if somebody wants to make a joke about the love that flowers between the Turkish president and a goat, he should be able to do so, in any European country, including Turkey'.

Awkwardly for Johnson, two months later he became the United Kingdom's chief diplomat, a job that required him to get along with countries like Turkey. His first visit there as Foreign Secretary could have been disastrous, but he managed to avoid calamity by not trying to defend his words in Ankara – and instead dismissing his poetic work as 'trivia'. He enthused for good measure about his 'Ottoman' grandfather and his 'proud ownership' of a Turkish washing machine. Words landed Johnson in potential trouble, but he managed to talk himself out of it. Many Romans landed themselves in hot water if they were as provocative as Johnson in their poetic efforts.

Slagging the emperor off could be treasonous, a crime which in Rome was punishable by death and a seizure of the convicted person's property. One budding poet, a well-to-do man called Gaius Cominius, was convicted of slandering Emperor Tiberius in a poem, and was only spared punishment because his brother pleaded for mercy. Another man of similar social status, Gaius Valerius Catullus, wrote poetry that was – as the historian Tacitus puts it – 'crammed with insults against the Caesars', but got away with it.

How? Catullus did not mince his words. He accused Caesar of having an affair with one of his officers, called Mamurra, and painted him as a 'shameless, insatiable gambler'. Caesar was tarnished in his view by his closeness to such a womanising and louche character as Mamurra, whom he nicknamed '*mentula*' (a crude term for the penis). But Catullus and Caesar soon made up; the poet apologised to the man he had taken to task and was then swiftly invited to dinner. It's not known whether Mamurra joined them. That approach does not mean Caesar was a soft touch. He could have easily gone after him, but such a reprisal would have made him a poetic martyr. As Tacitus puts it: 'For things unnoticed are forgotten, resentment confers status upon them.' Forgiveness was the ultimate display of Caesar's power, as those whom he spared knew they could have so easily been crushed.

Such a gesture appealed to Caesar's successors, including Nero. In 62 AD, he had to judge the first treason case of his reign. A praetor,

Antistius Sosianus, had been accused of writing and reciting verses lampooning Nero while at a banquet. The host insisted he had not heard the offending poetry, but several witnesses claimed they had. Some politicians were clamouring for Sosianus to be stripped of office and put to death. But Nero saved his life by intervening to veto such a sentence, but warned him that he would not tolerate mockery. The emperor wanted others to know that they did not have free rein to mock him, so made sure to give Sosianus the milder punishment of banishment to a remote island.

Rome's poets were not the only ones who risked their lives with their words. Cicero, a man who was unafraid to denounce politicians of all sorts of levels of importance, picked his most dangerous battle when he went after Mark Anthony. He had so much to say about Julius Caesar's former right-hand man, who had seized power after Caesar's assassination, that he spaced it out over twelve speeches, which he modestly chose to model on the legendary Greek orator Demosthenes' attacks on King Philip of Macedon by calling them the 'Philippics'.

Cicero delivered the first of his speeches on the floor of the Senate on 2 September 44 BC, lambasting Anthony's leadership at the time as consul. He caused so much uproar that he decided not to risk delivering his follow-up the following month in person, and put it out instead as a pamphlet. Given how vitriolic his message was, it is understandable why he ducked the chance to deliver it to Anthony's face in the Senate. Any rant that begins by praising themselves for 'abstaining from slander' previously is clearly not going to pull punches. Cicero goes back to Anthony's early days, accusing him of having been bankrupt and acting as a rentboy (literally, a 'boy sold for pleasure') in order to get by, calling him then a 'vulgar slut' whose 'price for whoring themselves around was not too small'. He repeatedly accuses him of sexual deviancy, mixing with pimps and prostitutes and being an out-of-control alcoholic. As an example, he accuses him of drinking so much wine at a wedding that he ended up vomiting in public the next day.

His attacks on Anthony built to a rhetorical climax when, in his last address, he successfully persuaded the Senate to declare Anthony a public enemy. But it started to be clear that he might regret his splenetic tone once Anthony made peace with Octavian. And Anthony moved into an ideal position from which to respond after he took power as part of a three-man rule with Octavian called the Triumvirate.

Anthony had not forgotten all the insults Cicero had thrown at him. And so when it was decided that a list would be drawn up of enemies to be hunted down and put to death, Anthony argued fiercely for his name to be included. Cicero was swiftly caught leaving his villa mid-escape to the seaside, where he planned to take a ship to Macedonia. He was beheaded and, under Anthony's orders, had his head and hands displayed on the rostra, where he had made many of the speeches against him, to show what happened to the emperor's critics. Anthony's wife, Fulvia, took revenge for the many jibes they had received from him. As the historian Cassius Dio writes:

Fulvia took the head into her hands before it was removed, and after abusing it spitefully and spitting upon it, set it on her knees, opened the mouth, and pulled out the tongue, which she pierced with the pins that she used for her hair, at the same time uttering many brutal jests.

Cicero's brutal putdowns show that politics has been so much coarser in the past. Trump has accused his opponents of many things, but has yet to suggest they are rentboys and pimps. But Cicero's demise is a reminder of what can be the price of such fierce rhetoric.

Johnson must feel lucky Turkey's president was happy to welcome him to Ankara and forget about the time he was called a 'wankerer'. Having to wax lyrical about washing machines is far less painful than what many writers have suffered for their offensive words.

POPULISM WORKS, BUT CAN GET MESSY

'I'm certainly not part of the aristocracy ... I'm a man of the people' Jacob Rees-Mogg told the BBC interviewer Andrew Neil in 2015, deciding to prove his populist credentials by adding: '*Vox populi, vox dei.*'

His snappy bit of Latin – which means literally 'Voice of the people, voice of God' – might sound like an observation from a great Roman statesman that the people should be heard as reverently as if it had come from the heavens. But it actually came centuries after the Romans during the Middle Ages. Latin teachers would leap in here to point out that this should be obvious from the reference to a singular god, rather than the plural ('*deorum*') that the Romans believed in.

To be fair, the people were regarded in Rome as a crucial part of the system of government. The acronym 'SPQR' (*Senatus Populus Que Romanus*) came to sum up who was officially in charge: the Senate and the people of Rome. The emperor wielded more power than any of them, but officially he was seen as another Roman citizen, albeit a pre-eminent one. His official title – '*Princeps civitatis*' ('First Citizen') – attested to that. Such symbolism can be seen around the modern world, with leaders of politics, business and religion all insistent to varying degrees that they are just 'first among equals' (*primus inter pares*).

Still, Rees-Mogg's preferred bit of Latin – '*vox populi, vox dei*' – cuts to a key truth in politics: people vote for those who most revere what they have to say. Only the popular get elected, and to be popular, you need to ingratiate yourself with the populace. Bill Clinton was celebrated for his ability to make voters feel special. One tale his supporters like to tell to sum up his campaigning approach came when he was passing through a town in a key American electoral battleground trying to drum up votes. His campaign battle bus zoomed past some voters, who were waving a sign at him with the phrase: 'If you give us four minutes, we'll give you four years'. On seeing it, Clinton was said to have brought the bus to a halt so he could hop out and talk to them. His eagerness to woo the electorate was rewarded with not just four but eight years as President.

By contrast, those politicians who are not interested in engaging with voters struggle to engage their interest in turn. Quintus Cicero recognised that in the catty advice he provided his brother Marcus about the electoral rivals he faced: 'Look at Antonius – how can the man establish friendships when he can't even remember anyone's name? Can there be anything sillier than for a candidate to think a person he doesn't know will support him?' The lesson he drew for Cicero was that he should strive to learn people's names and faces as 'nothing impresses an average voter more than having a candidate remember him'.

As glib a tactic as that might be, Roman politicians made it an art form. Many would rely on their special *nomenclator*, a slave whose job it was to remind their master of the people they had met, to grease the wheels. Emperor Hadrian marked himself out for not really needing such services, at times correcting his name specialist on who people were. Such behaviour proved to be much more effective than the manner other Roman politicians adopted. When the young aristocrat Publius Cornelius Scipio Nasica was running for the office of aedile, for example, he went out to press the flesh among the people he hoped would vote for him. But he was intrigued by the roughness of the hands of one man he met. 'My goodness, do you walk on them?' he quipped. His gag didn't go down well among those who overheard, as the man's hands were hardened from honest toil in the fields, and his haughty remark ensured he went on to lose the election.

It should go without saying that offending voters tends not to be a vote-winning move, but politicians cannot help themselves. When Gordon Brown was picked up on microphone venting in 2010 about the 'bigoted woman' who complained about immigration to him as he campaigned in Rochdale for the general election, he could not shrug it off. As soon as a recording of his remark had been played to him, which he listened to in a BBC studio with his head in his hands, he dashed back to her home in Rochdale to apologise in a desperate bid to draw a line under 'Duffygate'. Four years later, Emily Thornberry lost her position as a frontbench Labour spokesperson after being accused of snobbery for tweeting a picture of a house in Rochester, during a by-election, which was displaying an England flag. Both attempts at damage control failed to stop Labour, like our farmers' friend Scipio Nasica, from losing the election.

Whenever politicians become conceited and too lazy to listen, people start to warm to outsiders who pledge to represent their interests and shake up the status quo. Recent events have left many politicians and pundits breathless as they try to keep up with the outbreak across the world of what has been dubbed 'populism'. As the name suggests, populist politicians have thrived by promising to fight against an uncaring elite for what the people want. Donald Trump became President of the United States promising to stand up for the 'silent majority', seizing on the suggestion from his rival Hillary Clinton that he was supported by 'deplorables' as an attack on the average working American he wanted to champion. Emmanuel Macron was similarly maverick in France, starting his own party to blaze his trail – independently – into the presidency. The strength of their message meant that the first time they stood for office, they leapt to the top of the political ladder to become heads of state.

But populist politics is proving contagious. President Macron has already faced his own popular backlash, in the form of protesters taking to the streets of Paris in yellow vests. Hundreds of citizens were injured in these *'gilets jaunes'* protests, which saw petrol bombs flying around as well as tear gas from the police trying to restore order. They soon forced Macron to give ground, scrapping tax rises and increasing the minimum wage.

Such scenes make what has been going on in Britain seem as mild-mannered as a vicar's tea party. Anti-Brexit protesters have been painting their faces blue and going on marches, while pro-Brexit protesters have been waving signs outside Parliament demanding that MPs 'get on' with delivering 'the will of the people'. Who could possibly say no? This has been a powerful cause for Brexiteers to champion, with Remainers forced to try to ape this populist rhetoric. They have been shy about opposing Brexit for fear of inviting the wrath of the people by seeming to be determined to flout their will. Hence their decision to dress up their desire for another referendum in such democratically acceptable language as a 'People's Vote' and demand initiatives like a 'People's Assembly' (a role Parliament is already meant to fulfil, Brexiteers pointed out).

Establishment politicians have struggled to turn the tide. Tony Blair gave voice to that frustration in January 2019 when he decided to explain why the popular mood irked him. He chose to stand up for, rather than against, the elite by recounting a conversation about Brexit with a voter who snapped at him that he was 'trying to say to me that you know far more about this than I do'. In a rare show of elitist candour, Blair explained why he felt superior to the average voter:

I was Prime Minister for ten years. I want to say to people, I follow Newcastle United – if a game is on the TV I will watch it, but I know that Rafa Benitez has forgotten more about football in a day than I will ever know … It's because that's what he spends his life doing. You send people to Parliament and that's their day job. It's not your day job. So if they study the detail and say this is a bad idea they are not squabbling children. They are doing what you sent them to Parliament to do.

The Romans would not have been phased by such squabbles about populism. Indeed, they can claim to have invented it. One of the main political groups they had in the Republic were called the 'Populares'. As their name suggests, these liberal-minded individuals stood for people power and fought for the rights of the 'plebeians' against the conservative 'Optimates' (equivalent to 'the best men'), which fought for the senatorial elite. Those who sided with the Optimates found it hard to naturally connect with the average plebeian voter, namely because they could only claim to have the common touch if they were happy dealing with commoners.

The plebs were widely looked down upon by Rome's rich and aristocratic politicos, who saw them as part of the '*vulgus*' – the mob. Their general attitude is summed up neatly by the poet Horace, who declared in his odes his hatred for the 'uncultivated masses' (*profanum vulgus*) and that he preferred to 'keep them at a distance'. But the plebeian masses had numbers on their side, which meant anyone who sought elected office knew they had to be ready to put on their best smile and woo them to win. They had to break out of their patrician circle, as the dinner party circuit would not see them meet enough voters to ensure victory.

As someone born into a wealthy family, Cicero was inclined to be rather snooty in his attitudes towards the lower classes. But his brother urged him to try to be less haughty with voters in order to win their support. 'You can be rather stiff at times,' he was told. 'You desperately need to learn the art of flattery – a disgraceful thing in normal life but essential when you are running for office.' That meant shaking their hands, looking them in the eye and taking their concerns seriously. The Populares did not have so much difficulty, and indeed delivered a lot for their disadvantaged supporters, but not without upheaval. They had a starring role in the late part of the Roman Republic during what came to be known as the Conflict of the Orders. This blockbuster name is what has been given to the fight by the plebeians for full political rights, and the right to be treated on equal terms to their elite, patrician, overlords.

The big breakthrough for the Roman plebs came in 494 BC, when they were able to put forward their own representatives. These 'tribunes of the people' *(tribuni plebis)* were able to do a lot to protect the plebeian class, such as proposing new laws, and – most daringly – vetoing the actions of the Senate, a consul, or other public officials. They were protected by law from danger, with those who tried to harm or stop them at risk of being sentenced to death. That is a lot of power for one 'man of the people', which is why the Roman establishment sought to dilute it by having more than one in place, with the aim that any rogue tribune could be vetoed by their colleagues. And their legal immunity was phased out once they were out of office, so their enemies need only wait for their revenge. Later, the plebeians secured their own assembly (*'concilium plebis'*), which could pass laws.

Plenty of 'Populares' politicians stepped up to represent the people as tribunes. Some of those who fought hardest to deliver

137

results ended up causing chaos in the process. Perhaps the most controversial populist tribunes were the Gracchus brothers. Despite getting elected to posts designed to champion the masses against the establishment, Tiberius and his younger brother Gaius were just as blue-blooded as the patrician elite they fought against. Their father climbed to the top of the tree, being twice elected consul, and built up a large network of friends and contacts. Their mother was the daughter of a respected general, and could have become Queen of Egypt if, as a widow, she had not refused a marriage proposal from Ptolemy VIII, the King of Egypt, in order to devote herself to her sons.

Their eminent heritage and insider links will jar for some readers, given how the Gracchi went on to become notorious demagogues hell-bent on smashing the same system their family thrived in. But it turns out, populism is open to everyone. After all, Trump and Macron had elite educations and came to know the system – the former as a generous political donor, the latter as an adviser to Presidents and a minister in his own right – before they took power. To adapt Rees-Mogg's words, one can be part of the aristocracy and still be a man of the people.

Tiberius started off his career, like all good Roman men were meant to, by fighting for his country. He distinguished himself in battle, credited as the first one to scale the enemy's walls. After the army he was serving with suffered a string of major defeats while on campaign in Spain, Tiberius saved many of his fellow soldiers' lives by signing a peace treaty. But they had a problem on returning home. In the second century BC, the impact of Rome's constant wars was taking its toll on society. Soldiers had to serve until the very end of a campaign, no matter how long it took. Someone had to look after their property in the meantime. Those who lived in the countryside suffered, as while their wife and children could look after their farm, it would often go bust without them there to work the fields and to keep the money coming in. They would be forced to sell their property to make ends meet, with their bankruptcy a gift to wealthy speculators who wanted to build up a property empire. Snapping up these farms, and any land that the state had seized as an emergency move to support the war effort, allowed the rich to get even richer, while the poor suffered. Landbanking was rife, to the benefit of a few agricultural tycoons, and to the loss of those soldiers now left without a home. There was little these poor legionnaires could do. They could not make money by going on another military campaign, as only those who owned property could be in the army. Nor could they take on jobs like farm work, as the farmer tended to have brought in foreign slaves to do it more cheaply. Tiberius Gracchus decided to take matters into his own hands as a tribune of the people. After his election in 133 BC, he made a passionate plea in the Forum for his homeless brothers-in-arms. Plutarch records his furious speech as follows:

> The wild beasts that roam over Italy have every one of them a cave or lair to lurk in; but the men who fight and die for Italy enjoy the common air and light, indeed, but nothing else; houseless and homeless they wander about with their wives and children ... they fight and die to support others in wealth and luxury, and though

they are styled masters of the world, they have not a single clod of earth that is their own.

Tiberius sought to right this wrong by proposing a law to limit the amount of public land a citizen could own to around 125 hectares, with anything above that limit confiscated by the state and redistributed to Rome's poor and homeless veterans. But rich landowners ignored it, continuing to build up their empires by inventing fake names to buy new properties, and then not even bothering to hide their identities. He tried to soften the language in his law, and compromised by offering compensation to those who had to sell off their excess land, but it was still opposed. Rich senators hated him for pushing this change, claiming he was 'stirring up a general revolution' with his desire to redistribute Roman wealth.

Knowing the Senate would never approve a law that would hit its members' finances so badly, Tiberius tried to sidestep them by taking it through the People's Assembly, the alternative law-making body. Senators did not take kindly to being cut out of the process, deciding to try to stop him by asking another tribune – one who was less awkward – to go and veto the Bill. After shooting it down, Tiberius replaced the Bill with a harsher one, offering no compensation to the rich landowners who had to get rid of their excess land. But Tiberius and his tribunal nemesis were locked in a stalemate that dragged on for days. Tiberius heightened the stakes by using his own veto powers to bring the government to a grinding halt. He issued an edict banning his fellow officials from doing any public business and preventing them from using the state Treasury until his law was voted on, an effective government shutdown. When he finally called a vote on his proposed law, its rich opponents caused mayhem by storming in and stealing the voting urns people used to cast their ballot.

Eventually, Tiberius got his way. After trying to ask his rival tribune nicely to leave, a new law was proposed to kick him out of office that was swiftly voted on and approved. With the main roadblock cleared away, the Bill quickly passed, to the delight of Tiberius' supporters. He got his measure into law, with an official commission set up to enforce it by investigating landowners, measuring out how much excess land they owned and finding new tenants who could be equipped with the basic tools of the farming trade.

But that did not mean the Senate was any happier, as it still resisted the new land law by trying to starve the commission of the funds it needed. Events abroad gave Tiberius a chance to save his masterplan, as the King of Pergamon (in the north-west of what we now know as Turkey) died away and left his entire fortune to Rome. Tiberius seized his chance by proposing a Bill that would give the late king's inheritance to his agricultural commission, which senators were desperate to kill off.

That was the final straw for the Senate, and members plotted ways to get rid of the troublesome tribune Tiberius for trying to thwart their plans. Sensing danger, especially once his one-year term ran out, Tiberius stood for re-election. But rather than retreat from this fight, he doubled down on the populism by offering an even bolder pitch to the people for another year in office: promising to shorten the length of military service, to allow allies to become Roman citizens and – in a jibe at his foes in the Senate – to abolish their exclusive right to act as jurors, opening it up to people from other classes. Roman plebeians admired him so much that many, Plutarch notes, camped outside his house to ensure he was safe. But they could not protect Tiberius for long; he ended up being beaten to death in a public scuffle, his body thrown into the river Tiber.

Many of Tiberius' supporters met a similar fate. Those who survived were sent into exile without a trial or arrested and executed. One man had an especially grim death: being locked in a cage with poisonous vipers. To try to draw a line under this fallout, the Senate kept the land commission Tiberius had pushed through. If its members knew what his brother Gaius, who had his first job in politics serving on the commission, would go on to do, perhaps the senators would have rushed to shut it down.

After working on his brother's land commission, Gaius went on to serve as a junior official – a quaestor – in the Roman province of Sardinia. A far-flung posting had been typically seen by ambitious Romans as a chance to line one's pockets, safely away from the judgement and scrutiny of one's peers back home. The experience left Gaius deeply cynical about his fellow Romans, as he complained that he had been the only man who came back with all his money spent, while the rest had 'drunk the wine they brought and had returned with their wine-jars full of gold and silver'. And ten years after Tiberius' controversial tribuneship, his brother followed in his footsteps by becoming a tribune in his own right.

Gaius Gracchus used his new power to seek revenge on those who went after Tiberius and his supporters. One of his first proposed laws sought to ban any official who had been disbarred from standing for office again, a ready-made punishment for the tribune Tiberius had thrown out for trying to wreck his legislation. Another established the right for people to be prosecuted for exiling any Roman without a trial (as many of Tiberius' supporters had suffered).

Senators could not escape Gaius' fury. He proposed laws to break up their boys' club privileges, such as their right to be tried by juries solely composed of fellow senators and to collect taxes from the recently acquired province of Asia. He did not just take on the elite through laws, but through direct action. Wealthy Romans liked to make extra cash from gladiatorial games by setting up and hiring out temporary seating in the Forum, where they used to be held before the Colosseum was built. But Gaius Gracchus ruined their racket by having their seating dismantled, under the cover of night, before the festivities, so that ordinary Romans would have more space to watch – and not be obliged to pay for the privilege.

Gaius Gracchus needed to show the Senate that he meant business, as it was hell-bent on tearing up his older brother's crowning achievement: his land redistribution commission. As soon as Tiberius had died, senators rushed to neutralise his pet project by seizing the power to decide the legitimacy of how much land everyone owned for themselves. But Gaius fought back with a law reversing that. As a show of how serious he was in his anti-establishment verve, he defied the tradition public speakers tended to respect in the Forum of turning towards the Senate when they spoke, instead turning his back on the building. His defiant gesture was emulated more recently by Nigel Farage, likely unwittingly, when he led colleagues in the European

Parliament – twice – in protest against the European Union by turning their backs in the chamber as the bloc's anthem *Ode to Joy* was played.

Gaius' laws helped him build a broad coalition of support. Soldiers were wooed with a law that provided them with free clothes and equipment paid for by the public purse. Poor men had reason to be thankful, as it shortened the term they would spend in military service and outlawed the conscription of those under the age of seventeen. Another law required the state to bulk-buy grain to give it to citizens cheaply as a monthly dole. Such manoeuvres ensured the Senate realised the younger Gracchus would be just as troublesome as his brother. Gaius' political enemies worked to try to repeal as much of his legislation as possible. The divide in Rome over Gaius' populist crusade culminated in another ugly public scuffle, as had erupted in his brother Tiberius' time. On this occasion, the Gracchus brother was not killed in the fight, but instead he fled to a secluded grove, where he committed suicide.

The turmoil caused by the Gracchus brothers was brought to an end, but at a considerable cost. The consul who opposed Gaius, Plutarch records, appointed himself dictator and killed 3,000 Roman citizens without trial. He was later found to have committed fraud and taken bribes, and so spent his final days in disgrace – 'hated and abused by the people'. In a way, he represented the indulged elite the Roman people had decided deserved to be humbled by backing people like the Gracchi as their tribunes.

The Gracchi were not the only populists whose plans ended messily. The Emperor Commodus' right-hand man Cleander plotted to seize power by quietly diverting grain supplies in order to engineer a food shortage. He believed that the people would be so delighted by him stepping in to solve it that they would demand he become the next emperor as a reward. But his bid to secure power by mob rule went awry as the people turned against him and demanded his head – which Commodus duly supplied by having him beheaded.

Many of the laws proposed by the Gracchus brothers went on to be stripped away by their opponents. In a space of just fifteen years, the progress they had delivered, according to the writer Appian, was undone. Many people were left worse off and out of work. But some of the Gracchan legislation remained, namely Gaius' grain ration law. It set the model for Rome's bread dole that would become a mainstay of its welfare policy throughout its time as a Republic and Empire. The Gracchi were themselves honoured for their efforts to champion democracy with statues, which were worshipped by Roman citizens as if they were gods. Their time in office shows that populist politicians can get a lot done, but those determined to take on the establishment and deliver change will court controversy in doing so.

The Gracchus brothers' legacy shows that present-day populist politicians can expect any achievements to be mired in controversy. President Trump likes to say that he has delivered many things for his supporters, ranging from tax cuts to a buoyant economy, but his administration has been bogged down in inter-party skirmishes, admittedly exacerbated by his feisty use of the social media platform Twitter, and official inquiries into his affairs. As tempting as it might be to focus on events like the Mueller inquiry – infamously called a 'witch-hunt' by Trump – in assessing his presidency, his record of accomplishments – or lack thereof – should not be forgotten. The political soap opera around Brexit has often drowned out the good news stories cropping up about Britain's economy and business environment. Instead of dwelling on positive news like the fact that Norway's sovereign wealth fund is continuing to plough billions into the British economy, or that government borrowing has fallen to its lowest in seventeen years, our attention has been drawn irresistibly to the travails of Theresa May and Boris Johnson.

Modern populists are fighting not just to shake up the system, but to prove that they are doing so to their supporters. The controversy, just as the Gracchi brothers found, is inevitable for those taking on an entrenched establishment.

ENIGMAS WIN FEW FRIENDS

Theresa May did not want to give a 'running commentary' on the Brexit negotiations, saying that frequently at the outset. But she was soon forced to give a constant commentary, as anything she kept secret ended up being dragged out into the open. Her government complained at every point it was forced to cough something up, with MPs having to drag out basic details like its impact assessments of Brexit and even its negotiating strategy.

May's handling of the Brexit process proved frustrating for nearly everyone to follow due to how difficult it was to get clarity on the most basic points. 'I have just spent an hour with Theresa May and she has not told me a thing, she said nothing,' a friend of hers told BBC *Newsnight*'s political editor, Nick Watt. Amid mounting pressure to salvage her Brexit deal in February 2019, May expressed her frustration to reporters about their attempts to find out how she planned to handle the final stages of the process. 'Why is it that people are always trying to look for the next thing after the next thing after the next thing?' she fumed at them on a flight to Sharm El-Sheikh, where she made one of her many eleventh-hour appeals to European leaders.

Her colleagues would have been spoiled with the knowledge about what the 'next thing after the next thing' might be, as they found it hard enough to find out what the current 'thing' was. Cabinet ministers were often left exasperated by her tendency in meetings to sit in silence as everyone held forth, with it unclear what exactly she thought. Her favourite way of chairing those meetings was to go around the room and ask everyone their opinions, having made no indication of what she herself preferred. That was unnerving for ministers in the early days of her premiership, as they had to hold forth without any idea what she really thought, and therefore what they might risk saying that would incur her wrath.

Conservative MPs found that when trying to tease her out on the detail, they could come away with completely different interpretations of what she had said. One of her most notorious moments came in December 2018 after she told Tory MPs in a private party meeting that she was not going to quit before the next election, only for those in the room to emerge later with different interpretations of how specific she had been.

European leaders were similarly flummoxed whenever they dealt

with May. In January 2018, Angela Merkel regaled journalists privately at the World Economic Forum in Davos with her account of the
recurring conversation she had been having with her British counterpart since the referendum. The German leader would be asked
to make the UK an offer, but would reply: 'You're leaving – we don't
have to make you an offer. Come on, what do you want?' To which
May would reply again: 'Make me an offer.' And so, the German
Chancellor summed up, they were 'trapped in a recurring loop of
"What do you want?" and "Make me an offer."'

They had broken out of this loop by March 2019, however, when
May had tried to get her deal through Parliament twice, but needed
more time in the hope of having a third go at doing it. That required
European leaders to agree to delay Brexit in order to give her that
time, something they were only open to doing provided they felt the
time would be used well. They kept trying to find out if she had a
plan in the event her deal was voted down again, but she failed to
enlighten them. 'It sounded just as frustrating as being at Cabinet,' a
minister told me afterwards.

Ministers, European leaders and journalists all found May irritat-
ingly opaque to deal with. She was often compared to the Sphinx,
the treacherous mythical creature that was said to torment travellers
with riddles. But even that notorious trickster proved to be easier to
pin down. *The Times'* political commentator Matthew Parris wrote
in February 2019 about how those who had dealt with her across
government found she was 'extraordinarily uncommunicative', leading him to compare her to a 'political black hole … Nothing ever
comes out: no answers, only a blank so blank that it screams.' The

Telegraph's Michael Deacon noted that month how little effort she put in to answering questions in public:

> It's so blatant, it's almost impressive. Not just her refusal to answer the question, but her total lack of embarrassment about it. She doesn't blush. She doesn't gulp. She doesn't titter awkwardly and look down at her shoes. She knows she's dodging the question, and she isn't remotely ashamed. The fact is, she's not going to answer, and there isn't a thing you can do about it. Instead, she's just going to recite whatever line she and her advisers agreed on beforehand, irrespective of its relevance. And, while reciting it, she's going to peer at you, disapprovingly, down the full length of her nose, like a crow wearing a pair of pince-nez.

The Cabinet grappled with her evasive style for months, although their frustrations boiled over in March 2019 when May launched her third attempt to get her withdrawal agreement through the House of Commons. When the BBC's Nick Watt – fast becoming a confidant for despairing ministers – asked one member of the Cabinet to explain the thinking behind the Prime Minister's strategy when it seemed doomed, the sweary reply he received was revealing about the level of gloom. 'Fuck knows, I'm past caring. It's like the living dead in here,' Watt quoted the Cabinet minister as telling him live on *Newsnight* on 28 March. The rest of the minister's reply was less vulgar in nature, but still revealing of how despondent May's colleagues were feeling in their efforts to get any sense of direction from her:

Theresa May is the sole architect of this mess. It's her inability to engage in the most basic interactions which brought us here. Cabinet has totally broken down. Ministers say their bit. She gives nothing away. One side thinks X will happen, one side thinks Y will happen, and the Prime Minister decides on Z.

Stalwart Conservative supporters were left at a loss by her refusal to accept constructive advice. Senior Tory activists told me that month how they had dined with May and tried to offer some helpful advice on how she could endear herself, and her maligned deal, to her party members. They suggested she call together association chairmen to address them personally, arguing that they would appreciate the personal touch. At first May was resistant, pointing out that she had rung up a handful of association chairman to chat, but her dining partners insisted that more was needed. If she disagreed, they hoped she would show some spirit and argue back, but she did not. Instead, she offered the noncommittal promise to tell the party chairman about their idea, never to be acted upon. Her lack of action, or sign of any drive, led those despairing Tory activists to conclude she had run out of ideas and was crippled by indecision.

May was just the latest in a long line of secretive leaders. Gordon Brown spent years yearning for the top job, which left many expecting that he would have a detailed political blueprint ready to enact once he took power in 2007. But they were left at a loss and began to despair about a similar leadership void, while the man who aspired to replace him – David Cameron – branded him 'secretive, power-hoarding [and] controlling'.

Insurgent politicians are not necessarily any better at giving detail. When a band of MPs broke away from the Labour and Tory parties in February 2019 to form 'the Independent Group', interest was rife as to what they might stand for as independents. They all hated Brexit, but prominent figures were completely at odds over other issues, such as whether the Tory–Lib Dem programme of austerity had been a good thing or not. When two MPs, Heidi Allen and Luciana Berger, appeared on 24 February on Andrew Marr's sofa to show off their new grouping, the BBC's Sunday morning interviewer tried to find out where they stood on key political questions like tuition fees and nationalisation. But his enquiries were swatted down, with Allen accusing him of 'looking at this through the paradigm of the twentieth century'. Berger, in turn, suggested Marr was asking them questions 'through the prism of the old politics'. Over the following months, it became clear that they would refuse to be pinned down on policy. 'We don't just pull something out of our back pocket,' Allen declared at their European elections campaign launch on 23 April, warning journalists that it would be the 'same old' politics if she decided to 'pander' to them by outlining an agenda. Ironically, such coyness is not just the same old politics, but so old the Romans were practising it.

Emperor Tiberius would have been proud of how furtive modern politicians can be. He was a master at keeping his cards close to his chest. 'Now of all his self-described virtues, [he] cherished none more dearly than dissimulation,' the historian Tacitus wrote, adding that the emperor was such a natural that he did not have to try to conceal his thoughts as he was 'by habit or nature, always hesitant, always cryptic'. He lived by obscuring his true feelings and never being entirely clear what he wanted.

That love of equivocation manifested itself most absurdly in the wake of Emperor Augustus' death, when the path became clear for him to take over. All Tiberius had to do was indicate to the Senate that he was ready to assume power. But he affected modesty, making out he was unsure if he was ready to take on so much responsibility. So much power should not be invested in the hands of just one man, he intimated, suggesting that it should be shared. He was being deliberately coy, in an attempt to seem like a selfless public servant, only taking power – with a show of reluctance – after senators had begged him to do so. But the historian Tacitus suggests there was a more Machiavellian reason behind his act: he wanted to smoke his enemies out in the Senate by seeing who would demand that he took office with the least enthusiasm. Everything he got from them in response would be 'twisted into having some nefarious meaning', Tacitus wrote, and mentally filed away.

However, Tiberius' plan to stage manage his ascent went awry when senators took his show of reluctance seriously. If he was only happy to take on part of what Augustus took on, they asked him, what part of the Empire would he be happy to carve up for himself? That question stunned him into silence, as he wanted it all thrust upon him. After saying nothing for a few moments, Tiberius eventually insisted that he was too modest in the face of such immense responsibility to start carving out what bit he might want, and parts of government he would not take on. And he kept this act going for a long time.

His behaviour made the meeting even more farcical, as senators began dramatically gesturing and begging Tiberius to take over as Rome's head of state. Despite wanting to do so, his commitment to coyness meant that he responded by telling off senators for urging him to accept it. His argument, as the biographer Suetonius puts it, was that 'they did not realise what a monster the Empire was', but patience soon wore thin in the Senate.

'Let him take it or leave it!' one senator shouted during the increasingly stroppy encounter. Eventually, Tiberius gave in, but not with any apparent eagerness. He would become emperor, but insisted that his reign only last – as Suetonius records it – 'until I come to the time when it may seem right to you to grant an old man some rest'. Once in power, he was as secretive as ever, with Tacitus noting he would remain 'inscrutable', especially in a crisis. Despite his protestations before ascending to the throne, Tiberius proved to be in no rush to have any rest, staying in charge for twenty-two years until his death, at the age of seventy-seven.

The Senate did not earn the emperor's respect with its obsequious behaviour. When Tiberius once suggested that they all vote on an issue in an open ballot, one wily senator responded by asking if he could know how the emperor would vote, arguing that 'If you go first I shall have something to follow. If you go last of all, I fear I might find myself inadvertently on the wrong side.' Tiberius could not hide his scorn for the extent senators would go to vie for his approval. Every time he left meetings with the senators, he was said – according to the historian Tacitus – to mutter crossly in Greek that they were 'men fit to be slaves!'. Prime Minister May could only have wished for so servile a Cabinet and House of Commons.

Tiberius' successors were scarcely any better at pursuing open government, as Roman emperors had a variety of ways to avoid being clear about what they were thinking. They could hide behind the supernatural, asking for a prophecy on whether a potential decision augured well or not. Given they would be in charge of the state religion, they could ensure that the result – if the decision was sensitive – was known only to them.

Alternatively, they could hide behind the machinery of government. They tended to make official decisions with the help of their advisory council. The 'Consilium' came to be the highest decision-making forum in the Empire. That makes it sound like the Roman equivalent of a Prime Minister's Cabinet, but in practice it was closer to the smaller coteries they were criticised for preferring to consult, whether it be the 'Kitchen Cabinet' of Harold Wilson, Tony Blair's 'Sofa Cabinet' or David Cameron's 'Notting Hill clique'. Theresa May was not immune to this tendency either, as key decisions could be taken by just a few ministers in a sub-committee, or by her key advisers, before the wider Cabinet would get to discuss it. That came out infamously last July when she unveiled her latest Brexit plan to ministers at her countryside retreat of Chequers, and it proved so surprising to David Davis and Boris Johnson that they resigned soon after.

The Emperor's Consilium was fantastically secretive in the way it worked. Each of his advisers would be asked to summarise their view in personal notes for the emperor, who would then go away and study them overnight before coming to his own conclusion. That process limited the influence any potentially domineering member of the emperor's circle could have, and favoured those who could write – like modern civil servants – good memos.

Politicians publicly deplore decisions taken behind closed doors, yet they find it hard when in charge to avoid doing the same. Some prefer to do it officially in Cabinet, while others like to thrash it out among smaller coteries. The latter option has been increasingly popular among leaders, showing that they have come to realise – like Nero found – how useful it can be to ensure a grip is maintained of the eventual decision.

Such an approach to decision-making can encourage leaders to be frustratingly opaque about their thinking in public. But at least they are clear when a vacancy opens up that they want the top job. Compared to tricksy and secretive emperors like Tiberius, May can argue that she has been a model of transparent bonhomie as leader.

MEDDLE WITH MARKETS AT YOUR PERIL

After the financial crash, widely blamed on bankers' greed, the European Union sought to rein in their behaviour by bringing in a cap on their annual bonuses. It was set at the same level as their salary, although could be raised to twice as much if shareholders approved.

The measure was met with resistance, especially in the United Kingdom, which was keen to protect the City of London, Europe's global banking hub. The government fought the bonus cap through the courts, while London's Mayor Boris Johnson warned in 2012 that it would drive high-fliers out of the City and harm the national economy. 'This is possibly the most deluded measure to come from

Europe since Diocletian tried to fix the price of groceries across the Roman Empire,' Johnson declared.

Emperor Diocletian's chaotic attempt to regulate the Roman economy shows why Johnson thought he had history on his side in his opposition. By the fourth century AD, the economy was in a wreck. The state's free grain ration led to a growing number of dependants, as it encouraged many farmers to give up their work and live in Rome and enabled masters to free their slaves so they would live off the state. The rising number of unemployed people had damaging knock-on effects on the public accounts, as the state started to receive less in tax. Some emperors responded by inventing new taxes. In the first century AD, Vespasian went as far as imposing a tax on urine. It could be collected from public toilets to be sold as a source of ammonia for tanning leather and to keep wealthy Romans' togas nice and white. The depths plumbed by the emperor to find more cash disgusted his son Titus, who was said to have been shown a gold coin in response and told bluntly: 'Money doesn't smell.' Vespasian's tax became so notorious that his name became tied up in toilet humour, with the Romans using it to refer to their local lavatories. That tradition lives on today in the Romance languages; the French are among those to make use of what they call '*une vespasienne*'.

Such taxes proved not to be enough. The crushing level of taxation resulted in the imperial Treasury taking in even less. That meant emperors tried to sort the public finances by devaluing the currency, melting down base metal to produce coins of a lesser value than a *denarius*. What was once a silver coin ended up being issued on tin-plated copper, with the silver content reduced to one five-thousandth of its original level. These coins started to be worth less than their actual worth as metals, meaning the state was minting them at a loss. That sent inflation spiralling out of control, with knock-on effects for food prices and wages. So in 301 AD, Diocletian passed a series of edicts with the hope of calming things down, the most famous one setting a maximum price for common goods. The measure was aimed at combating the greed of merchants and speculators profiteering off the high food prices, as indicated by its moralising preamble:

> If the excesses perpetrated by persons of unlimited and frenzied avarice could be checked by some self-restraint – this avarice which rushes for gain and profit with no thought for mankind ... These measures are directed against the unscrupulous ... For who is so insensitive and so devoid of human feeling that he can be unaware or has not perceived that uncontrolled prices are widespread in the sales taking place in the markets and in the daily life of the cities?

It went on to detail over a thousand goods such as beef, grain, eggs, clothing and the retail prices 'no one may exceed'. Those who were tempted to break them were warned that they faced the death penalty. Chaos soon followed. Prices soared and people's savings ran short. Traders ignored the price limits and citizens, finding exorbitantly priced goods, formed angry mobs. Shops were trashed and tradespeople were killed. A black market quickly emerged, with the fallout colourfully described by the contemporary writer Lactantius: 'There was much bloodshed ... and the people brought provisions no more to markets, since they could not get a reasonable price for them and this increased the dearth so much, that at last after many had died by it, the law itself was set aside.'

The edict may have lasted no more than a year, with Diocletian's market interventions failing to bring stability. Less than four years after he began his economic reform programme, the price of gold had risen against the *denarius* by 250 per cent. By the turn of the century, that increase was eight times larger, at approximately 2,000 per cent. Diocletian's absolute failure to fix the Roman economy left him with no option but to resign in 305 AD, spending the rest of his life at his plush palace on the Dalmatian coast.

Those who succeeded him might have wanted to hide themselves away in their own luxurious retreats, but Rome's economic woes persisted, so further action was needed. Rome returned to its tried-and-tested tactic of devaluing its coins further, to little avail. More than half a century after Diocletian tried to solve it by meddling, another emperor, Julian, thought he could do better. The emperor, who was in power from 361 AD to 363 AD, tried to fix the price of grain, making a show of off-loading a large quantity of his own supply into the market at the price he had set. But the result was yet another black market, as the historian Edward Gibbon chronicled:

> The consequences might have been foreseen and were soon felt. The imperial wheat was purchased by the rich merchants; the proprietors of land, or of corn [grain] withheld from that city the accustomed supply, and the small quantities that appeared in the market were secretly sold at an advanced and illegal price.

This did not give Julian cause to rethink his masterplan; as Gibbon notes, he 'still continued to applaud his own policy', dismissing the rumblings of unhappiness about it as a 'vain and ungrateful murmur'.

The Roman Empire never recovered from failure to resolve this economic torpor, exacerbated by clumsy market interventions. That was one of the main reasons it crumbled over the century that followed. This was undoubtedly in Mayor Johnson's mind when he railed against the cap on bankers' bonuses. His suspicion was vindicated as the bonus cap proved, in many ways, to be as effective as Diocletian's food price controls. The banks, it soon emerged, worked out an easy way to get around the bonus cap, such as boosting their investment bankers' salaries and introducing new monthly allowances. This was to be expected in the financially innovative City, which knew how to deal with cumbersome charges. In the 1990s, for example, London-based investment firms got around high payroll taxes by rewarding high-flying staff with gold bars, fine wine and oriental carpets.

Politicians will always be tempted to meddle in the markets with the best of intentions. But they should tread carefully and think about the consequences, otherwise they might follow Emperor Diocletian and just make things worse.

PEOPLE LOVE FEELING GREAT

Positivity and popularity go together in politics, which is why politicians try to convince voters they are the one who can offer them and the country they live in the brightest future. The results of their efforts can end up sounding rather sappy.

'Let optimism beat pessimism,' trilled David Cameron in 2006, 'let sunshine win the day.' Barack Obama went further in his 2008 American presidential campaign, which was represented by slogans such as 'Hope', 'Yes We Can' and 'Change We Can Believe In'. As twee as such messages sound, they helped both men go on to enjoy electoral success. The effectiveness of such messages touches on a fundamental rule in politics: voters want a leader who makes them feel good. And those who seem like the best option for their country will interest them even more.

Voters tend to be patriots at heart. After all, if they did not like where they lived and grew up, they would have upped sticks and gone elsewhere in search of a better life. And so that national pride is what politicians over the ages have tried their best to tap into, with varying degrees of subtlety. Their tendency was satirised masterfully in the 1980s ITV sitcom *The New Statesman*. In one episode, Rik Mayall's slimy Sir Alan Beresford B'Stard MP is shown whipping Tory party members into a frenzy by delivering a speech full of nationalist platitudes, starting with the stirring declaration: 'Everyone in this audience knows in their hearts that England is simply the GREATEST. COUNTRY. IN. THE. WORLD!' Such stirring rhetoric lives on in current, actual, politicians. The best known example is Donald Trump, who swept to power promising to 'Make America Great Again'.

Who could object to greatness? Both sides of the EU referendum campaign sought to tap into that, with pro-Brexit supporters organised into various groups that stood 'for Britain', like 'Students for Britain' and 'Business for Britain'. The Remainers were not to be outdone, with campaign groups such as 'Labour in for Britain' and 'Lawyers in for Britain'.

Top-tier politicians recognise the importance of championing national pride, with the ambitious Matt Hancock telling fellow Tories in April 2019 that 'we need to sound like we actually like living in this country. We've got to be patriots for the Britain of now.' Even the newest political forces are offering it. The Independent Group, which sprang up after Labour and Tory MPs started joining it in February 2019, had a manifesto that was as vague as it was positive, declaring: 'Ours is a great country of which people are rightly proud.'

Such declarations would not have been out of place in Rome. The lavish games, the ornate festivals and the spectacular triumphal processions were all part of the pomp and ceremony designed to make citizens feel like, as Romans, they were part of the greatest civilisation on the planet. The proudest boast a Roman could make was that they were a citizen of Rome: '*civis Romanus sum*', a notion that was meant to guarantee safe travel, acting as an early version of the Geneva Convention in conferring basic rights. Much later on in the nineteenth century, Foreign Secretary Lord Palmerston snatched up the slogan to explain how the British Empire sought to keep its subjects safe around the world.

Ancient leaders knew the importance of making their people feel the same enthusiasm about their country. Quintus Cicero advised his brother when standing to be consul that 'the most important part of your campaign is to bring hope to people and a feeling of goodwill toward you'. They would have known the power such an approach could have on people from the famous speeches made by great leaders, with the Greeks recognised as pioneers of rhetoric. None would have been as renowned as the legendary funeral oration made by the Athenian leader Pericles.

His speech, coming a year into the Peloponnesian War in tribute to the war dead as a vigorous defence of the democratic system they died defending, is remembered as a masterpiece of oratory. It is full of lines that resound even to this day, such as Pericles' stirring defence of democracy: 'Our Constitution is called a democracy because power is in the hands not of a minority but of the whole people.' That was borrowed by French politician Valéry Giscard d'Estaing, who slipped it into the preamble to the draft constitution to the European Union in 2004. That Periclean sentiment has morphed into a slogan that is much used by democrats across the political spectrum, ranging from Boris Johnson (who keeps a bust of the Athenian on his desk) to Jeremy Corbyn: 'for the many, not the few'.

From the moment Pericles begins his speech, his sparkling rhetoric is clear. He begins, as the Greek historian Thucydides recorded, by praising the 'many brave men' who died, before going on to explain what they gave their lives to protect: Athens and its liberal values. 'If we look to the laws, they afford equal justice to all in their private differences ... if a man is able to serve the state, he is not hindered by the obscurity of his condition,' he says, going on to add by way of example: 'The freedom we enjoy in our government extends also to our ordinary life. There, far from exercising a jealous surveillance over each other, we do not feel called upon to be angry with our neighbour for doing what he likes.'

Pericles pays tribute to many other Athenian virtues, before rounding off by declaring: 'I say that as a city we are the school of Hellas; while I doubt if the world can produce a man, who, where he has only himself to depend upon, is equal to so many emergencies, and graced by so happy a versatility as the Athenian.' In other words, the soldiers died to keep Athens great. As he puts it: 'the Athens that I have celebrated is only what the heroism of these and their like have made her'. Given that, he concludes by urging the people of Athens to maintain 'as unfaltering a resolution' as those who died for them.

Roman leaders could not resist such tub-thumping rhetoric about their nation either. When a visiting delegation from the Middle Eastern region of Parthia came to Rome to ask for Emperor Claudius to return a member of their royal family he had taken hostage, Tacitus records that he gave them a lecture on 'Roman supremacy'. Such a tone worked wonders in elections. Those who believe a politician can offer them a better future will stick with them zealously, he argued, suggesting that voters preferred a candidate who promised them fabulous things – even if they were later broken – rather than one who did not promise anything attractive at all.

Politicians knew even then that they could not just scare their way into power. Voters needed a positive vision to back as well. Boris Johnson knew that during the 2016 referendum, boasting in one campaign speech: 'We will be vindicated by history; and we will win for exactly the same reason that the Greeks beat the Persians at Marathon – because [the Remainers] are fighting for an outdated absolutist ideology, and we are fighting for freedom.'

One can raise a few nitpicking points, such as that 'the Greeks' at the time were actually an alliance of independent sovereign states who had come together to face a common foe as part of the so-called Delian League. A Remainer with Johnson's rhetorical style could have twisted that into an argument for the UK to remain in its own European 'league'. But there was no time for that historical row to be picked, perhaps because it would not have changed his intended rhetorical point, namely that Leave stood for the positive prospect of freedom.

That shows the timeless rhetorical importance for politicians of giving voters something to feel positive about. As leaders such as Pericles and Claudius have showed, people love those they can believe will ensure their country remains great.

STICK WITH YOUR SOLDIERS

A government's basic – and minimum – purpose is to keep its people safe, so the men and women who ensure that rightly occupy a special place in the public's esteem.

Given their popular appeal, soldiers end up finding that politicians compete to be seen as their champions. This can come in the form of photo-ops, such as when Margaret Thatcher bolstered her warrior queen reputation in 1986 by jumping into a Union Jack-flying Challenger tank, a stunt Democratic presidential hopeful Michael Dukakis tried to emulate two years later but only succeeded in looking dopey and soft as he was dwarfed by his huge helmet. They do not all have to be seen riding around in heavy machinery. Leaders like to be seen mixing with the troops out in their camps, with the men particularly keen to be seen sitting and eating with them as if they were one of the soldiers. The Romans knew that was a good way to win support, with the ambitious Mark Anthony happy to sit down with his men to dinner, and eating at the common mess-table alongside them. That 'made his own troops delight in his company and almost worship him,' Plutarch records.

Such a prospect is why modern politicians go to such lengths to muck in with the troops, with men like Tony Blair and David Cameron whipping off their jackets when meeting with them out in the deserts of Afghanistan and Iraq. Despite the varying results they can have, some politicians go even further to try to look tough. Gavin Williamson excelled himself as Defence Secretary by being captured in February 2019 joining troops out in Norway, practising their 'ice breaking drill' by hauling himself out of freezing water. His successor Penny Mordaunt – a Royal Naval reservist – endeared herself to the armed forces well before she took on the job, by fulfilling a dare from military friends to say the word 'cock' several times in the House of Commons. She found an ideal excuse to do so in 2014 by slipping the word in six times into a debate on the welfare of poultry.

People in politics regularly pay tribute to the armed forces and cannot resist the temptation at times to borrow military rhetoric to present themselves as especially hardcore. Williamson once spoke of how he expected Britain to increase its 'lethality' after Brexit, reeling off a list of new high-tech equipment, such as drone 'swarm squadrons', that would enable this. That marked a more serious tone on his earlier efforts, most notoriously in 2018 when he suggested that Russia should 'shut up and go away'. He was not the first Defence Secretary to seem a bit foolish in the desire to seem tough, after

Michael Portillo rounded off a speech in 1995 by evoking the SAS' motto 'Who Dares Wins', declaring in a cocksure manner: 'We will dare, we will win.'

Politicians aspire to put money where their mouth is, as shown by the rows that erupted in recent years about whether the United Kingdom should spend 2 per cent of its national income on defence – a target ministers still say with pride is being achieved. By contrast, Jeremy Corbyn was accused of plotting to leave the country 'defenceless' after it emerged he had previously said in a speech that it would be 'wonderful' to be like Costa Rica, a country which 'abolished their army, and took pride in the fact they don't have an army'. He has been far from the only Labour leader to be mocked as soft on defence. His predecessor Ed Miliband was infamously accused during the 2015 election of plotting to 'stab the United Kingdom in the back' in his approach to national security.

The public reverence of the armed forces is nothing new; it was alive and well in Graeco-Roman times. The Greeks saw fighting in battle as a chance for people to show their courage, classing it as just as much of a public good (*agathon*) as paying taxes. The Romans felt the same about military service. One of the main ways a foreigner could gain Roman citizenship was by fighting in its army.

War and peace were a mainstay of political debate. In Greece, foreign policy was a compulsory item on the agenda whenever Athenians met in official assemblies. There was extensive debate over each move of a military proposal, and people voted routinely to sign it off not just in principle, but to approve the funds for it. War was a significant part of their official spending; several times more was spent on warfare than festivals (which the Greeks loved putting on) and state administration.

The Athenians and Romans were gung-ho in support of their boys. People took against anyone who criticised war. The Greek generals Aeschines and Andocides only pushed for peace on the grounds that it would buy Athens time to build up money so it could fight future wars much more successfully. Ancient sensitivity about criticising war was not a peculiarity of the era. After the Second World War, France chose to ban children's books from presenting cowardice in any positive light, creating an oversight committee to ensure that rule was upheld. Any publisher who broke it by depicting cowardice that way, or any other quality that was 'liable to undermine morality' among the next generation, could be punished with up to a year in prison.

The urge politicians feel to associate themselves with the military was felt by the Romans to an even larger degree. Emperors, and ambitious politicians, yearned to make their names with great deeds on the battlefield. Emperor Tiberius was a rare exception by choosing in first-century AD Rome to focus on consolidating the Empire's borders, rather than expanding them. The men who followed him, Caligula and Claudius, chose to push on and expanded the Empire. Their eventual successor, Nero, did not target new lands, which is one of the reasons the Roman political class took against him. Senators liked to see their emperor leading troops into battle, but he was more interested in improving Roman architecture and playing his lyre. To understand how odd Nero's passion for the Greek instrument rather than expanding the Empire appeared to many Romans, imagine how American voters would feel about their President obsessing more about mastering the ukelele than about governing.

Nero never bothered to visit a single military outpost anywhere near the border of his Empire. Any military conflicts that arose under Nero's watch would be delegated to someone else to sort out. He did consider an expedition to Ethiopia and thought more about leading an army into the east beyond the Black Sea, recruiting a legion of six-foot soldiers (a giant height at that time), which he named after Alexander the Great. But neither plan came to much.

Rome's troublesome neighbours gave Nero a chance to prove himself on the battlefield early in his reign, as the Parthians invaded Armenia. The Armenians were a vassal state of Rome, giving it just cause to respond. Nero sent troops to defend them under someone else's command, but the conflict ended in an effective stalemate, and a formal compromise was struck to end hostilities. If Nero had led his men personally into battle, perhaps he would be remembered differently as a ruler.

TREAD CAREFULLY ON FOREIGN SOIL

Boris Johnson once warned that modern leaders 'should have read about the experiences of Roman armies in Mesopotamia' before sending troops into battle in the Middle East. The region had become irresistible for Western nations like America, Great Britain and Russia to wade into, but to their eventual cost, as their interventions have been plagued by problems. The historian – now Tory MP – Rory Stewart warned how difficult the Middle East had been for leaders when he highlighted Afghanistan in a TV documentary as an 'easy country to enter but a difficult one to leave'. Leaders like Tony Blair and George Bush found their reputations were shaped by the mixed success they had in taking out Saddam Hussein's regime in Iraq and the Taliban in Afghanistan, while Anthony Eden was ruined by his disastrous attempt to regain control of the Suez Canal from the Egyptians.

The Romans had their own scrapes in the Middle East as they pursued military glory. Julius Caesar was dreaming up plans to invade Parthia (a region that covers modern Iran) just before he was assassinated. The Parthian Empire stretched as far west as the Euphrates river and as far east as the Indus, touching the Caspian Sea at its northern point and the Persian Gulf at its most southern. It was one of Rome's few neighbours who could put up much of a fight.

Caesar's lieutenant Mark Anthony decided to carry on what his fallen hero would not be able to accomplish by taking on the Parthians. He ended up finding out how tricky they were as an enemy when he tried to conquer them in 41 BC with a force of 100,000 men. But he was trounced, with thousands of Romans killed and thousands more taken prisoner, while their general was lucky to escape with his life.

Anthony could be thankful his campaign had not gone as disastrously as one of Caesar's political rivals had a few years before, whose grim demise he could claim to have been trying to avenge. Marcus Licinius Crassus had made his fortune as a property tycoon, owning silver mines and plenty of houses. He built up his property empire by behaving effectively as a disaster capitalist, buying properties that had come on the market – as Plutarch puts it – due to 'public calamities'. In moments of turmoil, enemies of those who had been in power would be sentenced to death in prescriptions and have their property taken off them to be auctioned off at a bargain. Crassus regularly snapped up such properties, and liked doing it so much that Plutarch records he even managed to get a man proscribed simply because he envied his belongings. He also purchased homes that had collapsed or were fire-damaged and rebuilt them. As generous as that sounds from someone who can also boast to have founded Rome's first fire brigade, he had a way to make it especially lucrative. Whenever Crassus arrived at the scene of a burning building with his firefighters, they would do nothing unless the owner immediately agreed to sell their building to him at a knock-down rate, which he would then rebuild and lease back to them as their new owner. If they refused, he – and his men – would let it burn down, safe in the knowledge that the city had no force of its own that would help. That trick allowed Crassus to become the richest man in Rome, with his wealth big enough to make him by modern standards a multi-billionaire.

But Rome was not enough to satisfy Crassus, as he still craved more. Not just more money, but more respect. His rivals had been able to boast of something that money alone could not bring him: great military success. Although Crassus could point to moments like his successful defeat of the slaves' revolt led by Spartacus, that was never going to put him on the same level as Caesar, conqueror of Gaul, and Pompey, the man who had saved Rome from populist rebels during a civil war and crushed an uprising in Spain. Crassus saw his chance to fix that by securing the governorship of Syria, which gave him an ideal staging post from which he could venture into the Middle East to take on Parthia. Thrashing Rome's Middle Eastern nemeses would have given him a lot to brag about. Despite his financial success, he would not be satisfied until he could boast of just as much success as a general. Crassus was said to keenly observe that no one was truly rich in his eyes unless they could be like him and pay for their own army. In his view, why pay for troops if you don't put them to good use?

That sensitivity lives on in modern tycoons like Donald Trump, who as President has revelled in his official role as Commander-in-Chief, appearing at rallies to address his troops in an oversized bomber jacket and declaring that he was building 'by far the most powerful military in the world'. His gung-ho approach was best summarised by how he explained his plan to defeat the ISIS extremists: 'bomb the shit out of 'em'.

Crassus hoped to take on his Middle Eastern foes with just as much force, but it quickly emerged after getting stuck in that he had little idea what he was doing. He was offered 16,000 cavalry and 30,000 infantrymen as support by the King of Armenia if he chose to attack from across the Armenian border, where the Parthians were massed, but instead he refused and ploughed on with the more direct route of crossing the Euphrates river to attack. His decision proved costly, as his troops ended up marching through vast desert, which left them short on supplies and water. Dehydrated, low on morale and proper training, his troops were in a poor state to take on a foe like the Parthians.

That was painfully apparent in 53 BC, when Crassus' disastrous campaign reached its climax at Carrhae (now known as the Turkish city of Harran), where his troops had their decisive clash. Crassus was proud to be able to pay for his troops' equipment, but it is hard to see how they could have been worse equipped: he had brought 35,000 foot-based swordsmen to a horseback bow-and-arrow fight.

Crassus could not have been surprised by the Parthians' approach to battle, as their penchant for horse archery was well-known. Indeed, their ability to keep shooting while retreating on horseback was so effective that we pay tribute to it with the phrase 'parting shot' – even if that just refers to aiming a witty quip, rather than an arrow, at someone. The result was that they could easily outmanoeuvre the Roman infantrymen, riding into shooting range, taking a shot and falling back before their enemy could get near. The few thousand Parthian archers were outnumbered considerably, but they were able to get around that by subjecting their Roman opponents to a constant hail of arrows. That meant any Roman infantrymen who tried to lunge at the enemy with their sword risked getting swiftly mown down.

The only way Crassus could stop the slaughter was by ordering his men to stay in a defensive '*testudo*' formation, which their shields raised around them like a tortoise, in the belief that the Parthians would eventually run out of arrows. But there was no sign that his gambit was paying off, as his men were still being picked off – including Crassus' own son – to their mounting despair. They insisted that Crassus should enter talks with the Parthians to stop the mayhem. He jumped on his horse to go out to meet them, and was about to do so until one of his officers feared that he was riding into a trap, grabbed his horse by the bridle to stop him, and their sudden scuffle led to the Romans all being cut down as hostilities resumed sharply.

The Parthians were said to have found the perfect way to mock the greedy Roman plutocrat in his death, according to historian Cassius Dio, by pouring molten gold into his mouth. His head was then used as a prop in a play put on at the Parthian king's wedding. And in one last trick, the Parthians decided to dress up one of their Roman prisoners of war who looked the most like Crassus in women's clothing and then parade him around in a parody of the triumphal processions Rome would put on. The Parthians proudly clung onto the military standards from Crassus' slain army as prize booty, until Augustus brought them back to Rome in 19 BC.

If modern leaders had learned from the errors of ambitious Romans like Mark Anthony and Marcus Crassus, they might not have had so many troubles by rushing headlong into the Middle East. The region will continue to draw the attention of political and military leaders in their own quests for glory. They might not risk as grisly a fate as Crassus if their mission goes awry, but – as Blair has found – living to suffer the fallout from a messy Middle Eastern campaign can be equally excruciating.

FOREIGNERS DON'T ACTUALLY EAT BABIES

Boris Johnson ran the gauntlet in October 2015 to attend the Conservative Party conference, as anti-government protesters crowding around the entrance hurled foul-mouthed abuse and large inflatable balls at him on his way in. This experience led him to muse on what drove people to be so angry, writing in the *Daily Telegraph* shortly after:

When a community is going through some period of stress – a war, or economic hardship – they are historically far more likely to identify and turn on scapegoats in their midst. Anxiety is transferred to some readily identifiable group: Jews, foreigners, homosexuals, gypsies – the victims of this kind of prejudice have in some cases been suffering for centuries. Sometimes, barely credible powers are attributed to these groups, and they become a catch-all explanation for everything that has gone wrong in a society. Your kids can't get a house? It's the immigrants. Can't get a job? It's the immigrants. Can't see a doctor in A&E? It's the immigrants. Traffic on the M4? It's the immigrants. Of course, these problems have multiple causes – but people are only too willing to project their anger on to a particular group, and some politicians, alas, are only too willing to assist.

Who did Johnson think were the politicians only 'too willing to assist' in whipping up anger about immigration? One of them clearly was Theresa May, who had stirred up Conservative Party members a few days earlier by declaring that the ongoing level of migration was 'unsustainable' and made it impossible to build a 'cohesive society'. Her hardline tone was familiar to those who had listened to her conference speeches over the years, as one MP acknowledged in his acerbic joke to Johnson's sister afterwards: 'Don't worry, Rachel, Tuesday of conference is always National Front day.'

Four years later, that MP might well conclude May was rather restrained compared to how provocatively other politicians – typically known as 'populists' – have been happy to speak about foreigners.

National leaders such as Donald Trump, Viktor Orbán and Jair Bolsonaro, as well as firebrands like Nigel Farage, are often accused of spreading xenophobia with what they say. Xenophobia is at its heart a fear of strangers. It comes from the Greek '*xenos*' (meaning stranger, or foreigner) and '*phobos*' (meaning fear). Yet for the Greeks, strangers were not necessarily people to be feared. Indeed, one of their highest virtues was *xenia*, effectively a quality of being a good host, which they could show by feeding and clothing a stranger who came to their house.

But that essential Greek quality is not so widely known as its negative counterpart: that the Greeks themselves were subject to xenophobia in their own right. Rome's ever-expanding Empire meant there was a stream of exotic treasure coming back to the city, and lots of new people. Prisoners of war were paraded through the streets by conquering generals, and then sold into slavery. Entrepreneurial travellers came to the city to find their fortune. The Roman conquest of the Greek peninsula during the second century BC resulted in the denizens bringing their unique style to Rome. The Greeks' sophistication, practising creative arts such as philosophy and poetry, alongside their exotic tastes, dabbling in mystical arts such as magic, both intrigued and irritated Romans.

Traditionalists tended to hate the Greeks in their midst. The arch-conservative Cato the Elder was deeply wary of what they had to offer Roman life. Greeks did not need to bear any gifts for him to be wary of them. He opposed the study of philosophy on principle, had nothing but disdain for their culture and looked down on everything else they had to say for themselves. He would complain that the great Greek philosopher Socrates was a 'troublesome windbag' and advised his son never to trust a Greek doctor. He would also be prone to making histrionic warnings about the perils of Greek influence, such as that Rome would lose its Empire if its people became 'infected' by its literature.

Others were even ruder about the Greeks. The satirist Juvenal aimed bile at many things in Roman society, among them the Hellenistic 'parasites'. In one of his works, he explains that the influx of Greeks and other foreigners have driven him out of Rome. It is clear from the very beginning that he will not pull punches, as he declares: 'My friends, I can't stand a Rome full of Greeks!' His complaint centres on the fact that they had become a 'most acceptable' race to wealthy Romans, worming their way – in his view – into their homes. He imagines them slyly offering to fill many roles 'in one person, whatever you need', ranging from teaching languages and oratory to being the in-house soothsayer or dancer. 'They know it all!' Juvenal complains, and he is only getting started. The Greeks are seen by him as social chameleons who used their acting and smooth-talking to work their way into Roman society, with the result that they 'own the secrets of the house, and so [are] feared'. As he puts it:

[The Greeks are] a nation of comics. Laugh, and they'll be shaken
With fits of laughter. They weep, without grief, if they see
A friend in tears; if you pine for a little warmth in the winter
They don a cloak; if you remark 'it's hot' they'll start to sweat.
So we're unequal: they've a head start who always, day or night,
Can adopt the expression they see on someone's face,
Who're always ready to throw up their hands and cheer…

Like Cato, who was said to complain that the Greeks spoke 'from their hips', Juvenal saw them as similarly sex-obsessed:

> Nothing's sacred to them or safe from their cocks
> Not the lady of the house, or the virgin daughter, not
> Even her smooth-faced fiancé, or the unbroken son.
> Failing that, they'll have the friend's grandma on her back.

Juvenal is far more bilious than the likes of Nigel Farage, who once warned that women were at risk of mass sex attacks from gangs of European and North African migrant men. 'It depends if they get EU passports,' he told the *Telegraph* on 4 June 2016, weeks before the EU referendum. 'It depends if we vote for Brexit or not. It is an issue.'

Ancient Rome's handling of immigration remains contentious to this day, as debate continues to rage about whether it led to the Empire's downfall. In December 2016, the prominent Brexiteer businessman Arron Banks ended up arguing about this on Twitter after declaring that Rome had been 'effectively destroyed by immigration'. None other than the classics professor Mary Beard waded in: 'I think you all need to do a bit more reading in Roman history before telling us what caused the fall of Rome. Facts guys!' Banks was unbowed, replying sarcastically that 'sacking Rome [had] nothing to do with the downfall (eyes to sky)'.

Needless to say, their row went on for a while. But Beard and Banks were not the only ones on opposite sides of the Brexit debate to fight a proxy war over Rome's downfall. A study published in the Journal of Social Archaeology in April 2018 found that Brexiteers tended to like talking about the Roman Empire on Facebook because they could then try to argue the UK was collapsing under a similar weight caused by foreigners. The exact circumstances of Rome's downfall have yet to be settled, although foreigners do come up a lot. The much-respected eighteenth-century historian Edward Gibbon pointed to invasions by a 'deluge of barbarians' and another factor: Christianity.

Despite the suspicion foreigners like the Greeks attracted in Rome, their treatment was nothing like that suffered by the Christians. Christianity was far from the dominant religion it is known as today. It started out as a mere 'pernicious superstition', as Tacitus put it. To the Romans, Jesus Christ was just a Jewish rabbi who stirred up trouble with his teachings in Judaea, and had to be put to death by the local governor to keep the peace. Christians continued to be regarded with suspicion because they were seen as disloyal to Rome, because their monotheism meant they refused to acknowledge the emperor's supremacy – or any of the Roman gods – as they could have no 'other gods' except their own.

Their repeated persecution at the hands of the Romans has been well-documented, with thousands estimated to have died in these purges. They began infamously after the Great Fire of Rome in 64 AD, when Nero blamed the blaze on them. He made a show of punishing them, as Tacitus records that they were torn to death by dogs or crucified and set on fire so that they would light up the night's sky 'as substitutes for daylight'. The suspicion remains, as touted by various ancient writers, that the emperor had been behind the blaze himself. But it did not gain sufficient traction at the time to bring a swift end to Nero's reign there and then, suggesting he managed to credibly enough blame the Christians. How so?

The Christians generally kept their heads down in order to survive in Roman society, so their minimal association with Romans meant rumours thrived about what exactly they got up to in their private acts of worship. Their lack of knowledge meant many scurrilous beliefs circulated in Rome about Christian worship, such as the idea that believers would sacrifice babies to eat their flesh and blood. That, as many Christian readers will know, is a tragic mangling of the religious rites that happen in a standard Eucharist service, when bread and wine is consumed as representative of Christ's flesh and blood. Christians were also suspected of regularly committing incest, with the incriminating proof in the Roman mind being how often Christians called each other 'brother' and 'sister'. The Roman rumour mill ran wild, forcing early Christian writers to seek to bust such myths in their work.

More dangerously for the Christians, any Roman who learned a bit about their beliefs risked coming to the conclusion that a key part was overthrowing the emperor. The Christians' belief in a 'new kingdom' coming would have led them to fear they were plotting against Roman rule. Christian talk of a divine fire cleansing away the old regime, as set out in the apocalyptic Book of Revelation, would have given them even more cause for concern. Jesus himself is quoted as saying in the Gospel of Thomas that 'I have cast fire upon the world and I am guarding it until it blazes'. Admittedly, that book is non-canonical, but it shows the sort of rhetoric Christians touted at the time. (The Romans would not have been able to overlook it as non-canonical anyway, as Christians only decided what was biblical canon in 325 AD.)

Roman suspicion of Christian pyromania meant that when their city was destroyed by the great fire, it was not hard for Nero to establish in the minds of many of his people that it was the fault of the small sect that was known to long for such a blaze. The Christians were not persecuted for their faith alone, but charged with arson. Followers who were arrested soon confessed to the crime, no doubt under torture, allowing the wider Christian population to be cast as guilty – as Tacitus puts it – of 'hatred of the human race'. That allowed Nero to punish them, using brutal methods the Romans would use to execute common criminals, to show his people that justice had been served.

Debate still rages over who exactly was behind the Great Fire of Rome. But Nero evidently had no trouble scapegoating the Christians because he already had enough prejudices to exploit. With some Romans already viewing them as child-eating incestuous Rome-hating monsters, it would be simple to pin arson on them as well. That is a symptom of the Christians being ghettoised in Roman society. If Romans knew how innocent much of Christian belief was, they would likely have been too sympathetic to see them as pyromaniac terrorists.

A similar lack of engagement emerges among voters who embraced the hardline anti-immigration rhetoric pushed by populist politicians like Nigel Farage. Those who have been most receptive are much less likely to live around lots of migrants. In the United Kingdom for example, the constituency that gave Farage's UKIP its first MP – Clacton – had a foreign-born population of just 4.3 per cent, several times smaller than the national average (13.8 per cent), according to census data from 2011 compiled by the Oxford Migration Observatory. The area that gave the party its second MP, Rochester & Strood, had 9.2 per cent, which was a similar proportion to other areas that have been deemed UKIP-friendly areas. By contrast, UKIP failed to break through in cities like Birmingham and London, some areas of which had foreign-born populations of over 55 per cent.

That is a sign that their limited exposure, if any at all, to immigrants meant they were easier for anti-immigration politicians to agitate. They would not have so much experience of immigrants, so their feelings about them would be more easily shaped by tub-thumping rhetoric. Charismatic politicians like Farage would have been able to tap into the most primal emotion: fear. 'The oldest and strongest kind of fear is fear of the unknown,' the horror author H. P. Lovecraft once said. And so it makes sense that the subject of the fear politicians like him would whip up in voters is of unfamiliar foreigners.

It is said that familiarity breeds contempt. But it could be said too that a lack of familiarity has the same effect. People have feared 'the other' since the Roman times, and that fear continues to be exploited. Liberal voices try to combat this, but entrenched beliefs – however mistaken – are hard for them to shake. No matter how offensive politicians like Trump and Farage are about immigrants, however, they at least do not try to accuse them of eating babies.

HEIRS TO BOUDICCA, BEWARE

In the heart of Westminster, there are plenty of statues standing tall. You would not quibble about why most of them are there, as they commemorate great leaders like Winston Churchill. But some would instinctively raise an eyebrow on hearing that one of the statues honours someone who burned London to the ground.

Indeed, that person has their own platform just by Westminster

Bridge, a stone's throw from the Houses of Parliament. It is easy to miss amid the London hubbub, not least because it is often hidden behind a souvenir stand. Their statue isn't some pop-up erected by anarchists in mischievous tribute, but a monument that has been standing for well over a century. Who is it? None other than Boadicaea, or, as she is better known these days, Boudicca. She has been standing there since 1902 on a large granite plinth, cast in bronze on a Roman chariot kitted out with scythe blades on each wheel, which is drawn by two powerful-looking horses rearing up as her two daughters trail behind.

Boudicca, Queen of the Iceni © EMMA DOUBLE

The inscription on the front of the plinth makes clear why the ancient British tribe leader is worthy of such veneration: 'Boadicaea (Boudicca) Queen of the Iceni who died 61 AD after leading her people against the Roman Invader.' The warrior queen's uprising against the Romans was so fierce that she blazed her way into the

British psyche as a symbol of Britain's fighting spirit. She has come to personify the qualities of defiance, independence and national pride as effectively as her Churchillian statue neighbour. And any female British leader doing battle with cocky Europeans tends to find her name invoked as an example of how to show strength.

Margaret Thatcher's style of leadership, crushing 'wet' Conservative colleagues in Cabinet, Labour at election time and Argentina when it had its eye on the Falkland Islands, encouraged people to see her as the heir to Boudicca. Labour politician Denis Healey quipped in 1982 as she fought the Falklands War that she 'has been charging about like some bargain-basement Boadicea'. Fellow Labourite Tony Benn followed up a few years later by branding her a 'tin-pot Boadicea'. Cartoonists had fun drawing her as the warrior queen, such as George Gale in the *Daily Telegraph* on 11 June 1987 – to illustrate her third successive election victory.

Caricature by the Daily Telegraph's *George Gale, 1987*
© BRITISH CARTOON ARCHIVE, UNIVERSITY OF KENT (40660)

Thatcher would not have been phased to be described as the new Boudicca. Undoubtedly it helped her cement her self-styled reputation as the 'Iron Lady', although her critics would have been using it to try to depict her as a rampaging power-mad queen. Maggie might have even felt some sisterly solidarity for Boudicca, given how they were both targets of male condescension and sneers. Thatcher decided that she needed to sound authoritative to make her way up the political ladder in Westminster, so she took voice coaching to learn to speak more deeply and slowly, in order to project greater gravitas. While she avoided being seen as whiny, critics instead carped that she was too strident in tone.

That turns out to be the sort of snipes any woman is at risk of, especially if they're overseeing a group of men. And it doesn't matter if the men are the Cabinet or Iceni troops. Boudicca was accused of having a 'harsh voice' by the Roman historian Cassius Dio, who also said that she looked 'most terrifying' and had a 'most fierce' look in her eye.

Such remarks were standard fare for Thatcher's critics. Perhaps the mildest jibe they ever made about her was to mock her decision in government to remove free school milk for seven-year-olds by branding her a 'milk snatcher' in a rhyme. One of her Cabinet colleagues, John Biffen, compared her relationship with ministers to a 'tigress surrounded by hamsters', while Labour's Tony Banks accused her of behaving 'with all the sensitivity of a sex-starved boa constrictor'. 'She's the biggest bastard we have ever known,' Danny Morrison, from Northern Ireland's Sinn Féin, observed. She could also exasperate European leaders with her approach to diplomacy. French President François Mitterrand famously described Thatcher as having the 'eyes of Caligula', while Jacques Chirac – who served as his Prime Minister – was heard complaining after dealing with her at a Brussels summit in 1988: 'What does she want, this housewife? My balls on a tray?'

The Romans were similarly shaken by Boudicca. Cassius Dio described her uprising as a 'terrible disaster', while Tacitus called it a 'grave misfortune' for the Empire. Tacitus had particular reason to appreciate the damage dealt by Boudicca, as he would have heard all about it from his family. His father-in-law had served on the staff of the general trusted to watch over Britain at the time, Suetonius Paulinus, and so would have had a close perspective on Rome's response to Boudicca's uprising.

Paulinus had been caught on the hop, as he had been busy campaigning just to the north-west of Wales on the island of Anglesey when Boudicca and her rebellious Britons made their first big impact: razing the city of Colchester to the ground. Once he caught wind of what was going on, he dashed to London (then known as *Londinium*) in the hope of crushing the revolt as it approached its next target. But he did not have enough troops to stand any sort of chance, so had to flee the city, leaving it for Boudicca and her forces to destroy. After razing London, she then torched St Albans (or, as it was known then, *Verulamium*).

She showed no mercy, torturing and killing anyone left behind in these cities. It was estimated that her forces massacred 70,000

Romans and Rome-sympathising Britons over the course of her uprising. 'Neither before nor since has Britain ever been in a more uneasy or dangerous state,' the historian Tacitus opined, going on to illustrate why even the recent state of Brexit-induced turmoil is not a scratch on the havoc Boudicca wreaked. 'Veterans were butchered, colonies burned to the ground, armies isolated. We had to fight for our lives before we could think of victory.'

Boudicca's death toll has not been forgotten by later writers. The British monk Gildas clearly had her in mind when he wrote in the sixth century witheringly about 'the treacherous lioness' who 'killed the rulers who had been left behind … to declare more fully, and to strengthen, the enterprises of Roman rule'. The great English poet John Milton wrote in his *History of Britain* about the 'wild hurrey' of a 'distracted woeman with as mad a crew at her heeles [*sic*]'. His term 'woeman' is not a Renaissance mangling of 'woman', as he uses the latter word several times in his work. It is a deliberate and unsubtle pun, emphasising how much 'woe' she caused on the British Isles.

Boudicca's bloody rampage ensured her place in Eurosceptic lore as an example of how strongly the British could fight back – under a strong female leader – when pushed around too much by overbearing continental oppressors. British leaders have constantly fought with their European counterparts. Money can be one of the biggest sources of grief.

Perhaps the most effective argument made by the Brexit campaign during the 2016 referendum on the United Kingdom's membership of the European Union was that Britons were paying too much into its coffers. They estimated the weekly membership fee to be around £350 million a week, a figure that their Remain opponents accidentally helped keep in the public consciousness by trying to argue it was inflated. They had a point, as it left out the rebate Britain got back, which ended up leaving the weekly bill at around half the mooted sum. But that would have resulted in a less dramatic figure for the Brexit campaign to push. The British people were convinced that the EU costed too much, and so decided to change that by rising up and voting on 23 June 2016 to leave the bloc.

It was obvious that arguing about money would strike a chord, as the amount going into European coffers had been a concern among the British people for decades. One of Margaret Thatcher's defining moments came in her dogged campaign to save the British from paying out so much to fund the political club known at the time as the European Community. As one of the biggest net contributors, the United Kingdom had to pay out huge sums. But on 25 June 1984, she seized her chance to correct it at a gathering of her fellow leaders in the imperial grandeur of the Palace of Fontainebleau in France. She told them all repeatedly: 'I want my money back', threatening to stop payments to the Community budget altogether unless she was given a rebate.

After such a display of her 'handbagging' diplomacy, so called because of her favourite accessory, which she would always have with her at such occasions, they gave in. Once the summit was over, Thatcher was able to boast proudly to the House of Commons that she had secured 'a fairer and more soundly based system' for the British taxpayer. 'This is a successful culmination of our long and persistent efforts to correct the budget inequity and to put the United Kingdom's refunds on a lasting basis,' she told MPs. This was one of her moments of triumph, which no doubt led her later when reflecting on her time in office to offer this withering verdict on those she had dealt with: 'They're a weak lot, some of them in Europe, you know. Weak. Feeble.'

Winning the rebate required her to be anything but weak and feeble. What the French referred to acerbically as '*le chèque Britannique*' saved the British taxpayer a significant amount of money. Since 1985, when it first kicked in, Brussels has refunded around £97.9 billion in total. That is roughly as much as the European Union spends in a year. It also became a significant symbol for Eurosceptics, helping to cement Thatcher's iconic status in their eyes. But that came under attack two decades later. Despite declaring on St George's Day 1997, the eve of his ascent to power, that England's patron saint had 'a new dragon to slay' in the form of Europe, Tony Blair allowed the Brussels dragon to take a huge bite out of the UK's rebate. The then Labour Prime Minister argued that it was an 'anomaly that has to go'. His viewpoint chimed with that of his French counterpart, Jacques Chirac, who insisted it 'could no longer be justified, it is from the past'. At the time, he was President of France. But he clearly remembered how furious he had been left by his past dealings with the Tories' warrior queen, as he cattily credited the securing of the rebate to 'Monsieur Thatcher'. The demand for British money had been, Thatcher trilled after securing her rebate, 'a constant source of friction in our relations' with the rest of Europe. She did not specify over what timespan it had been a provocative issue, but she did not need to, as it would have been impossible to limit such a concern to a select period.

This was not the first time Britons felt they'd had to kick back against foreign demands for their money; such fights raged nearly two millennia ago. The Romans were unrelenting in their efforts to extract enough cash from ancient Britain, but little did they know that their efforts would end up lighting the spark for Boudicca's revolt.

Yet it seems all too predictable with hindsight. The Iceni tribespeople she led, and their Trinobantes neighbours who joined her, resided just north of the Thames estuary in what we know these days as Essex and Suffolk. That region of East Anglia has distinguished itself as one of the most Eurosceptic regions in the country, a heartland targeted by UKIP and Brexit campaigners alike. Clearly, people there are less afraid than most to rise up and fight back.

A lot of money was sunk into the Roman conquest of Britain, which began from 43 AD. Emperor Claudius made substantial loans to his favourite local chieftains. Rome's largesse astounded them, not least when those who were taken captive by its army laid eyes on the sumptuous marble constructions in the Empire's capital city. 'If they have all this, what do they want with our mud huts?' one tribal chief remarked.

What they wanted ostensibly was the glory of expanding their Empire. In the same way Eurosceptics see the European Union's expansionist drive as a pursuit of 'More Europe', the Romans were determined to pursue 'More Rome'. Their ethos was captured by the poet Virgil, when he wrote in *The Aeneid*: 'Remember, Roman, your virtuous art shall be to rule with power the peoples, to impose lawful ways of peace, to spare those who submit and to crush the proud (who don't submit).'

The Romans believed that everyone's lives were better under their rule, as they learned how to be civilised. They saw themselves in the same way that Remainers see the EU: as a civilising force. The Iceni, however, would have seen Romans in the same way as Brexiteers see the Brussels elite: a high-and-mighty group that does not tolerate dissent. That belief is clear in how Tacitus describes the Roman occupation. It had troops stationed in Colchester – before Boudicca burned it down – to 'protect the country against revolt and familiarise the provincials with law-abiding government'. The natives, he adds by way of explanation, had a 'natural ferocity'.

Modern Eurosceptics would be inclined to argue that the EU sees itself as having a similar mission, enforcing its 'core values' on those who want to be in their club. The eighteenth-century poet William Cowper wrote an ode in which he imagined a druid giving Boudicca some encouraging words, urging her into battle as follows:

> Rome shall perish – write that word
> In the blood that she has spilt;
> Perish, hopeless and abhorred,
> Deep in ruin as in guilt
> Rome, for empire far renowned,
> Tramples on a thousand states.

A thousand states? Brussels bureaucrats would love that many to trample over, Brexiteers would think. Instead, it has to content itself with twenty-seven, and whoever it can find to replace the British as new EU members. The Roman mythologising about their role being to civilise an unruly world makes it easy to forget their ulterior motive: to secure more 'lucre'. Every person they captured could be treated as a piggy bank (Eurosceptic readers will not find it hard to relate). Anything valuable in their territory was seized upon. That was especially the case when the Romans needed to find money from somewhere to plug a hole in their accounts.

Conquering Britain did not come cheap. Emperor Nero is said to have considered pulling his troops out shortly after succeeding Claudius, a sign that the expense of occupying the far-flung island played on his mind. The Romans had to pay to cover the upkeep for those troops occupying this new territory. They could generate some wealth from the land's minerals, mining tin, gold, silver and lead, but not enough to stop them from targeting the natives to see how much they could shake out of them.

If British tribes wanted a peaceful life under Roman rule, their leaders were expected to pay for the privilege. Some might call it a protection racket, others would say they were expected to pay membership fees as part of the Roman club. The Icenian king Prasutagus hoped to ensure a trouble-free succession after his death by naming the emperor in his will alongside his two daughters. But his hopes were dashed as soon as he died, as his promise of a share of his estate proved not to be enough. Nero's chief tax collector, Catus Decianus, stepped up to seize his inheritance, declaring it to be henceforth the property of Rome. His demand came alongside a campaign to claw back the money Emperor Claudius had given tribal leaders, demanding that it be paid back with interest.

Why was he so money-grabbing? A big reason was that one of Nero's most senior aides had run up massive debts, which he sorely needed to pay off. Seneca was estimated to have around forty million sesterces in outstanding loans. It's hard to translate how much these were worth in modern currency, but it is safe to say they were the equivalent of many millions of pounds. And Nero's right-hand man decided, according to Cassius Dio, to call in his loans 'all at once'.

The Romans had a lot of money to collect, and the pressure on officials meant they resorted to ruthless methods. The late Icenian king's wife Boudicca, not unreasonably, protested against the taxman's attempt to seize her entire inheritance in the name of Rome. The response was brutal, as the historian Tacitus chronicles: 'all the chief men of the Icenians were stripped of their family estates, and the relatives of the king were treated as slaves'. Boudicca's daughters were raped, and she herself was stripped and publicly flogged for her apparent insolence. To make it extra painful, metal pieces and leather knots were added to the whips.

Boudicca and her fellow Iceni, bloody, but unbowed, hatched their plan for revenge. As Tacitus writes:

Driven by this outrage and the dread of worse to come – for they had now been reduced to the status of a province – they rushed to arms, and inspired to rebellion the Trinobantes and others, who, not yet broken by servitude, had entered into a secret and treasonable deal to take back their independence.

This will not be far off how Eurosceptics hope the Leave vote will be written up by historians, namely that a hard-pressed British people rose up against greedy continentals to throw off their shackles and take back control. Given how much Nero's taxman had done to provoke Boudicca, it was fittingly ironic that he was forced to flee the country due to her savage response. Her attack on London, where Catus had his base of tax-collecting options, left him with no choice but to flee back to Rome. His base, along with the rest of the city, was burned to the ground.

Eurosceptics might wish they could do the same to the European Commission building. Instead, the most dramatic step they have been able to threaten during the Brexit talks has been to walk away from the table, taking the £39 billion offered as a divorce bill with them. Both Brexit and Boudicca show how provocative money can be, especially when it comes between feisty Britons and their continental counterparts.

Boudicca has been impossible for Britain's first female Prime Minister to avoid as a comparison. And she has been no less resistible when people have considered the second female premier, Theresa May. Within weeks of her crossing the threshold of 10 Downing Street, she was being hailed as the new Boudicca. Perhaps it was her pledge to use Brexit to take back control of, among other things, 'our money' that invited such a comparison. The woman who used to have less fiery nicknames, like the 'Ice Maiden', had a new epithet. Sir Anthony Seldon landed on it in his review of her first set-piece speech to her party faithful at the Conservative Party conference. On 8 October 2016, he wrote in the *Daily Mail*:

> Theresa May stands like a Brexit Boadicea, breathing fiery words against fat cats, gas rip-offs, and her biggest bugbear – the privileged and the few – as she repositions herself as the Tory leader who is the tribune of the working classes. It is the most opportunistic manoeuvre by a woman who has quietly risen from a suburban rectory without trace.

Her fiery debut left Conservative MPs with high hopes about what she would be able to win for Britain after leading her troops to engage with their opponents in Brussels. MP Peter Bone held out the prospect in May 2018 that she could be welcomed in his constituency like a true warrior queen. He painted a scene reminiscent of a Roman triumph, suggesting that 'she will be carried shoulder high through the streets to the echoing of cheering crowds and I will be able to show her the site where a statue to the Brexit Queen will be erected'.

Sadly, the way the negotiations panned out with the EU fed doubts among May's colleagues as to whether she was fighting hard enough for Britain. The unveiling in July 2018 of her latest compromise to Cabinet colleagues at the countryside retreat of Chequers confirmed their worst fears. Boris Johnson was among the ministers who resigned over the so-called Chequers plan. Brexiteers were in uproar about May setting the country up for 'vassalage' under the yoke of Brussels, rather than freedom from its edicts. But one Eurosceptic MP tried to rationalise what she had put on the negotiating table. Michael Fabricant argued that it had to be deliberately bad and unworkable in order to force Brussels to make a counter-offer with something better. On 5 September, he suggested that EU leaders could end up saving her from political disaster and 'raising her to the heights of a new Boudicca'.

The weeks that followed yielded no change in her fortunes. Her former aide Nick Timothy decided it was time to issue a call to arms, urging her to seize her chance to be 'Brexit Boudicca'. He fleshed out his thinking in *The Sun* on 15 October:

> 'We need the PM to discover her inner Boudicca,' a friend said as we discussed Brexit recently. I could see where he was going with this. After all, as we remember from school, this ancient British queen rose up against the Roman Empire, winning battles, slaughtering enemies and forcing the Romans to contemplate leaving Britain all together. 'But, hang on,' I replied. 'Wasn't Boudicca eventually defeated?' Whatever the details, my friend was right.

Timothy should not have been so insouciant about the details, as his former boss could have learned lessons from how Boudicca's rampage against her European aggressors ended. Around 61 AD, her forces engaged the Romans for what was to be the last time. Their final battle is believed to have taken place in the Midlands, on the Roman road now known as Watling Street. Despite vastly outnumbering the Romans, it ended in bloody defeat. Around 80,000 Britons were estimated to have been killed in the massacre, whereas the Roman legions suffered only 400 lives lost.

How did that happen? Boudicca could have won if she had been more tactical. The Roman forces were well-positioned. They were protected from assaults from the side by a narrow gorge, and a forest shielded their rear, with open plains ahead of them. The warrior queen decided to lead her troops in a foolhardy charge against the front of the Roman battle line, precisely where they were at their strongest. The result was that they were funnelled into a tight mass and either cut down by javelin volleys or close up by the Roman soldiers with their blades. If she had held her troops back, luring the Romans out into the open, the result could have been vastly different.

In a similar sense, May did not trouble the EU much in the negotiations, as she was so eager to throw away any advantages. She rushed into the process, starting the clock on the talks by giving notice of Britain's intention to leave under Article 50 of the Lisbon Treaty before she had even decided with her ministers what the government wanted. One of the chief brains behind the Brexit campaign Vote Leave, Dominic Cummings, lamented that her hasty approach was tantamount to 'putting a gun in your mouth and pulling the trigger'.

May did not just skip over nailing down what her team wanted, but the preparations for what would happen if the talks collapsed

PART TWO: IN OFFICE

and she had to walk away without an agreement in place. The result was that her negotiating hand was severely impaired given that any time she insisted that 'no deal is better than a bad deal', her threat would ring hollow in Brussels.

The result of such an approach has left her Eurosceptic allies, who cheered her on at the outset, thoroughly underwhelmed. The statue-envisaging Peter Bone admitted on Sky News at the start of 2019 that the statue to the Brexit Queen was 'probably not' going to be built in her honour. Her former aide Nick Timothy was much angrier, writing in the *Telegraph* the previous month that 'Brussels has screwed Britain, Remainers have screwed the Prime Minister, and the Prime Minister has screwed the Leavers. And the result is the establishment has screwed the public, who voted in record numbers to leave the European Union.'

Such a verdict might not make May sound like the 'Brexit Boudicca', standing proud and thrashing her European opponents, but given how brutally the Iceni queen was defeated in the end, May might be the most Boudicca-like Prime Minister we have had after all. Boudicca's bloody end does not disqualify her from being put on her pedestal outside the Houses of Parliament. Jacob Rees-Mogg once hailed Alfred the Great as the 'first Eurosceptic' because he 'got rid of the Danes and made England independent', but the Iceni queen has a much better claim to that title, predating him by eight centuries by rising up to lead her fellow Britons in taking back control from their continental oppressors. Her forcefulness has been an example for modern female British leaders to emulate, and they have tried to live up to it. But British leaders would be wise to remember not to share Boudicca's impetuousness – storming into battle and fighting on their continental aggressors' preferred terms – or they risk their own tragic ends.

Romexit means Romexit

If the Romans had not cut down Boudicca and her forces in battle, she would not have stopped until she had hounded them out of Britain. Four centuries after their uprising, Boudicca's rebels got their wish, as the Empire's implosion forced the Romans to pull out of their lands.

The end of Roman rule in Britain is dated to around 410 AD, when the British were left to fend for themselves by Emperor Honorius as he had to redirect resources towards fighting off the Visigoths, who had been ravaging the western Roman Empire and were already laying siege to Rome. Given the immediate threat they posed, it no longer made sense for the Romans to devote time, money and energy to cling onto a far-flung province when their mothership was in jeopardy.

Despite the troubles flaring up and the economic torpor emerging in Western Europe, the British economy had been blooming. The Romans were effectively letting go of an economic dynamo. Archaeologists have found that buildings in Gaul at the time were being constructed austerely by reusing stone from previous structures. By contrast, Britons were using new stone in their buildings, refurbishing public structures and putting up new villas. Brexiteer readers might well feel that is to be expected, given how much joy they have found in the United Kingdom continuing to beat its European neighbours on several economic measures amid the Brexit process.

However, Rome's withdrawal was undeniably a blow to the British economic system. The Roman Army acted as a massive investor in the local economy, buying supplies and produce to maintain its own operations. The Romans hoovered up Britain's natural resources, like copper, gold, iron, lead, salt, silver and tin. They paid for materials like these with their Roman coins, meaning Britain was effectively in a currency union, so they could be swiftly purchased and spirited across the Empire to where it was required. Demand was so great that the Roman state was effectively Britain's biggest single customer, and it was no longer going to be shopping there.

Rome's exit from Britain marked the winding down of a huge economic stimulus, which was a big blow to many British towns that was only mitigated by it not having to pay any more tax into Roman coffers. But that was not enough to outweigh the impact of Rome's waning demand. Creative industries like pottery declined, while the centre of economic gravity shifted back to Britain's agricultural base. What can we take from how Britain coped with 'Romexit'? No doubt some Britons peddled doom and gloom, in what could be seen as a centuries-old precursor to what is now often described as 'Project Fear'. But their warnings have not survived, perhaps because the economy went on to prove them wrong, as it has now established itself as one of the biggest in the world.

However, the damage of what was essentially a no-deal Romexit cannot be glossed over. The turbulence caused by the collapse in demand from Britain's biggest customer had a marked impact. There was no Withdrawal Agreement in place between the newly liberated Britain and the moribund Empire. British industry had to adapt swiftly, with Britons trading more with each other rather than with their continental neighbours. The period that followed was not known as the 'Dark Ages' for nothing. The current British government has recognised a similar shift in trade would be necessary in a no-deal Brexit, indicating it would buy produce such as slaughtered livestock to help farmers cope with the fall in continental business.

The economic fallout caused by the fall of the Roman Empire shows the damage caused by trade waning with Britain's single biggest commercial partner, which Remainer readers might well think shows the peril that awaits in a no-deal Brexit. But their Eurosceptic counterparts will take heart from the fact that the economy was able to get over even a blow like that.

BUILD THAT WALL... AND MAKE THE PICTS PAY FOR IT?

Western leaders have been scrambling over recent years to find ways to secure their nation's borders. Differences of opinion between European politicians over how best to handle the influx of refugees and migrants from Africa and the Middle East have led them to try to solve the crisis with constant political fudge. Meanwhile, British politicians have been adamant that the Brexit vote means the United Kingdom has to 'take back control' of its borders.

Donald Trump capitalised on this popular unease most colourfully when he kicked off his presidential campaign in 2016 with a vigorous attack on those coming into America from Mexico. 'It is way past time to build a massive wall to secure our southern border,' he told voters. A wall – which he explained over the course of the campaign would be 'big, beautiful and powerful' – was needed to stop ne'er-do-wells pouring into America, who he claimed were 'bringing drugs … bringing crime'. 'They're rapists,' he rounded off. 'I speak to border guards and they tell us what we're getting.'

This marked the start of a campaign in which Trump regularly tapped into public anxiety about border security. Much has been written about the apparent novelty of that tactic, yet unease about what resided beyond national borders is far from new. The Ancient Greeks had just the word to refer to these strange folk who had not felt the influence of Greece's civilising influence: barbarians. These uncivilised foreigners earned the name '*barbaroi*' because all their utterances sounded like 'bar-bar'. Barbarians were not the only ones the Greeks knew lived over the border. They told each other horror stories about the people waiting to pounce on them if they ventured too far afield. And they were much worse than the criminals Trump tried to scare voters with; they were said to be cannibals hungry for human flesh – the so-called *Anthropophagi*. The Greek historian Herodotus described them in his writing as 'more savage than any other race … they neither observe justice, nor are governed by any laws'. These cannibals, according to Roman writer Pliny the Elder, drank out of human skulls and wore their scalps upon their chest 'like so many napkins'. People would expect to be safe and uneaten as long as they stayed in their known world around the Mediterranean, ideally within their city walls.

Walls like these played an important role, projecting strength to those looking on from the outside and providing reassurance to those within. Romans made walls an art form in more ways than one. They used them not just in their formidable architecture, but also as weapons to secure strategic advantage in battle.

Julius Caesar showed how effective they could be in war when he laid siege to the Gallic stronghold of Alesia in 52 BC. This required his troops to build eighteen kilometres of fortifications around the city to ensure the blockade was complete. And his army built a further wall, facing outwards, to stop Gallic reinforcements from sweeping in to attack the Romans from the outside. The Romans were outnumbered by as much as four to one, but thanks to Julius Caesar's construction of walls (with ditches in front of them) to control the flow of the battle, he secured his biggest military victory of his career and conquered Gaul.

A few decades later, the Romans built an even more ambitious wall. Unlike Caesar's siege fortifications, much of this structure is still standing. Just visit the north of England and you'll find the remnants from the banks of the River Tyne near the North Sea to the Solway Firth on the Irish Sea of what is known as Hadrian's Wall. The reason it was built, offered one biographer, is one Trump would undoubtedly thoroughly approve of: to 'separate the Romans from the barbarians'. It was the wish of Emperor Hadrian, according to restored sandstone fragments not too far from the wall dating from around the time of its construction, to 'keep intact the Empire'.

Emperor Trump checks out his wall © EMMA DOUBLE

Beyond the Empire's northern border resided ancient Britons, known as Picts. They lived on the edge of the Romans' known world, so it was deemed necessary for them to face something suitably robust as a threshold if they wanted to approach Roman civilisation.

The complete structure might have been only eighty miles, a fraction of how long Trump's wall would be if built across America's 1,933-mile border with Mexico, but it has one big advantage over the President of the United States' masterplan: it was successfully built. Construction took around six years, with three legions of Roman soldiers – each around 5,000 strong – providing the main workforce.

By contrast, after two years in office, there has been scant progress on Trump's wall. Debates have raged about how solid it needs to be, amid ideas that parts would be see-through or even a 'digital wall'. Another key question has been whether other things, like fencing, could suffice. 'The President still says "wall" – oftentimes frankly he'll say "barrier" or "fencing", now he's tended toward steel slats,' his outgoing chief of staff John Kelly told reporters. The President, meanwhile, veers between saying that fencing and steel slats could work to insisting that 'the wall is coming'. If only the President had learned from Emperor Hadrian, he would have avoided such flip-flopping over the building of his own wall.

The plan at the outset was for the Romans to build their wall mostly with stone, at a maximum height of around 15 feet (4.6 metres) and 3 metres in width, with the final thirty miles composed of turf at 6 metres in width. A guarded gate would be in place every mile, and there would be two observation towers in between them. The plans changed radically, however – a sure sign that the emperor decided to stick his nose in. Gates were added much more regularly, indicating that those overseeing it wanted to ensure greater ease of movement through the Empire's northern border. Work is likely to have overrun, given that it was then decided to reduce the width of the wall to 2.4 metres or less, with lighter standards of craftsmanship, in order to get the job done.

Construction might have had to be rushed, but the Romans could at least boast to have made their massive wall, as solid a piece of evidence as any of the Empire's might. After walking the length of Hadrian's Wall, the peripatetic politician Rory Stewart suggested that its purpose may have been just to serve as a symbol of Roman might, writing:

> Perhaps ... it was a mistake to take the Roman strategy too literally – to ask how the wall was really supposed to function, or what exactly prevented the Romans from pacifying the North or creating a sustainable state across the Island. For there to be a wall, it was enough that someone powerful in the capital had believed in one.

The wall eventually fell into disrepair, leading to its current fragmentary state today, but over the years it stood tall as a propaganda tool.

That symbolism clearly appeals to President Trump in his own pursuit of a border wall, although his critics have cottoned on. 'It's like a manhood thing for him,' Democrat politician Nancy Pelosi quipped at a private gathering. But symbols are rarely cheap.

President Trump struggled not to get bogged down in a more awkward question about his wall: who would pay for it? Mexico dug in and refused to fork out, leaving him to dig into American coffers. But opposition politicians have been doing their best to starve it of sufficient cash; the government ground to a halt for thirty-five days early on in 2019 due to the protracted political stalemate – the longest government shutdown in American history. The President tried to get out of the quagmire with the money he wanted for the wall, at one point resorting to justifying his case by pointing out to his Catholic interlocutors that there was a wall around Vatican City.

Did Hadrian manage to get the Picts to pay out for his wall? How it was paid for is as unclear as how President Trump has proposed to afford his own one. In the past few years, he has tried to suggest it will be paid for variously by 'playing with the trade deficit', tax reform, and the North American Free Trade Agreement (although it doesn't mention wall funding at all). The clearest summary Trump offered on how his wall would be paid for was: 'It will be in a form, perhaps in a complicated form.'

There was no free trade deal between the Roman Empire and the Picts to cover their own wall, but it is possible they would have had to pay fees if they wanted to cross either way. If so, they would have chipped in a bit. The President gave his own twist on that by arguing that Mexicans would pay 'indirectly' for his wall through the restyled trade deal between the United States and Mexico. Either way, he is finding – just as the Roman emperor did – that if he wants the wall, he'll have to dip into his own pockets to make it happen.

If the self-described master dealmaker somehow manages to secure enough money to make his wall a reality, Hadrian's experience shows his problems are far from over, as future leaders can have vastly different priorities.

After Hadrian died in 138 AD, a new emperor took over called Antoninus Pius, and he was not satisfied with the northern part of the Empire being marked with a border built under a previous regime. He wanted to make his own mark. So the 'Antonine Wall' was built by Roman soldiers through what is now the central part of Scotland, stretching from modern Bo'ness on the Firth of Forth to Old Kilpatrick on the River Clyde. While at thirty-nine miles in length it wasn't as long as his predecessor's project, he could however boast to have gone much further north. The Picts were left in even less doubt about who was in charge of British territory, with Rome's control expanding into Scotland.

So President Trump might well find his successors want to make their own mark by building it their way, whether in a different location, a different style or a different size. At least he can console himself with the fact that Antonine's Wall was only manned for around twenty years, before being ditched in favour of Hadrian's original.

As previously mentioned, Trump has marked himself out as someone who puts his name to everything he can, a trend he has continued in the White House. His changes to American healthcare have been billed as 'Trumpcare', while no other politician can claim to have pushed for a wall with more enthusiasm than him. 'Build the wall' is one of the key slogans his supporters chant at him whenever he mentions border security. And so he would want any border construction to be firmly identified with him, and to remain that way after his presidency.

But Hadrian had his own struggles to stay identified with the wall built under his reign. Such projects need maintenance, and the advent of new technology and materials means that a new leader can leave a massive wall like Hadrian's looking in a completely different condition. That was the case less than a century after its completion, when then emperor Septimius Severus stepped in to rebuild it with new mortar. Being the last person to shape the wall, Emperor Severus started to be identified closely with the wall. The medieval writer Bede paid homage accordingly in 730 AD, writing in his histories about 'a strong stone wall from sea to sea, in a straight line between the towns that had been there built for fear of the enemy, where Severus also had formerly built a rampart'.

Trump seems to be aware he is not the first to dream up the idea of building a border wall. 'They say it's a medieval solution, a wall. That's true,' he recently remarked. 'It's medieval because it worked then and it works even better now.' He could have gone further, though, by billing it as an ancient solution, given the example Hadrian set. Like the Roman emperor, he feels such a construction would show off the might of his regime. If he learns from the Roman rulers' examples, he would know how hard it is to actually build one, and how especially tricky it is to get other people to pay for it.

Perhaps what should worry President Trump most, as a man whose penchant for slapping his name on buildings so that they are remembered as his own, is that even if his wall is built, others could be recognised for it instead. Just as Emperor Severus came to be praised for the wall Hadrian first built, Trump's successors could make the wall their own. All they would need to do is change the building material – not an impossible idea given how much Trump's mind has changed on what he should use – or add a new feature, to seize ownership of it. If more of the wall is built by his successors, all adding their own touches, the less his original input would be remembered. The biggest embarrassment would come if, years later, the final parts were to be set in place by Chelsea Clinton – or one of Barack Obama's daughters – as President, because then it would be remembered as the 'Clinton wall' or the 'Obama wall'. If Trump's successors stopped him from being remembered for his wall, what then would he have left as a legacy?

PROVIDE VALUE FOR THE PUBLIC'S MONEY

Politicians cannot expect to climb the career ladder and secure more responsibility without showing they can be trusted with public money. Spending wastefully is a good way to put one's future advancement at risk, especially if they try to profit by fiddling the books.

Westminster learned this to its cost in 2009 when a slew of revelations emerged, serialised in the *Daily Telegraph*, about British politicians using their expenses to splash out on bizarre luxuries. A floating duck house, moat cleaning, helipad maintenance and new toilet seats were among the most controversial spending decisions. Any politician who tried to explain themselves had to face a stormy public, ready to heckle and boo them. A decade on, their reputation has still not recovered. If they're especially successful, they can hope only to do better than bankers, lawyers and estate agents at winning the public's affection.

Romans would have been just as outraged by the lavish spending that was uncovered in the Houses of Parliament. Simple living was a virtue, and those who followed an ascetic lifestyle were idealised. Anyone who stood for election took pains to play up for voters their apparently modest manner, as Plutarch records how they behaved in the early days of Rome:

It was the custom at Rome that the candidates for office should address their fellow citizens and appeal to them personally for their votes, and they would walk about in the Forum dressed in a toga, but without a tunic underneath it. They did this in some cases to emphasise their humility by the simplicity of their attire.

Later on, emperors tried to curry favour by making gestures to seem in touch. Augustus was known to eat simple foods such as figs and bread, which he would dip in cold water in order to make it tastier. He was 'most restrained' in how much wine he drank, Suetonius notes approvingly. His unfussy living was seized upon by Boris Johnson in February 2008, who told reporters – including Andrew Gimson – over lunch at the House of Commons press gallery that he intended to reign in London's City Hall as mayor 'like the Emperor Augustus, living in a simple room'.

After taking his third wife, Livia, Augustus presented her to the public as a traditional motherly figure, going as far as to insist that she weave clothes for him and her on the family loom. And she was made to do so in their front hall in full public view, playing the part in what was effectively an ancient version of a photo opportunity, just so Roman society could see how relatable they were as a family. He also passed laws to inhibit displays of wasteful luxury, with caps on how much money a host could spend on dinner parties, although they were regularly ignored.

By contrast, Emperor Nero showed 'riotous extravagance' in the eyes of the historian Suetonius in that he never wore the same outfit twice. Mark Anthony caused similar outrage among the Roman people by living it up while Julius Caesar was toiling on campaign; Plutarch records that he would travel about with an entourage carrying expensive golden drinking cups and would constantly be seen hosting 'lavish meals'. And when the general Pompey commissioned a model of his head to be made entirely of pearl in order to be paraded around in celebration of his military successes, the writer Pliny the Elder lamented nearly a century later that it marked 'the defeat of austerity and the triumph, let's face it, of luxury'.

The scorn Roman writers have for such behaviour might lead us to think politicians had to live minimalist lifestyles, but there is plenty of evidence of the sumptuous living standards most tended to enjoy. Instead, it touches on a timeless political hypocrisy. Those in politics usually live well, but they cannot be seen to be living it up. Critics will find any excuse to tut, while their fans will be inclined to see their spending as good value, or a sign of good taste.

That balance politicians try to strike was highlighted in 2016 when Nicky Morgan, a Conservative politician who had been removed from the Cabinet by Theresa May shortly after she became Prime Minister, decided to take issue with the premier publicly for posing in snazzy £995 leather trousers for an interview. 'I don't have leather trousers. I don't think I've ever spent that much on anything apart from my wedding dress,' Morgan said, claiming that her 'barometer' in deciding what she wore was to ask herself how she'd explain it to voters in Loughborough market. Morgan was later forced to apologise for her jibe, but the row she caused highlighted the modern sensitivity about the standards politicians maintain.

Such sensitivity can be traced back to the expenses scandal, which left politicians feeling as if they could only escape public criticism by

living in as downmarket a way as possible. That was captured acutely by the television satire *The Thick of It*, when the foul-mouthed
spin doctor Malcolm Tucker explains why a new minister should
throw out their nice new chair. 'People don't like their politicians to
be comfortable. They don't like you having expenses. They don't
like you being paid. They'd rather you lived in a fucking cave.' The
minister plaintively replies: 'OK, fine. So what should I be sitting on?
Should I just get an upturned KFC bucket?'

Politicians do not have to live in caves to get by in this climate, but
some did earn credit when showing off how humbly they lived. 'I
don't spend a lot of money, I lead a very normal life, I ride a bicycle
and I don't have a car,' one Labour MP boasted to *The Guardian* in
2015. Indeed, that MP – Jeremy Corbyn – found his frugal lifestyle
helped him build an image as a true man of the people, paving the
way for him later that year to leapfrog established rivals to become
leader of the Labour Party. His modest lifestyle – making his own
jam and tending to an allotment – would have earned him plaudits
in Rome, with Cicero once musing that 'nothing is better' for a man
than agriculture. Green fingers showed a politician's earthiness, and
Corbyn was eager to demonstrate that he was not afraid to get his
hands dirty. He went as far as to offer gardening tips on Twitter in
April 2019 to Alexandria Ocasio-Cortez, an American left-wing politician who is similarly celebrated by fans for seeming in touch with
people, after she asked for advice on what she should plant at her
own allotment. 'Best way to be healthy is to get your hands dirty – in
the soil!' he rounded off.

Corbyn's supporters were euphoric about just how ordinary he seemed to be. They could become painfully gushing in their delight, as illustrated by one fan posting a photo of him on social media late at night on a bus and making clear how they felt about it by quoting Joan Osborne's song lyrics: 'What if God was one of us? Just a slob like one of us, Just a stranger on the bus, Tryin' to make his way home?'

Such a rapturous review is par for the course in how Corbyn is treated by his supporters, but it is far from new for a politician to win the public's affection for how ordinarily they live. The statesman Marcus Porcius Cato showed how it was done way back in third-century BC Rome. Cato the Elder made a name for himself as a relentless campaigner against corruption, whose integrity was whiter than white and frugal to the point of outright miserliness. Whenever he drank water in his early days as a soldier, he would, as a treat, add vinegar. This was a popular mix, as the sharpness of the vinegar would mask the dubious quality of the water. And only when he was exhausted would he add a little wine to spruce up his drink.

When Cato later entered politics, he would not let the fact that he rose to be as senior as a consul stop him from drinking only the cheapest wines, tending to drink the same wine as his slaves. Anywhere he lived was kept to the basics, with plaster on the walls deemed too much of a luxury. And any land was used strictly for farming, rather than anything fancier like a garden.

As a politician, Cato never missed a chance to try to make people behave like him. He never missed a session of the senate and was a staunch critic of those who were absent. When he became governor of Sardinia, a sort of posting that many of his predecessors would use as a cash-cow, he charged nothing to the public purse and toured the province on foot. Rather than having a large entourage of servants and friends accompanying him – all living it up on the state's expense – he would be accompanied by just one servant, who carried his robe and his cup for pouring libations. Nothing was too small a gesture for the sake of saving the public purse some money for Cato. After travelling to Spain to stamp out a rebellion, he made a point of leaving his steed behind 'to save the state the cost' of transporting it back.

He was merciless in his crusade against public waste. One of his early jobs was to serve as an official auditor (known as a 'quaestor') scrutinising the renowned general Publius Cornelius Scipio's operations on the eve of his invasion of Africa. But Plutarch records that he was unable to overlook the lavish spending he saw, with Scipio's troops paid 'extravagantly high' amounts and treated to special games and festivals. The general tried to fob him off by arguing that what would matter in the end was how many battles he won, not how much he spent to do it. But Cato was not convinced, leaving Scipio's camp – which at the time was in Sicily – to dash back to Rome and denounce him before the Senate. His claims of corruption and profligacy prompted two tribunes to go out and question Scipio, who were reassured that his spending was vital for military success. Duly convinced, they left and allowed him to set sail for Africa, where he achieved such great success that he was anointed 'Africanus' in recognition. But Scipio Africanus was not forgiven by Cato, who continued in his campaign to be Rome's one-man answer to the National Audit Office.

The Roman establishment was rife with corruption. His zeal to stamp it out shone through once when he managed to persuade a group of election candidates to allow him to judge their campaigns' probity, as they promised to forfeit a large sum of money to him if he caught them cheating. Marcus Cicero was delighted that the zealous Cato had turned his attention to electoral corruption, as he thought his influence could be more effective than the laws that had by then been passed – only to be ignored. 'If the election proves free, as it is thought it will, Cato alone can do more than all the laws and all the judges,' he wrote. But his hopes were dashed when Cato announced after the election that one of the candidates had broken his rules, which clearly blindsided those who were running for office. His rivals gathered and decided that the guilty man should be let off and allowed to keep his money – a typical move that summed up how the political class felt about Cato.

The prospect of unpopularity did not stop Cato's quest to stamp out public waste. When people clamoured for state handouts, namely free corn, he railed against the idea. 'It is difficult, my fellow citizens, to argue with the belly,' he told the crowds, 'since it has no ears.' Never one for gluttony, he had no time for those who enjoyed their food too much. After laying eyes on a knight who had put on the pounds, his view was acerbic: 'How can a body like this be of any service to the state, when everything in it from the gullet to the groin is devoted to their belly?'

His outspoken evangelism for austerity and prudence meant, after many years in politics climbing the ranks, that he was considered a perfect candidate to stand for the position of censor. It would mark the crowning achievement of his career. The job came with a lot of responsibility. Keeping the general survey of Roman citizens, known as the census, up to date was just the start of it. He would also be in charge of the membership roll of the Senate, possessing the power to kick out anyone who fell beyond the pale. And he would have licence to stick his nose into all corners of life, being duty-bound to stamp on any bawdy behaviour and impropriety. Punishments could include being stripped of voting rights and even citizenship. Such powers meant the prospect of him becoming censor sent shudders through the Roman establishment, so naturally the great and good of the Senate plotted against him.

Some were driven to act by feelings of downright snobbery; they hated the idea that a man of Cato's background could occupy such a senior position in public life. He had not been born with a silver spoon in his mouth, nor had he been helped up the career ladder by being part of an elite family (his father was a humble soldier). Instead, he had made his own way, which meant he was what the Romans called a 'new man' – just like his fellow *novus homo* Cicero. Others wanted to stop Cato because, as Plutarch notes, they had committed 'shameful misdeeds' and dreaded the idea of what he would do to them as censor. So they decided to put up seven other people to stand against him, all promising to be very lenient and forgiving in office. Far from backing down, Cato doubled down in response. He made impassioned speeches threatening miscreants and urged the Roman people to choose the most earnest candidate, not the nicest. Voters welcomed what he had to say, viewing him not 'like someone seeking office, but like someone already in office issuing his decrees'. And so he was duly elected.

The political elite's efforts to stop Cato taking charge showed that the establishment had an instinctive aversion even then to anyone who threatened to shine too bright a spotlight on their activities. Westminster's 2009 expenses scandal came after Parliament spent four years fighting requests to cough up the details. The government tried to pass a motion exempting MPs' expenses from coming out, but backed down in the face of the immense opposition that emerged. The farce only ended after the *Telegraph* got its hands on the expenses figures in the summer of 2009 and started reporting on the most outrageous claims, with the full details grudgingly released within weeks. Four MPs were prosecuted on criminal charges of false accounting, each of them ending up in jail.

Parliament's desperate fight to keep the expenses secret was the culmination of MPs' increasing efforts to avoid too much scrutiny over how they did their jobs. In 1999, Elizabeth Filkin became the parliamentary standards commissioner, and she quickly made enemies just by doing her job. She investigated powerful politicians such as then Deputy Prime Minister John Prescott and Cabinet ministers like Peter Mandelson – a confidant of Prime Minister Tony Blair – and John Reid. Probes were launched into the financial affairs of other members of the governing Labour Party, such as Keith Vaz. Some of them didn't like the scrutiny and sought to fight back.

Whispering campaigns were started against Filkin. Rumours were spread that she wanted to get a book deal out of her time as a watchdog, solely based on the fact that she would be seen taking extensive notes at meetings about parliamentary standards. Some of those targeted by her were reported to have privately contacted journalists to spread scurrilous stories about her family. Others complained to the Speaker of the House of Commons about her zealous behaviour. Efforts were generally made to make her job as hard as possible to carry out. Despite official reviews concluding that she needed more staff, she was only allowed a part-time typist as support. She had expected to be reappointed once her initial three-year term was over, but the money she would have had if she stayed on for longer was cut. MPs managed to push her out, and she left her post in early 2002. Filkin found, as Cato did, that the establishment was terrified of scrutiny.

Despite angering senior politicians and civil servants, Filkin was adored by the public for her tireless work. She told *The Guardian* in 2002, shortly after stepping down, about the response she had been getting: 'Hundreds of letters, hundreds. I've been inundated with people who say please keep doing what you're doing. Everywhere I go, it's lovely. People come up to me in shops. I never expected any of this just for doing a public service job, which is what I've always done.'

Filkin concluded that effective scrutiny only worked if 'the people in the key positions of authority ... want it to succeed and want to protect it'. Cato would have come to the same conclusion after he got stuck into his job as censor. He cracked down on big spenders by carrying out a review of how many expensive possessions everyone owned, and hit those who owned pricey objects with special taxes equivalent to ten times what they were actually worth. His hope was that they would decide it was better to give up their baubles and pay less tax, and those who were affected hated him for it. He nailed crooked practices, cutting off the pipes for those who liked to siphon off the public water supply into their homes and demolishing overly big homes that encroached on public land. And he finally satisfied a grudge by exacting sweet revenge on his old foe Scipio Africanus, expelling him as a member of the equestrian class.

Rich senators hated him for doing all this, although Plutarch notes that he was 'wholeheartedly admired by the Roman people'. They erected a statue in his honour, commemorating his 'wise leadership, sober discipline, and sound principles'. Rome's answer to Robin Hood was loved by the people for his fearless scrutiny of the elite's finances and behaviour, in a manner Elizabeth Filkin experienced centuries later as Parliament's enforcer. Cato's unstinting integrity rubbed off on his son, who was immortalised by Dante in his *Divine Comedy* as the guardian in purgatory:

> I saw close by me a solitary old man, worthy, by his appearance, of so much reverence that no son owes more to a father. Long was his beard and mixed with white hair, similar to the hairs of his head, which fell to his breast in two strands. The rays of the four holy lights so adorned his face with brightness that I saw him as if the sun had been before him.

Those who desire accountability from MPs will be tempted to see Filkin in similarly celestial terms. Cato's experience shows that prudence with the public's money is a timeless political virtue for politicians. They do not have to replace their chairs with KFC buckets to survive. They just have to remember that their job is to serve the public, not to use their money to make themselves even richer.

TAKE PREDICTIONS WITH
A PINCH OF SALT

Predictions are like drugs for politicians: as dangerous as they know they are to indulge in, they just cannot get enough of them. There can be quite a rush if they are proven right, as the Liberal Democrat politician Vince Cable experienced after being lauded as a sage for predicting the 2008 economic crash – although critics liked to joke that all he had done, like most gloomy economists, was predict nine out of the last two recessions. Even if they are proven wrong, it is only a matter of time before politicians get caught up in speculation about the future. Winston Churchill captured the irresistibility of predictions when he quipped that 'a politician needs the ability to foretell what is going to happen tomorrow, next week, next month, and next year. And to have the ability afterwards to explain why it didn't happen.'

Sometimes, people resist the temptation to make predictions. Speculation was rife at the start of 2019 about how well Theresa May's Brexit deal would be received by MPs when she presented it to the House of Commons for their consideration. Given the vast numbers of people in Parliament who had made clear beforehand their intention to vote against it, nearly everyone had written off her chances of success and simply speculated as to the extent of her impending humiliation. 'I don't know whether or not we'll win,' said one of her Cabinet ministers, Michael Gove, that morning, adding that he was 'not an astrologer'. The size of her defeat, by 432 votes to 202, a majority of 230 votes, will have no doubt left May wishing she had taken advice from the heavens.

Astrologers were the closest thing Ancient Rome had to pundits and pollsters, dispensing insight – however dodgy it might be – about what the future held. They became a guilty pleasure in Ancient Rome, a city which Tacitus said 'found a meaning in everything' – much like the Westminster bubble. The astrologers' dabbling with the occult meant they skirted the edge of Roman law and propriety, but Romans could not help being intrigued by their exotic backstories and otherworldly talents, honed abroad in places like Egypt and Greece. Their stories helped take people in, as the satirist Juvenal captures:

> They will believe every word uttered by the astrologer has come from Hammon's fountain [somewhere said by legend to have been found by the god Bacchus in the Libyan desert] for … man is condemned to darkness as to his future. Chief among these was one who was often in exile … For nowadays no astrologer has credit unless he has been imprisoned in some distant camp, with chains clanking on either arm; none believe in his powers unless he has been condemned and all but put to death.

It did not take long for astrologers to gain favour in first-century Rome. The Emperor Tiberius took one on, an Egyptian man of Greek descent called Thrasyllus, as his in-house forecaster. He was lucky to have got the job as the first court astrologer, given the measures his new boss liked to take in case he received an unsatisfactory forecast.

In search of the best celestial guidance, Tiberius would invite the best astrologers around so he could test them out. They would be required to meet him in secret at the top of his cliffside residence, the historian Tacitus records, escorted along a steep and uneven path by a burly henchman. If their predictions fell flat, they were thrown into the sea on their way out so no one could reveal what had gone on in their meeting. When Tiberius took Thrasyllus down this perilous path, he asked him what the heavens were telling him. 'They tell me I'm in mortal danger,' he replied. As much as that sounds like a statement of the obvious, the emperor was hooked, not least because the astrologer went on to warn starkly that Tiberius, too, was in danger. Tiberius 'marvelled that he could foresee' the plots against him, Cassius Dio records, and Thrasyllus became an indispensable member of the imperial entourage. The emperor's in-house stargazer was relied upon hugely, to the extent that he saved the lives of some noblemen Tiberius suspected of plotting against him after telling him he would live for another ten years, leading him to believe he did not need to act, as he was destined to outlive any conspirators. His prediction proved to be false; Tiberius perished the following year. Before that happened, however, Thrasyllus had been rewarded by the emperor for his service with the highest honour a foreigner could expect: Roman citizenship for him and his family.

Astrologers did not just have to worry about upsetting emperors, but also wider Roman society. Their predictions could often land them in hot water, especially if they were making forecasts about matters of state, such as when the current emperor might die, or who might be destined to replace him. Such predictions were easy to believe, as astrologers claimed that their conclusions were born out of celestial insight. If astrologers were not employed by the emperor, or other members of the Roman elite, they could ply their trade in public. These 'street astrologers' would offer their prophecies to whoever was curious, and could pay. That meant times of uncertainty and political instability were extra lucrative, as people sought them out for a sense of what would happen. Their views were lapped up. But they had to be careful not to unsettle too many people with their bold forecasts.

The occupational hazards of doing so were dramatic. Public astrologers were constantly being kicked out of Rome in turbulent times. Admittedly, they weren't the only profession to be exiled. Tiberius at one point banished ballet dancers from Italy, Tacitus records, because he argued that their 'frivolous' and 'degraded' behaviour risked undermining public order. Astrologers still had a much worse time than ballet dancers, though. They were thrown off cliffs, not just the one on which Tiberius' home was perched, but also off the Tarpeian Rock in Rome, and some were executed outside the city gates. Their clients were not by any means safe. The politician Publius Anteius was accused of funding an exiled astrologer, and asking him to forecast his fortune as well as to predict how long Emperor

Nero would last. Speculating about the emperor's lifespan was seen as tantamount to treason, and this charge resulted in Publius Anteius being sentenced to death.

Any astrologer who wanted an easy life tended not to ruffle feathers with their predictions, given the hazards they faced. It proved safer to behave as a yes-man, promising long lives and happy futures to whoever they were asked to hold forth about. The young Augustus took astrology so seriously that he was said by the Roman historian Suetonius to have gone with his mother to the house of a soothsayer called Theogenes when he had reached adulthood to find out what the future held for him. After his mother was promised 'almost incredibly good fortune', he feared that his own prospects had to be worse. But the forecaster's euphoric response – rising and flinging himself to Augustus' feet – gave him no reason to worry. He was so pleased with his horoscope that he published it, so everyone could see he was destined for great things.

Astrologers' desire to please did mean their predictions could easily be wrong, and Roman society noticed. In the marvellously titled satire about the Emperor Claudius, *Apocolocyntosis* (literally 'The Pumpkinification of Claudius'), the character Mercury notes that astrologers had been predicting every month when Claudius would die. 'Do let them tell the truth for once!' the god exclaims with exasperation in the play. Like a modern pollster, astrologers had to accept they would be mocked – in their view, unfairly – for how wrong their predictions could be.

Astrologers had long been the butt of jokes due to their desperation to please with predictions. One joke, recorded in the Ancient

Greek collection *Philogelos* ('Laughter-lover'), tells of how an astrologer once told a man that he was unable to father children, only to be informed that he had seven kids. In response, the astrologer said without a beat: 'Look after them well.'

Some writers tried to stick up for the maligned stargazers. Cassius Dio records that soon after taking charge in 69 AD, the Emperor Vitellius issued a decree ordering astrologers to depart Rome, and the whole of Italy, by a certain day. They fought back, he notes, by putting up in the night a notice of their own, predicting that Vitellius would die before the day was over. But Cassius Dio did not mention that the emperor went on to live for another couple of months, dying on 20 December – rather than 1 October, as they had predicted.

Pollsters would insist that they have a much better track record of accuracy than astrologers, but their impact on public life is not much different. Admittedly, none of them have had to fear death after reporting something controversial about what the public thinks. Nor has anyone put their lives at risk for fraternising with a pollster, but their conclusions have been able to cause just as much commotion as a punchy horoscope.

In the September 2014 referendum on whether Scotland should break away from the United Kingdom, the No campaign had built up a consistent lead over the previous months. Surveys of public opinion showed for most of the campaign that voters were more inclined to vote to remain part of the UK than for independence, at times by as large a margin as 22 per cent. But that notion was shattered in the final weeks of the campaign, when a poll by YouGov for the *Sunday Times* at the start of September suggested that Yes had pushed ahead to lead by 2 per cent. Despite the efforts by the pro-independence campaign's leader Alex Salmond to play down the significance of 'just one poll', it caused mayhem.

The poll sent financial markets into a panic, with sterling falling by about 1.3 per cent against the US dollar and shares tumbling in some big Scotland-linked businesses. The panic spread across Westminster. The leaders of the major parties launched a mad dash up to Scotland to put in some last-ditch campaigning, and the Prime Minister made several emotional pleas to voters to think again. David Cameron teamed up with Ed Miliband and Nick Clegg to jointly promise Scottish voters that a range of new powers would be devolved to them if they voted to stay in the United Kingdom. Their pledge was trumpeted as 'The Vow' on the front page of the Scottish newspaper the *Daily Record*, which depicted their promise as if it had been made on old parchment paper, to underline its solemnity to voters.

That one YouGov poll upended the referendum campaign, scaring No campaigners into doubling their efforts to stop Scotland voting for independence. Their fears did not come to pass, as the pro-unionist campaign won in the end by 55 per cent to 45. Cameron and his colleagues will argue that it had gone exactly as planned, but the panic caused by the poll showed how seriously they feared things could go awry.

Cameron suffered another scare at the hands of the pollsters less than a year later. Ahead of the 2015 general election, he and his Conservative colleagues had thrown everything possible at stopping the advance of the man who stood the best chance of replacing him as Prime Minister: Ed Miliband. The polls suggested that the then Labour leader had a serious chance of winning power, but not by enough of a margin to form a government by himself. So the Conservatives warned that he would be forced to cut unseemly deals with parties like the Scottish Nationalists, putting out posters depicting Miliband in Salmond's pocket to emphasise this point. But with four weeks to go until people voted, three polls came out that suggested their campaign was destined for disaster.

Less than a month before election day, *The Guardian* trumpeted on its front page that this was 'the day the polls turned'. On 7 April, the newspaper reported that three different companies – Survation, Panelbase and TNS – had found Labour was leading in the popularity stakes, by a margin of as much as 6 per cent. But the polls had turned back a month later to Cameron, and decisively so on election day, as he won around 7 per cent more of the vote than Miliband's Labour. How did Cameron save himself from grim defeat? The polling shock a month from election day, might just have done the job, as the Conservatives' election pitch relied on people taking seriously the idea that Miliband could get anywhere near power, and so voting to keep Prime Minister Cameron in office. Voters would have had little reason to believe that idea after seeing the fresh polling suggesting that Miliband was in the lead in the race for Downing Street.

The following year, 2016, brought even more drama for political forecasters, and quite possibly the biggest shock polls in history. The EU referendum on 23 June seemed for so long like it would be a comfortable win for the Remain campaign. A few surveys suggested at times that Leave had more support, but surveys overwhelmingly indicated that Remain would glide to victory. 'I really wish we had managed to dampen the hype,' a senior figure on the Remain campaign told me, bewailing how it proved 'impossible to contain'. Their own research might have led them to believe there was nothing to worry about, as the polling firm run by Remain's official guru Andrew Cooper revealed, hours after voting started on referendum day, that Remain was ten points ahead. There seemed to be so little to worry about that it was reported that the Prime Minister would not bother to stay up for the result, as he expected to sleep early and wake up to toast his victory.

'Well, that didn't go to plan!' Cameron observed to his aides the morning after, with it clear that Leave had won 52 per cent compared to Remain's 48 per cent. The man who many were led by the polls to think would stay safely in power for many years after his election victory, and who they believed would renegotiate better terms of membership for Britain after winning his promised referendum, ended up swiftly resigning.

The referendum result surprised a good few of my colleagues in the *Telegraph* newsroom, who had predicted that Remain would win in our office sweepstake – an understandable position given how many polls suggested it was ahead. Our letters editor was one of the few to enter the office that morning thoroughly vindicated, as he had predicted it would be a 52/48 per cent split exactly in favour of Brexit. He concluded proudly soon after that you didn't need the United

Kingdom's top pollsters to understand what the nation thinks, when the *Telegraph* postbag did a much better job.

Months later across the Atlantic, America had its own lesson in how reliably politics could be predicted. The 2016 presidential election seemed as if it would be a slam-dunk success for Hillary Clinton. Every bit of serious analysis kept pointing that way. The grandly titled Princeton Election Consortium gave her a 99 per cent chance. The Huffington Post website concluded she had a 98 per cent chance of success, while the *New York Times* newspaper's election-watchers seemed apocalyptic by contrast in giving her only a 91 per cent chance of success. Her Republican rival, Donald Trump, seemed destined for a return to the world of reality TV and business, but on 9 November, he defied the consensus and clinched victory.

The past few years have been tough for the polling industry, with critics mocking them for being about as accurate as astrology in their predictions. Some British politicians, such as Labour peer Lord Foulkes, have called for political polls to be banned during election time because of how much they can shape the public debate.

They are not demanding anything unprecedented. The Italians ban the publication of polls in the two weeks before a general election to avoid influencing voter behaviour. Commentators manage to get around the ban, however, by writing up their poll findings as if they apply to a fictional horse race, rather than the political horse race. The relevant candidates are written about as if they are jockeys or horses, with special epithets to obscure their real identity. And so election-watchers in recent years could check in on how the former centre-right Prime Minister Silvio Berlusconi was doing.

Astrologers were the pollsters of their day in Ancient Rome: popular, but regarded with suspicion. Showered with money and appreciation when they're right, but mocked and cast out when they are not. While politicians like Cameron may wish they could punish pollsters for their misleading predictions by throwing them off Big Ben, they should restrain themselves.

Ancient and modern history shows that it is much healthier to take pollsters' pronouncements with a pinch of salt, as the Romans did, knowing how often events can defy what had been foretold.

PART THREE

LEAVING OFFICE

True glory takes root, and even extends itself; all false pretensions fall as do flowers, nor can anything feigned be lasting. (*Vera gloria radices agit atque etiam propagatur, ficta omnia celeriter tamquam flosculi decidunt nec simulatum potest quicquam esse diuturnum.*)

MARCUS TULLIUS CICERO, *DE OFFICIIS*

BOW OUT BEFORE YOU'RE PUSHED OUT

All good things must come to an end, but politicians find that hard to judge when it comes to their careers. Veteran British ministers can be encouraged to step down with the promise of a peerage, while any leader who wants to get rid of someone kindly can normally work with them to find an appropriate excuse to justify their exit – such as that they are 'going away to spend more time with family'. Emperor Claudius found that a good way to get rid of bad members of the Senate was to urge them to voluntarily step down. If they refused, he would seem less brutal in kicking them out as their names would be released alongside those who had agreed to retire, thereby giving the public the rosy impression that they had selflessly decided to quit.

Others do not have to go through such rigmarole in the process of bowing out. Cincinnatus is a model of leadership not just because of his action-hero-like decision to come out of retirement twice to save his fellow citizens from a crisis, but because he quit as soon as he had done the job each time. The first time the former consul was called upon to serve as dictator, he had been nominated for a term of six months. He could have done a lot with such power in that time, but he resigned after just fifteen days and returned to his farm. His second taste of supreme power lasted a bit longer, at twenty-one days. He clung onto his office for not a day longer than absolutely necessary.

If only modern politicians learned such self-restraint. America decided in 1951 to enforce it in their constitution, by banning anyone from being elected to the office of President more than twice. France followed suit in 2008. By contrast, China cleared the way for its President to stay on for life last year by abolishing term limits from its constitution.

With no set limits in the United Kingdom, the Prime Minister can carry on governing as long as they keep winning elections – and their party still wants them in charge. Theresa May acknowledged that in the wake of her anticlimactic 2017 election performance, telling her party she would stay on 'for as long as you want me'. Her time in office following that was dogged by questions over when she might finally resign. 'I'm in this for the long term' was all May would say. Every bump in the road fed speculation that her time would be over, with every period of calm eliciting speculation that she might go on longer. It was only at the eleventh hour, as she struggled to convince her critics to let her Brexit deal pass through Parliament, that she had to accept it was not possible for her to go on any longer.

Few of her predecessors escaped speculation about how soon they might be off. From the moment Tony Blair, the man who won three elections for Labour, said that he would not serve a full third term, the clock was ticking on his final few months before handing over.

That announcement was hard to avoid, as the signs were mounting that his magic had long worn off with the voters, prompting debate about who could next take over the reins.

Those who try to shrug off the critics and fight for survival can either appear dogged or pig-headed. When plotting was rife in the Labour ranks during the 1960s, party leader Harold Wilson remarked: 'I know what's going on. I'm going on.' And he made good on that, staying on and fighting four elections before he bowed out in 1976. By contrast, Gordon Brown – Blair's successor – insisted in an early interview that 'I'm starting a job that I mean to continue.' He ended up lasting only three years, as colleagues panicked about how to remove someone who was feared to be 'Labour's worst PM'.

It's hard for politicians to resist the allure, as Margaret Thatcher once told a television interviewer, to 'go on and on'. They start to feel that their time in office has been so beneficial to the nation that it is in the national interest to stay on. But others would suggest they are more motivated by self-interest. David Cameron proved to be a rare exception when he reached for a cereal-based simile to explain, before winning a second general election in 2015, why he was unlikely to pursue a third term as Prime Minister: 'Terms are like Shredded Wheat – two are wonderful but three might just be too many.'

If politicians avoid biting off more than they can chew, a risk Cameron recognised in his Shredded Wheat analogy, they can aspire to end their careers on a high note. That is the political ideal, with the leader's exit dominated by admirers gushing about how they are leaving too soon, rather than critics scoffing that their departure had been long overdue. The best way for them to ensure that is to follow Cincinnatus' mentality: never forget what you are in office to do, get on with it and then depart once the job is done.

As basic as that sounds, it is too easily forgotten. Those who flounder in office end up inviting attempts to put them out of their misery. Those who show no sign that they'll ever let go of power can also encourage attempts to prise it out of their hands, as Julius Caesar found after deciding it would be appropriate to be appointed 'dictator in perpetuity'.

PROPER PLANNING PREVENTS
POOR PUTSCHES

'*Et tu, Brute*, is my comment on that,' Stanley Johnson told a BBC journalist in June 2016, shortly after the EU referendum. What had inspired the media personality to reach for Julius Caesar's dying words on discovering his friend and protégé, Brutus, among his assassins? The shock assassination of his son's hopes of being Prime Minister.

Boris Johnson seemed widely to be the heir apparent after David Cameron indicated he would bow out. After winning two terms as Mayor of London, he had found himself a seat in Parliament and was one of the most – if not *the* most – popular politicians in the country. Leading the Vote Leave campaign, alongside his fellow Tory Eurosceptic Michael Gove, to victory left them in a position where the prize was theirs for the taking. Gove had made repeatedly clear, vehemently so, that he did not want the top job, at one point offering to write that pledge 'in parchment' with his own blood to make that point. 'There are lots of talented people who could be Prime Minister, but count me out,' he insisted on television during the referendum. 'Whatever poster you put up, do not put up one of me!'

His vehemence meant it had been safe to assume that he would stick with his Brexiteer brother-in-arms for the leadership race. But expectations were dashed within days when Gove announced that he would not support Johnson as he had concluded 'that Boris cannot provide the leadership or build the team for the task ahead'. His withdrawal of support dealt Johnson's leadership hopes a fatal blow, as Gove was an influential figure, whose support encouraged many Tory MPs to row in behind the pair. Without him, Johnson was damaged and doomed to fail. The timing of his betrayal was especially brutal, as it came just hours before Johnson had been due to announce his campaign. He was left with no choice, having been cut down by his former ally, but to admit he would not be throwing his hat into the ring. Johnson's allies were livid over this turn of events. 'Gove is a c**t who set this up from the start,' one friend of the betrayed politician texted a journalist. Another ally, Tory MP Jake Berry, tweeted publicly that there was a 'very deep pit reserved in Hell' for people like Gove.

Fresh from stabbing Johnson in the back, Gove left them to seethe as he announced his own candidacy. Despite claiming to have thought up his leadership bid over the previous few days, his essay-length 5,000-word discourse led many to suspect he had been thinking about it for much longer. As well-considered as his pitch was, Gove's leadership campaign floundered as Tory MPs were shy of backing someone who had entered the race amid such controversy.

'He couldn't wipe the blood off his dagger that quickly,' one MP put it to me.

In an act of swift political karma, the eventual winner of the Tory leadership – Theresa May – sacked Gove soon after she entered office. 'I would have sacked me too,' he later admitted, acknowledging the 'mistakes' he had made. In recognition of how brutally he scuppered Johnson's ambitions, an act of treachery came to be jokingly known as 'doing a Gove'. He was only allowed back into government after spending a year in the political wilderness, showing he knew how to be loyal by touring the media studios slavishly defending ministers at every opportunity.

Impatience, and a fear of what a man with Johnson's foibles would do if he became Prime Minister, led Gove to take a decision that made him a political pariah for months. Johnson's father's casting of Gove was fitting, given that the betrayal had come from someone his son – like Julius Caesar – had thought of previously as a long-term ally. Although Gove must count himself lucky that the fallout has been not nearly so bloody.

Brutus and his conspirators were driven to act because they feared that Caesar was going power-mad and was acting like a wannabe king. They were incensed by the pomp and ceremony that surrounded him. He had a statue placed next to those of Rome's past kings, who represented an era many senators saw as the bad old days. Coins were issued bearing Caesar's image, and he even had a golden chair to sit on in the Senate and could wear the gaudy triumphal costume of an all-conquering general whenever he wished. One episode in particular spurred them to decide to take action: when Caesar was

repeatedly offered a crown in public by his lieutenant Mark Anthony. Although he refused it each time, Caesar's sceptics feared it was
just a show to mask his desire to seize power and rule as a monarch.
Plutarch records the display as follows:

> After he had dashed into the forum and the crowd had made way
> for him, he carried a diadem, round which a wreath of laurel was
> tied, and held it out to Caesar. Then there was applause, not loud,
> but slight and preconcerted. But when Caesar pushed away the
> diadem, all the people applauded; and when Antony offered it
> again, few, and when Caesar declined it again, all, applauded.

That was enough provocation for Caesar's assassins. The equivalent
moment for Gove came when Johnson decided on the weekend after
the Brexit vote to spend his Saturday playing cricket with members
of his family and Earl Spencer's XI at Althorp House. Such chillax-
ing after a historic referendum result convinced him he lacked the
required seriousness to lead. While Caesar's assassins decided to act
for fear he was too hungry for power, Gove was driven to act for fear
that Johnson was not hungry enough.

Brutus' plot came together on 15 March, 44 BC, better known in
Rome as the Ides of March. He and his fellow conspirators planned
to kill him when he came to a meeting at the Senate, and it could so
easily have gone wrong.

Caesar was running late. The plotters were terrified that their
scheme had been unravelled when one was approached by a man
who took him by the hand and remarked that they had 'kept this a

secret from us ... But Brutus has told us everything.' The conspirators 'stood there speechless', Plutarch writes, only to find out that the gentleman merely wanted to know how one of them had made enough money so quickly that he could afford to stand for public office. At another point as they waited, a senator bounded up to Brutus and one of his fellow conspirators and whispered to them: 'My prayers are with you. May your plan succeed, but whatever you do, make haste. Everyone is talking about it by now.' He walked away, leaving them to sweat over whether they had been exposed. Their fears did not come to pass, as Caesar eventually came, and was leapt upon by the scores of senators as they advanced to stick their knife in.

They managed to get rid of him, but had clearly not considered how to manage the fallout. Confident that the public would see them as liberators, they called on their fellow citizens to enjoy their new-found freedom. But instead, 'they were greeted only by cries of fear, and the general confusion was increased by people wildly running to and fro in the terror'.

Their efforts to win around the public in the aftermath became further unstuck once the contents of Caesar's will had been revealed. He had promised every Roman citizen nearly three months of their daily income as a gift, and allowed them to use his private gardens. The extent of his generosity caused, as Plutarch writes, 'a great wave of affection for Caesar and a powerful sense of his loss', scuppering the conspirators' hopes. Their failure to take the public with them was confirmed by the euphoric response their nemesis Mark Anthony received from the crowd with his funeral oration.

The result was that Rome became too dangerous for Brutus.

Soldiers who fought with Caesar in his campaigns, still harbouring affection for their former commander, were ready to kill him if they spotted him in the city. So the conspirators' figurehead escaped the city and found safe refuge in Crete. Tensions were already fraying between the plotters, with Brutus' meetings with his closest allies ending in shouting matches. As Plutarch writes about one key meeting:

> The doors were shut, and with no one else present the two men first began blaming one another and then fell to recriminations and counter-charges. These soon led to indignant reproaches and tears, and their friends, who were amazed at the vehemence and bitterness of their anger, were afraid that the quarrel might end in violence.

Things got even worse for Brutus and his allies, as Caesar's anointed heir Octavian took over and, in 43 BC, he had those who killed his adopted father branded murderers and enemies of the state. Brutus and his allies were encouraged by reports of a war between Caesar's top supporters, as Octavian clashed with Mark Anthony on the battle-field. They were led to believe that Rome was ripe for them to take control of because Octavian did not have enough troops to defend the city, and so marched his forces back. That turned out to be a fatal mistake, as the news of Brutus' imminent arrival drove Octavian to bury the hatchet with Anthony so they could combine forces. To-gether, they crushed Brutus and his fellow conspirators' forces, which led to a pitiful end for the arch-conspirator as he fled into the nearby hills, where he ran himself through with his own sword to avoid being taken alive.

Political plots can easily go wrong. When conspirators tried to bump off Emperor Claudius by having him eat a poisoned mushroom, Tacitus records that their plan did not work for very basic reasons. Namely, that he was so drunk that he did not feel the effects of the poison at first, and was safe once he had evacuated his bowels. One of the plotters, we are told, was 'horrified' by his survival.

Brutus and Gove cannot blame their failure on bowel movements, but rather, their own haste. If Brutus had bided his time, he could have had a happier ending. Plutarch writes that he could 'easily have become the first man [i.e. leader] in Rome if he had had the patience to serve for a time as Caesar's deputy' and waited for his star to fade. Instead, killing Caesar caused him to become so cherished that he was declared a god after his death. Someone else took over, and Brutus died as a reviled social pariah.

Gove made a similar error by rushing to betray Johnson in his own bid for power. The brutal way in which he upended Johnson's 2016 bid to be Prime Minister brought the latter much sympathy, while Gove long struggled to shake off the stain of treachery on his reputation. If he had remembered what had happened when politicians had been betrayed by their allies, as Caesar was by Brutus, he might have held back. Waiting, and sticking with Johnson, could have left him firmly established as the government's second-in-command and heir presumptive. But that was all ruined by his hasty decision. Three years later, Gove tried again to stop Johnson taking power by launching his own leadership campaign, promising Tory MPs that he would put up a decent fight if he was sent through to the final round to face off against him. He initially shrugged off questions about his past betrayal, but soon embraced it in a bid to show how willing he was to fight him. 'Mr Johnson, whatever you do, don't pull out … I know you have before,' he teased at the launch of his second leadership bid, conveniently glossing over his own role in derailing Johnson's entry into the 2016 race. But his colleagues baulked, fearing the psychodrama they would risk by sending Johnson's Brutus to face him, and culled him from the race. He had to content himself with serving as one of Johnson's right-hand men in government, in a magnanimous gesture from the man he once double-crossed.

It can be nerve-wracking for plotters to wait for the right moment to strike. Those who plotted to kill Caligula, including senior officers of his own Praetorian Guard, missed many potential moments. That might be because they were biding their time, but the historian Josephus blames it simply on the 'sloth of many of those involved'. For example, he points out, when Caligula stood up on top of the palace to throw coins out to those waiting down below in the marketplace, he could have easily been pushed off. One of the key members of the conspiracy, the emperor's chief Praetorian Chaerea, became fed up about the opportunities they were letting slip. His fellow plotters urged patience, arguing that a bungled attempt on the emperor would be worse than no attempt at all.

The plan they settled on in 41 AD was to pounce on him somewhere discreet at the theatre, where he was watching games and festivities. Senior members of his Praetorian Guard were part of the plot, which was important as they were on duty as his close protection.

That meant there were assassins stationed in the viewing gallery near Caligula, and outside waiting in the corridor that connected the theatre – through an underground passage – to the palace. The passageway was narrow, making it an ideal place to launch an ambush, as the emperor was exposed to those immediately around him, squeezing out the few still loyal guardsmen who would protect him. On top of this, the hustle and bustle through the theatre corridors of attendees there for the show would make it even harder to run in to help.

During the performance, one of the conspirators, Caligula's chief Praetorian Chaerea, slipped out of the emperor's box. That unnerved another plotter, called Minucianus, who sat alongside the emperor trying to hide his panic about whether Chaerea had got cold feet – or worse, if he had remembered his duties as the emperor's supposed bodyguard and was about to betray the conspirators. And so the nervy conspirator decided to rise from his seat, planning to pop outside and check in with his fellow plotters, possibly to urge them to break into the box to kill Caligula there and then. But Caligula grabbed him by the toga and told him to sit back down, which he duly did out of respect for the emperor. The plotter eventually slipped away after trying again shortly after, but only because the emperor thought he was desperate to go to the bathroom (as the historian Josephus puts it, to 'perform some necessities of nature').

Once the show broke for an interval, Caligula finally popped out, although he had been dithering over whether to do so. Josephus suggests he was torn as to whether to sit tight to see the rest of the show, or pop back to the palace for a bath and some food before seeing the rest of the entertainment. The historian Suetonius has a different theory about his delay: he had an upset stomach after eating too much the day before, so was not keen to get up and have lunch. Caligula was persuaded by those around him, many of whom were involved in the plot, to pop out so he could freshen up for the rest of the day's entertainment. But he never got to have that bath; he was run through with swords on his way back to the palace.

The fear of failure will not stop ambitious politicians like Gove from plotting. But they should learn from the experiences of Brutus, and what other Romans concluded. 'Everything will be clear and distinct to the man who does not hurry,' the historian Livy warned, 'haste is blind and thoughtless.' Successful plans to topple leaders can be cobbled together quickly, but they tend not to end well for those carrying them out unless they have thought ahead.

HOW TO AVOID GOING FROM HERO TO NERO

No matter how illustrious a career one leads in public service, it has to come to an end at some point. Leaders like to think they can, as Margaret Thatcher said, 'go on and on'. Her Roman predecessors would understand that inclination.

A career high for many Romans is to be celebrated as the star of their own triumphal procession. This sort of ceremony – typically thrown to celebrate great military victories – saw them treated like they were living Gods, or, failing that, rockstars. They would wear a crown of laurel and an all-purple gold-embroidered toga and have their face painted red. Riding in a horse-drawn chariot, with their army, captives and war spoils in the procession, they would be rapturously received by the populace.

Few people would not let such a welcome get to their heads, so the triumphant leader had someone on hand to remind them that they were still a mere mortal. No one knows for sure what exactly they would have told these politicians as a reality check, but their intended message is clear: all good things must come to an end. The Romans were so obsessed with mortality that they even had a term to express a person's potential lifespan – a *saeculum*. What niggles away at politicians contemplating what follows their career is how they will be remembered once their *saeculum* is over. If a politician achieves a great deal but no one remembers that, have they really made an impact?

Once they have died, debate about their record hits fever pitch as a historical consensus starts to emerge. Brutus hoped that after he and his fellow conspirators killed Julius Caesar that they would be celebrated as saviours of democracy, but Mark Anthony turned the tide of public opinion with his spirited funeral tribute. Caesar's posthumous anointment by the Senate as a god, giving rise to his own popular cult, showed how well he would be remembered.

Leaders can still depart the mortal coil, but not quite leave the political fray. One of President Donald Trump's many critics was the Republican senator John McCain. That was in part due to Trump's own criticisms of the former prisoner of war, infamously accusing him of not being a 'war hero' during the Vietnam War because 'I like people who weren't captured'. Before McCain died on 25 August 2018, he aimed one last swipe at the President in a farewell message, which his aide read out posthumously:

We weaken our greatness when we confuse our patriotism with tribal rivalries that have sown resentment and hatred and violence in all the corners of the globe. We weaken it when we hide behind walls, rather than tear them down, when we doubt the power of our ideals, rather than trust them to be the great force for change they have always been.

The funeral service that soon followed built on this message, with President Trump pointedly not invited. His name was never mentioned explicitly, but he was under constant attack by those who spoke at the event in front of the 2,500 people in the church. The *New Yorker* magazine described it as the 'biggest resistance meeting yet', adding: 'The funeral service for John Sidney McCain III, at the Washington National Cathedral … was all about a rebuke to the pointedly uninvited current President of the United States, which was exactly how McCain had planned it.'

Trump's predecessor, Barack Obama, used his tribute to denounce 'insult and phony controversies' in public life, something he was often associated with. McCain's daughter pulled no punches with her own critique: 'We gather to mourn the passing of American greatness, the real thing, not cheap rhetoric from men who'll never come near the sacrifice he gave so willingly, nor the opportunistic appropriation of those who lived lives of comfort and privilege while he suffered and served.'

As if the target of her remarks was not clear enough, Meghan McCain inverted Trump's election campaign slogan 'Make America Great Again' to offer this conclusion: 'The America of John

McCain has no need to be made great again because America was always great.' Despite the solemnity of the occasion, the applause she provoked among the 2,500 people in attendance showed how much those in attendance agreed. Trump's fans were apoplectic in response, with one commentator on the Breitbart website calling it a 'going-away grudgefest'.

Some politicians, like McCain, did not have to worry about how well they would be remembered in the history books. Others can't help obsessing about whether their time in office will be regarded as well as they hope. The core of their worry is that they will be remembered as a flop, in the same way that Emperor Galba's short-lived reign in 69 AD led the historian Tacitus to come up with a brilliantly pithy review that could sum up many disappointing leaders. '*Omnium consensu capax imperii, nisi imperasset.*' In short, everyone thought he was capable of ruling, until he tried ruling.

Not all politicians can be as confident about their place in history as Winston Churchill, who predicted: 'History will be kind to me, as I intend to write it.' Others have had to be more sanguine in view. Enoch Powell, no stranger to controversy, once warned his fellow politicians that complaining about how they were covered by the press, a key shaper of public opinion, was as pointless as a 'sailor complaining about the sea'.

The classical scholar – who became a professor at twenty-five years old – would have known how fiercely Roman politicians had been battered by the waves. Emperors were certainly not safe. While they could expect to be written up well while alive, the Roman historian Tacitus notes how the writers could stick the knife in – 'influenced by still raging animosities' – after they had gone. He also acknowledged the risk of what President Trump likes to call 'fake news', urging readers to look for the 'truth unblemished by marvels' rather than 'the falsity of hearsay gossip and … incredible tales – however widely current and readily accepted'.

Such gossip and incredible tales have shaped how we see many emperors today. Filmmakers were able to run riot when they made films about Caligula because of the variety of filthy and bonkers stories involving him. The BBC's 1976 series *I, Claudius* depicted Caligula as someone who was happy to eat a foetus torn from his sister's belly, a deed that was totally dreamed up by the screenwriters. Three years later, the hardcore pornographic biopic *Caligula* came out. It went even further, revelling in all the gore, sex and salaciousness it could depict on screen – with eminent actors like Sir John Gielgud and Dame Helen Mirren all playing their part appropriately. Caligula has been so widely depicted as an insane and debauched tyrant that it meant filmmakers could let their creativity run wild – as no detail would be too absurd to add to his portrayal.

Yet so many of the tales now assumed to be fact about Caligula are based on reports not of what he actually did, but what others claimed he would do, or was thinking of doing. One of his supposed standout moments is when, as the imperial biographer Suetonius records, he planned to make his favourite horse *Incitatus* ('Swift') a senator. But it could well be argued that this was not a sign of madness, but rudeness. In other words, Caligula just wanted to belittle senators by arguing that they were so pointless even his horse would be as effective in their job, rather than actually suggesting he should sit alongside them.

Power clearly went to his head, as it would for many politicians if they were awarded supreme command of the Roman Empire at the age of just twenty-four. Once, three elderly senators were woken up in the middle of the night and marched into his palace under the watch of his armed guards. They understandably feared the worst as they were taken into a big hall and made to sit down on a row of seats in front of a stage. Suddenly, there was a blast of music and Caligula rushed on – with a flowing cloak – whereupon he performed a little song and dance before dashing off. He made them fear for their lives just because he could. At another time, he suddenly burst into laughter at a dinner party. On being asked to share what had tickled him so much, he replied: 'I've just thought that I've only to give the word and you'll all have your throats cut.'

Caligula is not just said to have been bad, but also sexually depraved. Much has been written about his bacchanalian dinner parties and incestuous relations, but how debauched was he really? Dame Mary Beard is highly sceptical, pointing out that the 'clearest evidence' of incest with his sister Drusilla was the 'deep distress' he demonstrated over her death, 'which is hardly clinching proof'. The classical scholar goes on to argue that the tales of his orgiastic parties are based on the mistranslated notion that his wife and sisters sat 'on top and below' him, when Suetonius was merely describing where they sat around a dining table.

Of course, that is not to say Caligula was a saint who was unfairly written up by historians. But he could claim to have been victim of a few historical hatchet jobs. That said, the man who took over from him could claim to have been treated even worse in the history books.

Any politician who fears their greatness might not be fully recognised should be thankful they have not been as poorly recorded as Emperor Nero. There is a lot of good Nero can claim responsibility for. A few decades after him, Trajan, who was emperor during the turn of the first century AD, is said to have often opined that Nero did better in five years than any other emperor.

That verdict comes from one of Rome's most successful emperors, who left the Empire the largest it ever was in history by the time of his death. The clearest sign of his eminent record can be seen in the column that still stands tall in his name in Rome. Yet it is understandable why some would be astonished that seemingly sensible people like Trajan would suggest Nero had any redeeming qualities, because many people have come to regard his name as a byword for evil incarnate.

But for every charge Nero faces over his recorded infamy, there is a case that can be put in his defence, or at least in mitigation. Among Christians at the time, Nero was widely believed to be the Antichrist. That said, his persecution of the Christians – then an obscure religious sect – was not strictly a bad thing in the eyes of Roman historians. Even his sharpest critics, such as Suetonius, chalked it up as a rare point in his favour.

Needless to say, whatever he is associated with during his fourteen-year rule – from 54 AD to 68 AD – tends not to be favourable. No moment defined him more than in 64 AD, when he is commonly said to have not just started the Great Fire of Rome, but then reacted by getting out his fiddle to play as his people suffered. That incident gave rise to the idea of Nero 'fiddling while Rome burns', a phrase which has since caught on to describe any leader reacting to ongoing catastrophe by carrying on as normal. It's no wonder it has been taken up as a political attack line, given how arresting a scene it conjures up of a leader – backlit by flames – blithely indulging themselves rather than dealing with the crisis on their doorstep.

Any modern act of self-destruction attracts comparisons to Nero's handling of the fire. In the final days of the Second World War, Adolf Hitler issued a 'scorched earth' policy on 19 March 1945, demanding that anything be destroyed that could be helpful to Allied forces as they made their way into Germany. German troops had to destroy 'all military objects, including traffic and communications installa- tions', with 'industrial and supply installations, as well as … other objects of value' such as works of art, destined for the scrapheap too. The order was officially termed the Demolitions on Reich Territory Decree (*Befehl betreffend Zerstörungsmaßnahmen im Reichsgebiet*), but it quickly became known as the much snappier Nero Decree (*Nerobefehl*).

Nero's purported pyromania has become a staple in popular culture. In a classic episode of *Doctor Who*, William Hartnell's time-traveller is shown giving the emperor some inspiration after accidentally setting alight his plans for a new Rome. Initially, he reacts in horror:

A lifetime's work! I'll have you both killed over and over again! Guards! Guards! Fool! Idiot! Traitor! Pig! I'll stick you both in the arena, on an island with water all round, and in the water there will be alligators and the water level will be raised and the alligators will get you! Fool! Traitor!

But gradually, the emperor warms to the idea:

> Brilliant! You are a genius! A genius! I will make you rich! Rich! So the Senate wouldn't pass my plans, eh? Wouldn't let me build my New Rome? But if the old one is burnt, if it goes up in flames, they will have no choice! Rome will be rebuilt to my design! Brilliant! Brilliant!

The Doctor touches on that episode, broadcast in 1965, many decades later on a return to the Ancient Roman era (broadcast in 2008). The Great Fire of Rome, a city he describes as 'like Soho, but bigger', had, he claims, 'nothing to do with me', adding: 'Well, a little bit!' Nero's involvement, and musical response to the fire, have become part of the modern political lexicon. Even *Doctor Who* points the finger at him. So should we assume Nero's handling of the Great Fire of Rome lived up to its nefarious billing?

There are some good reasons to question it. The most basic one is that the fiddle did not exist at the time. It would not go on to be invented for at least a millennium, when the eleventh century came along.

That does not mean Nero could not have expressed himself musically. He was a keen player of the lyre. But where would he have found one, and a stage costume to dress in, for his supposed performance? On the night he learned of the blaze, he was by Tacitus' account at his holiday resort in Antium, around thirty-five miles away from Rome. He is not recorded as having packed them before jumping onto his horse to ride through the night to the city so he could personally take charge of the response to the fire. He can't have retrieved them from his imperial palace, as it was already ablaze by the time he arrived, so anything inside would have gone up in smoke.

Even if he had found his musical apparel, where exactly did he perform? Ancient historians cannot agree. Suetonius thinks he performed on the Tower of Maecenas on the Esquiline Hill. Cassius Dio suggests it took place on the palace roof, while Tacitus claims he 'had mounted his private stage' but concedes it is just a 'rumour'. It's quite possible that Nero, who fancied himself an artist-in-the-making, quoted some of his own poetry to express his sorrow. That could have been good enough to puff up into a juicier-sounding set-piece performance.

The fact Nero was miles away from Rome when the fire started might seem like too convincing an alibi, so Tacitus records that there were gangs of men roaming around Rome feeding the flames and stopping people putting them out who were claiming to be acting on official authority. But he cannot be sure they were carrying out Nero's orders, as he adds they could equally have been doing so 'in order to have a freer hand in looting'.

Why would serious historians have reported such things if they could not be confident in what they were recording? On one level, it is likely to have been because they wanted to entertain. Such nuggets would be, as a cavalier journalist would say, too good to check. On a more serious level, these writers would have been aware that Nero ended his reign being declared a 'public enemy' by the Senate. With his troops threatening mutiny, he committed suicide before his enemies could finish him off.

There was an official interest in making sure his memory was as reviled as possible, in a process the Romans called '*damnatio memoriae*'. His statues were removed from public places, and unlike previous leaders such as Julius and Augustus, Nero was not proclaimed a god after his death. The calendar was also de-Neroised, with the month of 'Neroneus' becoming what we now call April.

Ancient historians would have had an interest in sticking the knife in. Nero and his family were gone and there a new dynasty in power, so there was every reason to put the boot in to show those in charge how much better it had become under their watch. Despite their bias, the hatchets Roman writers took to the likes of Emperor Nero dealt long-lasting damage to his reputation, particularly as their works tend to be the main sources we have to rely on centuries later to understand what went on. We are in the same state that future historians would be in if they tried to interpret Boris Johnson's premiership with access just to the official records of what decisions and laws he pushed, along with some press cuttings from the vibrantly anti-Tory *Morning Star* newspaper to help shed light. The free-for-all against Nero meant there was little point in scrutinising critical stories, so writers could make the most of juicy tales – as Cassius Dio did around a century after the fire – of how Nero 'secretly sent out men who pretended to be drunk or engaged in other kinds of mischief' to set Rome alight.

Talking up malicious rumours allows these writers to balance out their acknowledgement of positive things Nero did, like how much he did to fight the fire, without risking accusations they were trying to eulogise and whitewash his rule. He went as far as offering up his own gardens in order to provide temporary accommodation and shelter for homeless citizens. The price of grain was slashed, with emergency supplies imported from nearby towns and regions. Such crisis management could have earned him heroic write-ups, with his dash to save Rome chalked up as his finest hour. One of his predecessors, Tiberius, received a glowing review from the historian Tacitus for his firefighting skills, who noted that he 'acquired prestige' after a serious fire 'devastated' Rome by paying out 100 million sesterces to cover the rebuilding of the houses and apartment blocks that had been burned down. That emperor is let off lightly at another point by Tacitus, who records how he 'disarmed criticism' after leaving Rome following an 'exceptionally destructive fire' by throwing around enough money to cover the losses. 'This earned him votes of thanks in the senate by eminent members, and, as the news got round, a feeling of gratitude among the general public.'

By contrast, Nero's response to a bigger fire was sullied by the many suggestions that he'd had a hand in it. His villainous aura was not just shaped by those rumours, but by so many others from his years as emperor. Historians dug up enough dirt to fill several series of *Game of Thrones*. There were tales of familial strife – Suetonius making the rather bold claim that his own father was condemning him to his friends soon after he was born. Nero's father was reported as saying: 'Anything born to me and Agrippina has got to be ghastly and a public misfortune' (*detestabile et malo publico*), as if he had been an early version of the demon child Damien in *The Omen* film series.

Nero's second wife Poppaea died after suffering a miscarriage, which gave ancient writers licence to speculate liberally over whatever suffering he might have added. Both Tacitus and Suetonius claim that he kicked her in the abdomen, the latter claiming it happened after a quarrel caused by him coming home late from the chariot races. That bit of colour might have made their rows extra relatable to the average reader, but given that the emperor and his spouse lived in separate apartments, would they really quarrel over something like that?

Historians run riot with stories of all the people Nero might well have bumped off. It was 'generally claimed', Tacitus recounts, that he had ordered the poisoning of his chief aide and prefect of his Praetorian Guard, Burrus. The supposed method of execution was to have his throat daubed in poison, 'ostensibly as a remedial measure', but Tacitus admits he does not know if that was true, or if he merely died of illness.

Nero is widely credited by ancient historians with masterminding the death of his mother, but Agrippina was far from innocent. She thought the young emperor would be her puppet, but took against him once it became apparent that he had his own mind. She threatened to use her influence to remove him in a coup by persuading the soldiers to install her stepson Britannicus, whom Nero had pipped to the throne, instead. This was no ordinary family affair, but a high-stakes political power struggle.

Faced with such a threat, it is easy to see why Nero is so widely believed to have orchestrated the poisoning of his adoptive brother Britannicus over dinner. To get around his food taster, Tacitus recounts that 'a cup as yet harmless, but extremely hot and already tasted, was handed to Britannicus; then, on his refusing it because of its warmth, poison was poured in with some cold water'. When he keeled over at the table, short of breath and mute, Nero told shocked diners calmly that it was one of his usual fits of epilepsy, something he had been suffering since childhood. Britannicus' sister Octavia was similarly insouciant about it.

The truth, Cassius Dio recounts with macabre relish nearly two centuries afterwards, was revealed at Britannicus' funeral. His skin had been left darkened by the poison, he notes, so it was smeared with gypsum to cover it up. 'But as it was being carried through the Forum, a heavy rain that fell while the gypsum was still moist washed it all off, so that the crime was known not only by what people heard but also by what they saw'.

However, this has since been debunked by modern toxicologists, who have pointed out that the only known poison that could have turned the face dark was strychnine, which was not in use at the time. Such tales of imperial intrigue aim to ensure those reading are in no doubt about how they should feel about Nero. Yet there is evidence that he had some popularity. His death paved the way for Rome's very own Lord Lucan episode. The 'Nero Redivivus' legend took root, with speculation rife about whether he was actually alive and would pop up somewhere to take back power. It was especially popular in the eastern parts of the Empire. 'Seeing that even now everybody wishes [Nero] were still alive. And the great majority do believe that he still is,' wrote the Greek philosopher Dio Chrysostom. The belief in his return was fed by a series of imposters who arose claiming to be him, often sparking mayhem in the process.

How could he have built up such appeal? It isn't due to Nero's musical prowess, as much as he might have hoped it would be. Being emperor seemed to be a distraction from his real ambition of being a pop star, something he sought to fulfil by touring Greece performing with his lyre. 'Only the Greeks appreciate my music!' he later complained. He was so grateful to the crowds that turned out across Greece that he later gave it financial independence, no longer requiring it to pay its taxes to Rome. While his act of generosity delighted the Greek people, it infuriated taxpayers across the rest of his Empire. Nero did not mind, as the act seemed to him to be wholly appropriate as a way to recognise fans who had the good taste to enjoy his music. That obsession was captured in his supposed last words, when he was said to have gasped on his deathbed: 'What an artist dies in me!'

The Romans might not have been quite so interested in Nero's music recitals, but they came out for whatever entertainment he put on. He hosted mock sea battles, filling the stone and wood amphitheatre with saltwater to do so, and put on Greek-inspired entertainment like dancing and poetry recitals. The games he oversaw were a chance for Nero to show how much of a softie he could be. As discussed earlier in this book, he shied away from the battlefield, a place many glory-seeking Romans had made their name. When presented with the first execution warrants for him to sign as emperor, he is recorded by Suetonius as having wailed in response: 'I wish I'd never learned to write.' And that lack of bloodthirstiness came out in the gladiator games Nero encouraged, which were much less dangerous to human life than what Roman spectators had previously seen. In one year, Tacitus recounts with ill-concealed horror that he 'had no one put to death, not even criminals'. Instead, he had senators and other grandees – instead of slaves and prisoners – face off, even though, as Tacitus bewails, 'some of them we were well to do'. Traditionalists like him were horrified, as they had been used to simple and grisly gladiatorial bouts, but they were outnumbered by the audiences that came to lap up the Neronian revels.

Nero was not just good at putting on a show; he can be credited with significant improvements to the quality of life of the average Roman. After the disastrous Great Fire, he instituted a variety of measures aimed at ensuring it could never happen again. It could be said that it had been just a matter of time before such a blaze would happen, as the city was rife with fire risks. A typical Roman lived in a block of flats, which tended to be held up by wooden props. These buildings could be several storeys high, with the top floor posing the greatest risk for residents as it was the hardest to escape from in the event of a fire. Such safety issues meant that part was the cheapest to rent, so the poorest in Roman society tended to live at the top. This state of affairs was colourfully captured by the satirist Juvenal when he mused on how Romans lived in 'perpetual dread of fires', fuming that 'smoke is pouring out of your third-floor attic, but you know nothing of it; for if the alarm begins in the ground-floor, the last man to burn will be he who has nothing to shelter him from the rain but the tiles'.

And so Nero decreed that the maximum height of these apartment blocks would be cut to 17.75 metres, and that they ought to be built free-standing in future rather than leaning against each other. Building regulations were tightened to ensure greater use of flame-retardant material, with the emperor paying at his own expense for each apartment block to have a special portico built at the front.

His record spanned more than fire safety, however; he also popularised pampering by building a huge bathhouse at his own expense. The Neronian Baths, completed in 62 AD, set the trend for future imperial baths for centuries to come, boasting Greek-inspired features like a gymnasium. They were a marvel for social mobility. Rich Romans could afford – and enjoyed – baths in their own homes, but Nero's baths were said to be free to enter, allowing everyone to enjoy them. Such a facility was a great leveller, as everyone – rich or poor – would be luxuriating alongside each other. If everyone is naked, after all, how can you tell how wealthy they are? The only obvious way is the size of the entourage they would have, with slaves – who themselves would use the baths – holding towels and body oil. The oil itself was complimentary. Such perks undoubtedly ensured it went down a storm, leading the likes of the poet Martial to declaim: 'Whose baths were better than Nero's!'

Building such a lavish bathhouse was a daring move on Nero's part, as Roman traditionalists – already having to cope with less blood and guts in the arena – were wary of what these new bathing facilities would mean for society. Warm water, they believed, softened a good citizen's moral fibre. A year after the bathhouse opened, it was struck by lightning, the blow reducing a bronze statue of Nero inside it to a shapeless melted mass. Nero rushed to rebuild it, for fear that critics would seize on the lightning blast as a clear omen that the gods saw the baths as a den of iniquity.

Taking bathing mainstream was a big part of Nero's programme to modernise Rome. He was drawn to anything advanced, Suetonius reporting that he became so obsessed in his later years that he invited senators around to show off his new water-powered organs he had received. These hydraulic musical instruments had left him as excited as a boy with a new toy, as he eagerly set about 'explaining their several features and lecturing on [the] theory and complexity of each of them' to his bemused audience. His obsession with new technology inspired him to start using the groundbreaking new material of concrete for buildings. That was important for his crowning architectural glory: the *Domus Aurea* (Golden House). His new residence was big enough to house a 120-foot statue of himself in its entrance, and boasted a huge pond along with rooms decorated with marble, ivory, gold and gems. It was not just sumptuous, but architecturally innovative. There was a dome over the main banqueting hall that was said to revolve in sync with the sun and moon to resemble the heavens, and panels in the dining room ceilings which could be slid aside to allow flower petals or sprays of perfume to be showered down on guests.

Despite the Golden House's impressiveness, it was left to crumble into dust under his successors and their respective plans. In 69 AD, the Golden House was a victim of Nero's see-sawing reputation under the various different people that took over after him. Otho, one of the four emperors who took charge that year, put aside money for work on it, but within months Vespasian had pulled the plug, drained its lake and begun building over it a huge gladiatorial arena that we now know as Rome's Colosseum.

When Emperor Nero was not trying to build swanky new parts to Rome, he was cutting back the reach and burden of the state. He put an end to secret trials and extra-judicial killings and returned legal powers to the Senate that his predecessor had taken away. He also made efforts to cut back the tax burden on entrepreneurs. The Empire was a massive marketplace for people to trade within, but not an encouraging one for ambitious traders as their goods were hit with customs duties in every region that they passed through on their way to their final intended destination. That meant any businesspeople hoping to export from one corner of the Empire, say Parthia, to the other, Britain, would struggle to turn a profit.

Their complaints about greedy tax collectors were heard by Nero, who contemplated abolishing all indirect taxation, which – as Tacitus notes – could be seen 'as the noblest of gifts to the human race'. But his radicalism was curbed by Rome's great and good, who warned that scrapping indirect taxes risked the collapse of the Empire, as it would encourage people to demand the abolition of direct taxes as well. Plenty of those complaining were the consuls and tribunes who had gone on to make more money by setting up tax-collection businesses, ostensibly to help the Empire balance its books. A cynic might suggest their concerns were not driven so much by the national interest as by what would best protect their personal income. But their pleas, mixed with 'loud praise for his noble generosity', hit home.

The emperor ended up having to compromise, but he was still able to deliver some results. He struck a blow for public account-ability by demanding that all tax rules were published, rather than kept under wraps as they had previously been. That meant taxpayers could at least have an idea of what the regulations said when forking out their dues. Complaints against tax-collectors were fast-tracked;

praetors and provincial governors had to give them 'special priority'. Claims for arrears, it was decided, would lapse automatically after one year. Some spurious duties demanded by tax collectors when shaking down Roman entrepreneurs were scrapped.

Such steps show that Emperor Nero did try to do some good, which explains why some people could actually like him. But that view, and the very idea that he did anything praiseworthy, would strike many people understandably as ludicrous given how well-established his villainy has become. Modern politicians should not rest easy and assume they will be remembered with acclaim provided they do not get tied up in anything as grisly as what happened under Nero. Of course, few would ever be involved with as cutthroat a level of politics as he was caught up in during his time. But many of his predecessors and successors did similar things to Nero, and have been understandably hauled over the coals by historians. Yet in their cases, they have attracted much less vitriol, if any at all. How did they escape it and emerge with pristine and gleaming reputations?

Infamy, infamy, they've not all got it in for me

The emperor now known as Constantine 'the Great' could have so easily have gone down in history as anything but great. He not only killed his wife Fausta, but also his eldest son Crispus. Lurid claims swirled around both deaths; one writer suggested the empress was dispatched in an overheated bath, while Crispus was dealt with using 'cold poison'. However, Constantine became the first Roman emperor to convert to Christianity, doing so on his deathbed in the belief that he would get into heaven, and he was effectively forgiven by historians.

Tony Blair might have hoped to clean his own slate when he converted to Catholicism two years after leaving office. But the former Prime Minister is still struggling to shake off the stain on his reputation left by the war he waged in Iraq. Is there any hope for Old Tone? As Prime Minister, he said after reaching a career high in his breakthrough in the Irish peace process by agreeing the Good Friday Agreement to have felt the 'hand of history' on his shoulder. Will he be grateful for how it holds him? Perhaps, if he follows the Caesars' playbook.

Julius Caesar, alongside his adopted son and successor Augustus, is hailed as one of the greatest leaders the world has ever seen. But if he fought the military campaigns that made his reputation today, he would find himself hauled before the Hague to face charges of war crimes. Over the course of more than thirty pitched battles in the Gallic Wars, he is estimated to have captured more than 800 towns across what we now know as France and Germany. He killed more than a million men, women and children, with a million more captured and sold into slavery. It was genocide ostensibly for the glory of Rome, but in truth in service of his own future.

What pretext did Julius Caesar have for launching such a campaign? Not much beyond a desire to boost his political career and to pay off his massive debts. The former consul had as weak a pretext for invading Gaul as Hitler did for invading Poland in 1939, in his case portraying it as a pre-emptive strike in defence of Rome. That excuse may be as shaky as Blair's claims about WMDs in Iraq, but at least the former Prime Minister can still try to argue that it was worth removing the country's dictator, Saddam Hussein, from power.

Caesar's campaigning (both militarily and political) sparked increasing alarm back in Rome, with senators preparing to prosecute him on his return from Gaul for abuse of his authority, a process which could have not just stripped him of his wealth and Roman citizenship, but further humiliated him by rolling back all the laws he passed as consul. How did he stop this? By fighting a propaganda war.

Caesar was a master of public relations. He had a knack for the perfect soundbite, as demonstrated by the famously pithy way he summed up a quick victory in battle to the Senate, writing: '*Veni, vidi, vici*' ('I came, I saw, I conquered'). That phrase has been endlessly referenced over the ages, such as when Hillary Clinton chose to mark the death of Libya's leader Muammar Gaddafi in 2011 by quipping: 'We came, we saw, he died.'

Another way Caesar showed his PR mastery was in his awareness of message control. He decided in one of his first acts as consul to release what was effectively the world's first newspaper, so that citizens could be kept abreast on what had been going on in the Senate. The '*Acta Diurna*' (Daily Deeds) served as an official government gazette, informing the public about what they needed to know. Initially it focused on hard news, such as the results of official debates, military victories and legal proceedings. Then it went on to include news on the markets (specifically, the price of grain), Roman society (notable births, marriages and deaths), and even entertainment (details about the latest gladiatorial battles and games as well as the latest gossip).

By that time, Caesar had his fair share of enemies in the Roman establishment, some out of jealousy and others motivated by fear of how far he would go in his pursuit of power. They had a mutual interest in stopping his popularity from snowballing any further by hindering his ability to stir up the Roman people with tales of the battles he was winning in Rome's name. This meant many of the official channels Caesar could have used to make his case were unavailable. Obviously, he could not turn up in the Forum and mount the rostra to speak to the people directly because he was many miles away on campaign. He could not use the official newspaper he had pioneered to share word of what he was up to, as his enemies in the Senate controlled it and could suppress what he had to say. They also tried to obstruct the reports he sent back, seeking to stop them from being opened and read out.

But Caesar's allies sought to wrest back control of the narrative about what their man was doing, and so Mark Anthony used his powers at the time as tribune to read the letters out himself. He won many people around to Caesar's side, as Plutarch records, because people could then conclude his activities were 'moderate and just'. Meanwhile, Caesar himself put out his own work so that the average Roman citizen would be able to hear his take on what he was doing in Gaul. Caesar's 'Commentaries on the Gallic War' form a masterpiece of political propaganda, in which he offers a swashbuckling narrative about his own campaigns. They're written in the third person, telling the audience of what 'Caesar' did. Some might take that as a sign of his pomposity, but scholars argue that it was intended to make it even easier for his allies to read out and to inform the public of what their champion was getting up to.

Taking charge of how the Gallic invasion was perceived back in Rome allowed him to sell his efforts in the best terms possible. And so he cast himself as on a mission to defend and further the glory of Rome. As both commander and chief reporter on his own army, it's no surprise that he came across as consistently calm and in control, no matter how fiendish his foes might have been. The more fearsome he could make his enemies, the greater he seemed in defeating them. His enemies in the Senate tried to sow doubt in the public's mind about his intentions, but how could they cut through to the average citizen when they had such riveting tales of derring-do to enjoy? The popular support he built up left him unassailable, and his accounts are still being studied by aspiring tacticians in the present day. Sharp message control allowed Julius Caesar to save his career from burning out before it had begun amid Senate recriminations and allowed him to blaze a trail of epoch-defining success.

Caesar's step-nephew Octavian, who when he succeeded him as emperor took on the name Augustus, showed he had learned the importance of controlling the narrative. His imperial name has become synonymous with dignified nobility, yet he personally was anything but 'august'. He scandalised Roman society by 'stealing' (as Tacitus puts it) the wife of another man, 'and asked the priests the farcical question whether it was in order for her to marry while pregnant' with someone else's child. In his politics, though, he was even more controversial. His modern-day fans are willing to look past it, though. 'Basically, through a really harsh approach, he established 200 years of world peace,' Mark Zuckerberg once explained. 'What are the trade-offs in that? On the one hand, world peace is a long-term goal that people talk about today, [but] that didn't come for free, and he had to do certain things.'

The Facebook founder, who went as far as naming one of his daughters after the emperor, might not want to dwell on the 'certain things' Augustus had to do, but it is worth considering them in order to see how much is glossed over in favour of how he would prefer to be remembered. We can get a very clear sense of that from the autobiography he published after his death: *Res Gestae Divi Augusti* (The Deeds of the Divine Augustus). It skips over messy periods like the fallout from Julius Caesar's assassination, during which Augustus was part of a three-man regime that ostracised, ruined or sentenced to death hundreds of senators and thousands of other dignitaries as part of a programme of 'proscriptions'. Many of those on the list of 'pro-scribed' people were hunted down and slaughtered out in the open.

Many parts of the self-glorifying look he gives his own rule show his penchant for 'alternative facts', as the Trump administration would call them. Early on, he recounts how he responded to Julius Caesar's murder by raising a private army at nineteen years old to 'restore liberty to the Republic when it was oppressed by the tyranny of a faction'. Curiously, he forgets to mention that it was a criminal offense under the law to raise private militias in order to overthrow the state.

Augustus goes on to pose as the selfless saviour, writing: 'When I had extinguished the flames of civil war, being in absolute control of affairs by universal consent, I transferred the Republic from my own control to the will of the Senate and the Roman people.' Far from extinguishing them, he helped keep these flames burning for much longer in his pursuit of Caesar's chief assassins, Brutus and Cassius, and then in his fight with Mark Anthony to be Caesar's true heir.

Despite his claims to have given the authority invested in him back to the Senate after saving the Republic, it was promptly returned to him on a huge ten-year term. Senators went on to compliantly renew his term without question each decade, Augustus justifying it on the grounds of various external military threats and ultimately consolidating his grip on power. That confirmed his status as an autocrat, although he was savvy enough not to take on the formal title of 'dictator' given how badly it went down when Julius Caesar took it on.

Augustus did not just have an eye on the example set by his predecessor, but also the example his successor might set. Tiberius, his nominated heir, was a calculated choice. Instead of choosing someone he liked, or thought would be a good ruler for Rome, he went for someone who would not show him up. Augustus was familiar with Tiberius' arrogance and filthy temper, and so he sought to make himself look even better by setting himself up as a contrast, as Tacitus puts it, to Tiberius' 'extreme wickedness'. Such qualities could only make Augustus look like an even better emperor.

Of course, if all a politician had to do to ensure the public remembered them admiringly was to publish a rave review about themselves, and make sure to be succeeded by someone worse, we would be constantly agog about the calibre of great leaders presiding over us.

An official account from a politician about their time in office is important, but it tends not to change people's minds radically about the author because it is too easy to dismiss as self-serving and score-settling prose. The key thing ambitious Romans recognised was to have other people writing about you as glowingly as you might do about yourself.

The ever-bumptious Cicero wanted everyone to know how much he did for Rome as consul, namely defusing a conspiracy in the summer of 63 BC by the senator Catiline to overthrow the Republic. He would rarely miss a chance to shoehorn it into any of his public speeches afterwards, using the slightest excuse to tell his audience about how he faced down the plotters. When defending his fellow politician Lucius Murena against charges of electoral bribery, he used the fact that the defendant had stood against Catiline in an election to remind the court about his involvement in defusing the Catalinarian conspiracy. That meant he could not resist retelling how he turned up at the polls Cataline hoped would sweep him into power with an armed guard and a military breastplate under his toga. 'Not in order to protect me,' he hastened to add, 'for I knew that Catiline would aim at my head and neck, not at my chest or body, but in order that all good men might observe it, and, when they saw their consul in fear and in danger, might as they did, throng together for my assistance and protection.' His scare tactic, equivalent to a Prime Minister turning up at an election count with a police escort and a stab vest on, helped put voters off electing the firebrand populist Catiline.

Cicero was irrepressible in his desire for everyone to know how he had 'saved' the Republic, and did not hold back in reminding his audience about how much he was applauded for his time in office once it was over:

On that day, the entire Roman people gave me in that assembly, not a congratulation to be remembered for the rest of the day, but they gave me immortality and eternal glory, when they themselves swearing also, with one voice and consent approved of my oath couched in such proud and triumphant words. And on that occasion, my return home from the Forum was of such a nature that there did not appear to be a single citizen who was not in my train. And my consulship was conducted throughout in such a manner, that I did nothing without the advice of the senate, – nothing without the approval of the Roman people; that in the rostra I constantly defended the senate, – in the senate-house I was the unwearied advocate of the people; that in that manner, I united the multitude with the chief men, and the equestrian order with the senate. I have now briefly described my consulship.

Cicero promised to talk about his consulship only 'briefly', but he wanted everyone to be able to relish it at greater length in the form of an epic poem. He wanted a skilled writer to take it on, naturally, in the hope that it would be as celebrated a work as Homer's *Iliad* (focusing on Achilles in Troy) and Virgil's *Aeneid* (all about Aeneas). Unfortunately, his own opinion on how significant his actions as consul had been was not echoed by Rome's literati.

Cicero begged the city's writers to wax lyrical about him. When writing to his friend and historian Lucius Lucceius, he tried to sell his story to him by arguing that it offered 'much variety' and plenty of plot twists, which meant it would have a 'strong hold' on an audience's imagination and be 'very enjoyable' seeing the good guys (i.e.

Cicero) win in the end. He offered to help supply evidence so his potential biographer was clear on the facts, but urged him to 'praise those actions of mine in warmer terms than you perhaps feel'. Above all, he wanted the work to come out promptly so that people could 'learn what I am from your books while I am still alive'.

Lucceius evidently did not take him up on his offer; nor did a whole host of other writers. 'Thyillus has deserted me and Archias written nothing about me,' Cicero wailed to a confidant in a letter. He ended up deciding that if no one would be willing to rhapsodise about his life in verse, he would have to do it himself. The work on his consularship – *De Consulatu Suo* – was predictably glowing, as we can tell from the extracts he insisted on quoting to his friends in letters he wrote to them after it was finished. Ironically, he told his friend Lucceius that if he was forced to write about his own achievements, he would be boringly restrained in his tone. 'Men are bound, when writing of themselves, both to speak with greater reserve of what is praiseworthy, and to omit what calls for blame.'

Cicero's biographical struggle shows that politicians know sycophantic write-ups are much better and more believable when coming from other people than from their own pen, and that they cannot expect other writers to be just as convinced about their own greatness.

Blair used the power of third-party writers to great effect in office. The key messages for journalists on a day-to-day level were presided over with masterly control by his team. Meanwhile, biographers such as John Rentoul brought out books even in Blair's early years trumpeting his significance in office, in initial attempts to shape how he would be remembered. Those who had worked with him, like Alastair Campbell and Peter Mandelson, went on outside of government to publish their own biographies offering further positive takes on the Blair premiership. There have been a fair share of hostile accounts about Blair, whether by sceptical journalists like Tom Bower or by those close to Blair's friend/enemy Gordon Brown, such as Paul Routledge. That is why Blair has been busy working to salvage as positive a legacy as he can, to avoid being for ever tarnished in the history books.

There are a few events that could leave a lasting stain on Blair's reputation, such as the 2007/08 credit crunch. David Cameron routinely blamed the Blair government's management of the UK's finances for leaving the country vulnerable to the 2008 economic crash, although Labour-leaning defenders insist that it was a massive global crisis that the party could have done little to avoid.

What will be harder for Blair to shake off is the war he oversaw in Iraq, a decision only his staunchest allies are willing to defend him publicly over. Blair has acknowledged that he could be for ever tarred by Iraq. 'Be careful your opponents don't all define your record,' he advised listeners of the *Remainiacs* podcast in March 2019, lamenting that 'for the left it's all about Iraq'. He was shunned by the ill-fated breakaway party Change UK, with its then leader Heidi Allen remarking that 'once you are tarnished, you are tarnished'. Hence his determination to ensure people think about more than Iraq when assessing his premiership, especially when writing about it for the history books, by mounting – for example – an energetic campaign against Brexit.

Historical debate will rage about him, in the same way that many Roman emperors such as Nero and Caligula have experienced. There will be writers who will inevitably continue to pile in on him, castigating him for Iraq and other aspects of his leadership, while others will continue to defend him. Certainly, some people will come to a more sympathetic conclusion if they take into account what else he did in office. Take the Kosovo War, for example, one of his less controversial foreign incursions. That left him a hero among local Kosovan Albanians to this day (with some naming their own children after him – 'Tonibler'). He was confident enough to chalk it up while in office as something that would make him look good in the history books. But he could not deny, when talking to *The Guardian* in March 2003, that generally he would have to 'be prepared to be judged by history'.

Blair's domestic record tends to attract more favourable reviews, with even his political foe Jeremy Corbyn now forced to acknowledge his achievements, such as the introduction of the UK national minimum wage (even if Corbyn goes out of his way to praise everyone else in Blair's government except the man himself for doing so).

Constantine didn't necessarily need to convert to Christianity to ensure he would be heralded as 'the Great'. He had enough military successes to claim it in his own right, reunifying the Empire under one leader and winning big victories over the Germans in 306–308, 313–314, the Goths in 332 and the Sarmatians in 334. But the significance of his conversion to Christianity meant that he did not need to do much else to ensure he was glorified in the history books.

Modern politicians take pains to put together their own accounts of their time in office, in the hope that future generations will come to agree with them. One can scoff at their vainglorious attempts, yet their efforts continue a long tradition of political self-aggrandisement and fanfare that goes as far back as the Caesars. If they don't do it, a void is left for their critics and enemies to shape how they are seen in history.

Blair has made his case in his own memoirs, *A Journey*, for why he feels his greatness should be recognised in the history books, and he continues to defend his record whenever he has the chance in public. As controversial as his name might be now due to Iraq and his indefatigable campaigning against Brexit, depending on how events pan out in the future, he could still be remembered as 'Tony the Great'. Historians in Brussels would be only too happy to think of him that way if he manages to help keep the United Kingdom closely tied to the European Union.

CONCLUSION

Reg (played by John Cleese): All right, but apart from the sanitation,
the medicine, education, wine, public order, irrigation, roads,
a fresh-water system, and public health, what have
the Romans ever done for us?

People's Front of Judea Commando: Brought peace.

Reg: Oh. Peace? Shut up!

– MONTY PYTHON'S LIFE OF BRIAN

As John Cleese and the rest of the Monty Python crew explored in their masterly 1979 comedy, there are many things the Romans have done for us. If only their exchange had gone on further, they could have fitted in another big achievement – namely, setting up the template for modern politics.

While the Greeks invented many key political concepts, the Romans turned them into a model that we are still building on in the present day. Back then, politicians were rabble-rousers: cutting deals, slinging mud at each other and desperately trying to protect their image. And they show no signs of stopping now. Even the way politicians campaign is recognisably Roman. Despite all the advances of modern technology that allow political campaign teams to study the electorate in increasingly complex ways, elections are still won essentially by whoever can reach out and woo the most voters.

For all the buzzwords modern campaigners use, ready with talk of voter engagement rates, hitting the doorstep, and election-day 'get out the vote' operations, the core principle remains – as the Romans understood – to get out among the public and impress. As Quintus Cicero advised, a good candidate needed to be in the public eye as much as possible, 'speaking constantly with voters, then talking with them again the next day and the next'.

Candidates in Ancient Rome behaved in similar ways to how they do now: promising voters the earth, knowing they would inevitably be unable to deliver on all their pledges in office. That mentality is laid bare by Cicero's proto-Machiavellian advice: 'A candidate must be a chameleon, adapting to each person he meets, changing his expression and speech as necessary.' He added: 'If a politician made only promises he was sure he could keep, he wouldn't have many friends.' Whether right or wrong, some of the most successful campaigns we have seen recently have been those that have not worried about the deliverability of what they had been promising, as long as it was sufficiently inspiring for the electorate.

Romans were so ahead of their time in political campaigning that outsiders were left astounded by its professionalism. The

Greek historian Polybius records how the Syrian King Antiochus IV Epiphanes, on returning home after spending a decade as a prisoner of war in Rome, showed exotic habits he had picked up from watching years of Roman electioneering. He would tour the capital city of Antioch, talking with whoever he met, hand out presents such as dates and money and join his citizens in the public baths. The monarch would poke his nose into the workshops of silversmiths and goldsmiths, and even go as far as drinking at the same places his citizens went to. Onlookers were most confused by his penchant for putting on a white toga in order to go around the marketplace like he was running for election, shaking people's hands and begging for their votes – even though he was an unelected monarch. Clearly, the excitement of a Roman election campaign was contagious.

Such behaviour lives on in modern politicians, with some like Boris Johnson rightly paying tribute to how much he and his peers owe to the Romans. No matter how much we think politics has changed since their peak, we are still doing as the Romans do, except we have swapped togas and swords for suits and smartphones.

By looking back to the Ancient Romans, we can see the same desire among the electorate for dynamic leaders with stout principles who'll bring in better days. Politicians have constantly tried to embody that ideal, with mixed results. They could not all be the new Julius Caesar or Augustus, but that did not stop them trying to get as far along the *cursus honorum* as possible. Their modern counterparts are still participating in that scrabble to the top. Such ambition is timeless, and it helps explain why many of us are drawn to watching dramas about Ancient Rome, namely that what goes on can be just as relevant to modern society as an episode of *EastEnders*.

We cannot rely solely on colourful characters like Johnson and Rees-Mogg to champion the relevance of the Romans and other figures from the past. As Marcus Tullius Cicero said: 'To be ignorant of what occurred before you were born is to remain always a child.' Hopefully, those who have followed the Romans onto the political stage, especially those reading this very tome, will remember that.

ACKNOWLEDGEMENTS

After writing a book dedicated to acknowledging the debt we owe to the Romans, it would be wrong of me not to acknowledge my own debt – in this case, to those who helped me with this work.

Firstly, I'd like to thank my wife, Emma, whose illustrations you will have seen scattered throughout these pages. I am enormously grateful for her encouragement, and her patience in not just reviewing what I wrote but putting up with my hours locked away with piles of books. This book would not exist without her, as she inspired me to knuckle down to write my first one. The least I could do given this is to dedicate this book to her, with my love.

Thank you to the Biteback Publishing team, especially James Stephens, Olivia Beattie and Stephanie Carey, for their diligence and help in getting this together. Thanks also to my *Telegraph* colleagues Rob Winnett, Tom Welsh and Ian Marsden – I have balanced the writing this of book with my role of making sense of the Brexit process for our readers. I'm also delighted that one of the *Telegraph*'s top cartoonists, Bob Moran, was able to design the front cover.

Thank you to my friends and family for their advice, for reading and commenting on my various manuscript drafts, especially Sara Jones, Adam Sammut, Valerie Gibson, Charles Orton-Jones and Paul Gamble. Thanks also to Rachel Cunliffe for her tips.

Thank you to my school and university teachers who instilled, guided and developed my fascination with the classical world. Thank you to my mother Rosanna for all her support, and my brother Ivo, whose diligent introductory Latin lessons over our holidays meant I could hit the ground running when I started studying it at school.

Last, but certainly not least, thank you, dear reader, for picking up this book and getting stuck into my *Romanifesto*.

BIBLIOGRAPHY

For those who are still hungering for more classical or political insights, here are the resources I've scoured in the process of writing about the Romans (and the Greeks) for this book. I am of course grateful to each and every author for their endeavours.

Ancient
Bede, *Ecclesiastical History of the English People*
Cassius Dio, *Roman History*
Catullus, *The Poems*
Dio Chrysostom, *Discourses*
Herodotus, *Histories*
Horace, *Odes*
Juvenal, *Satires*
Lactantius, *On the Deaths of the Persecutors*
Livy, *The Early History of Rome*
Macrobius Ambrosius Theodosius, *Saturnalia*
Marcus Tullius Cicero, *Letters and Speeches*
Marcus Tullius Cicero, *On Friendship*

Ovid, *The Art of Love*

Marcus Tullius Cicero, *On Obligations*

Pliny the Elder, *Natural Histories*

Plutarch, *The Makers of Rome*

Polybius, *Histories*

Quintus Tullius Cicero, *How to Win an Election*

Strabo, *Geographica*

Suetonius, *Lives of the Twelve Caesars*

Tacitus, *The Annals of Imperial Rome*

Titus Flavius Josephus, *Antiquities of the Jews*

Modern

Anthony A. Barnett, *Caligula: The Corruption of Power* (Routledge, 2001)

Mary Beard, *Julius Caesar Revealed* (documentary broadcast on BBC Four, 18 April 2019)

Mary Beard, *SPQR: A History of Ancient Rome* (Profile Books, 2015)

Alan Clark, *Diaries: In Power 1983–1992, Volume 1* (Phoenix, tenth impression edition, 2003)

Michael Cockerell, *Boris Johnson: The Irresistible Rise* (broadcast on BBC Two, 9 November 2013)

Bernard Donoughue, *Westminster Diary: A Reluctant Minister under Tony Blair* (I. B. Taurus, 2016)

Andrew Gimson, *Boris: The Rise of Boris Johnson* (Simon & Schuster, 2016)

Richard Holland, *Nero: The Man Behind the Myth* (History Press Ltd, 2002)

Tom Holland, *Dynasty: The Rise and Fall of the House of Caesar* (Little, Brown, 2015)

Tom Holland, *Rubicon: The Triumph and Tragedy of the Roman Republic* (Abacus, 2004)

Boris Johnson, *The Dream of Rome* (HarperCollins, 2006)

Rachel Johnson, *The Oxford Myth* (Weidenfeld & Nicolson, 1988)

John Milton, *History of Britain* (Paul Watkins Publishing, 1991; facsimile of 1677 edition)

David M. Pritchard, *Public Spending and Democracy in Classical Athens* (University of Texas Press, 2015)

Gareth Sampson, *Rome, Blood and Politics: Reform, Murder and Popular Politics in Late Republic* (Pen & Sword History, 2017)

Rory Stewart, *The Marches: A Borderland Journey Between England and Scotland* (Mariner Books, 2017)

Stephen Williams, *Diocletian and the Roman Recovery* (B.T. Batsford, 1985)